A Sinner's of the Second Oldest Profession.

One thing…

In the 21st century, prostitution occurs across cultures and political systems, even operating in socialist societies. The originator of the phrase "the **world's oldest profession**" was Rudyard Kipling. His 1888 story about a prostitute begins, "Lalun is a member of the most ancient **profession in the world**."

…led to another.

The advertisement (arguably, an example of the second oldest profession), shown above from ancient times.

The *Lupanar of Pompeii* is an advertisement for the most famous brothel in the ruined Roman city of Pompeii. Lupanar is Latin for "brothel".

**"Forgive me, Father, for I have sinned.
I've written advertising for tobacco, alcohol, tampons (blame the Irish Nuns), sugar and more."**

The curse of being raised a Catholic and the wardrobe of hair shirts, some of which fit me, that go with it.

The upside is I've worked with some very clever and amusing people; some of whom you'll get to meet as we wander down my Memory Lane.

ISBN 078-0-646-82145-0

layout and typography; Mike Doyle. Artwork by Mark Salwowski.

Typefaces: Headings: **Franklin Gothic**, Text & Captions: Garamond.

Cover design by Paul Carpenter.

dc**P**

Published by Doyley Carte Productions.

Produced by
York Publishing Services Ltd

web: www.yps-publishing.co.uk

Printed in the United Kingdom on paper from sustainable forests.

FOREWORD

By Sir John Hegarty.

John, as always, an advocate of less said the better, had this to say about my book, for which I thank him.

'This is a story about how to write your way to the top.
And have lots of fun at the same time.'

Sir John Hegarty. "The Heg."
Photo of John by Opal Turner,
taken from his book,
Hegarty on Advertising.

INTRODUCTION

This book is about the thrills and spills of my life in advertising. Like Sir John Hegarty (of whom more later), he and I were born in an auspicious year.

To quote John from his book 'Hegarty on Advertising', ***"I've been very lucky to be in the right place at the right time enough times. The first stroke of luck in my life was being born in 1944. You might not think it so lucky to be born in London as it endured the closing months of World War 11, but it was lucky in that I was born at the start of what became known as the 'baby boom' and was part of a generation that would emerge from the hardships of war and reap the rewards of change that would sweep through Western society."***

The second 'Elizabethan Age'?

The country was being rebuilt and so were the social mores. Mobility was now possible; you weren't condemned to be forever part of a social class.

With the coronation of "Her Maj" as she is sometimes referred to in Australia, pundits predicted a second Elizabethan age.

The First Age *seeing the remarkable body of work by Shakespeare and Marlow, and also the discoveries and adventures of Sir Walter Raleigh and Sir Francis Drake (they all seemed to be Knights of the realm then).*

The Second Age*, the 1960s, did see a similar remarkable era of creativity in Britain. We saw artists such as David Hockney, the Beatles and the Rolling Stones, Orton's plays and the 'Kitchen Sink' theatre phenomenon. While in cinema we enjoyed classic movies by the likes of David Lean followed by Ridley Scott, Hugh Hudson and Alan Parker from the advertising world.*

And, let's not forget the comedians such as the Goons and comic actors coming out of universities leading to work like Monty Python's Flying Circus. The list could go on, and on.

Simultaneously, and not by accident, British advertising came to be considered amongst the best in the world. Heady days .

Clive James[†], author, poet and essayist (and Australian) was reported to have written in The Observer, *where he was TV critic at the time, that he thought the commercials were often better than the programs.*

School days.

Despite all the dreadful scandals revealed about the Catholic priesthood, I must give some credit to the Dominican Nuns who taught me at St James' Secondary Modern in London's Burnt Oak.

Dominican Nuns.

Sister Catherine, the school Principal took a shine to my Mum, who was from the same part of Ireland. When I was in Year Four, they tested all of us and three, including me, were jumped up to Year Six (Years ten to twelve in Australia). I panicked, but Sister Catherine assured my Mum that I was capable and I did end up with two 'O' levels (Art and English) and two 'A' Levels(History and English Literature) in the General Certificate of Education (GCEs), which could have got me into university. However, with a widowed mother I felt obliged to go out and earn a crust.

Sister Rose taught me English Literature and History, and Sister Imelda taught me Art. I loved this subject so much I confess to faking injury to avoid the building, metalwork and carpentry classes. The art lessons took place in the stables building of a house where the Wright Brothers are said to have lived when they were in England.

2i's Coffee Bar. Where friends and I used to go as teenagers in Soho, listening to music that was called 'Skiffle' such as Lonnie Donegan, Chas McDevitt and Nancy Whiskey, while making a cup of coffee last forever.

I was a skiffle* and then a Soul Man.

And then along came R&B and Soul music with the likes of Georgie Fame and the Blue Flames at the Flamingo in Soho where American troops would drop in to hear sounds from home. And then there was The Who at the Marquee in Wardour Street. For me, it would also include nights at the Refectory in Golders Green and the Manor House Blues Club, at the pub of the same name, watching Rod "The Mod" Stewart, who appears later.

✱ Skiffle is a musical genre with influences from jazz, blues, and American folk music, generally performed with a mixture of manufactured and homemade or improvised instruments. **Wikipedia.**

7

Earning my keep.

I used to deliver newspapers for the newsagent across the road from us and he started to get complaints that deliveries were late, the reason being I was reading the papers and magazines. Half in humour, he offered to get me an armchair so I could read in the shop.

Never the less, he put me forward for a job on the Hornsey Journal *as an apprentice proofreader, but a major printing strike (remember those?) meant the job was lost.*

However, I was qualified, having passed the entrance exam. So I got on my bike and knocked on every door of every printing company in North London. By good luck, The Hendon & Finchley Times *Group of newspapers hired me as an apprentice compositor, starting my love of typography.*

In my final year, after five years, I became a journeyman in 1965. I also gained the City & Guilds of London Full Certificate in Typographic Design, with a possible future as a Typographer.

Life as an apprentice compositor.

Back to school.

In 1965 I started as a full-time graphics student at the London College of Printing* (LCP) on the Vocational course. However, my Shop Steward (or 'Father of the Chapel') had me down as becoming a union official as I'd already been 'Father' of the Apprentices.

I use the term loosely, but I had to negotiate terms for the newspaper delivery boys with management; an interesting insight into 'politics'.

While still a 'Comp' I continued my general studies at evening classes with History of Art at the Worker's Educational Association and American Literature at our local grammar school in Finchley.

Some examples of my work at the LCP. Best I stuck to words?

A special dedication.

This book is dedicated to all the wonderful people and teachers that I've been lucky enough to work with, learn from and had the pleasure of knowing, over my career.

Hopefully, you know who you are. Apologies to anyone who might feel I haven't done justice to them.

But I would like to make special mention of the man I never knew, but for whom, I would not be here. My Dad.

He ran for the bus coming home from work in 1946 and died on the top deck from valvular disease of the heart leaving his new wife a widow and me just two years old.

It's worth noting that I could have suffered a very early exit as Mr. Hitler and his friends dropped a bomb on the North Middlesex County hospital's maternity ward in Enfield in 1944.

As good luck would have it, they had moved all the mums to a bomb shelter otherwise this book may never have existed, for which you might have been grateful. I hope not and that you enjoy my memories.

James Anthony Doyle, my Dad.

My UK Employment:
a potted history.

1960 – 1965 Trained as an apprentice Compositor on the Hendon & Finchley Times Group of Newspapers, achieved a Full Technological Certificate from the City and Guilds of London Institute in Typography.

1965-1967 - Studied at the London College of Printing as a fulltime 'Mature' student on the, Vocational Course in Graphic Design, where we were supposed to be trained for studio work. But I knew nothing when I started as an Intern during the Summer holiday at CDP in 1966.

1967-1968 Pritchard, Wood.
Junior Copywriter, Salary: £900 pa.

1968 – Doyle Dane Bernbach.*
Junior Copywriter, Salary: £1,500 pa.

1968 – 1969 – Papert, Koenig, Lois (PKL).
Copywriter, Salary: £2,500 pa. Agency resigned major accounts.

1969 – 1970 – Colman, Prentis & Varley (CPV).
Copywriter, after the resignation of half the billing at PKL four of us moved as a group to CPV. Salary: £3,500 pa.

1970 – 1973 – Collett, Dickenson, Pearce (CDP).
Copywriter, Salary: £3,000 pa.

1973 – 1975 – Dorland Advertising.
Associate Director, Group Head, Copywriter (Just got married and more than doubled my salary but hated the agency). Salary: £8,000 pa (including a car to the value of £1,600).

1975 – 1977 Samuels, Jones, Isaacson, Page/BMP.
Deputy Creative Director, Copy Chief, Salary: £8,000 pa (including a company car to the value of £1,500, and a colour TV).

1977 – 1978 French, Gold, Abbott.
Copywriter, Salary: £No record.

1977 – 1978 – BBDO (1).
Copywriter, Salary: £9,750 pa, (including a company car).

1978 – 1980 – The Kirkwood Company.
Group Head, Copywriter, Salary: £13,000 pa (including company car to the value of £4,000).

1981 – Freelance, various agencies.

1981 – 1984 - Wright & Partners.
Partner, Co-Creative Director, Salary: £13,800 pa, plus £1,200 perks).

1984-1986 Colman RSCG & Partners.
Director, Group Head, Copywriter, Salary: Initially hired for four months at £2,500 pm then hired full-time after that at £30,000 pa (including company car).

1986 – 1988 - Garret, Doyle, Fugler.
Partner, Copywriter, Salary: No record. Declared agency bankrupt.

1988-1989 – BBDO (2).
Associate Creative Director, Copywriter, Salary: £60,000 pa (including a company car to the value of £18,000 plus a TV and video player).

1989 – 1990 – Laing, Henry, Hill, Holliday.
Head of Copy, Director, Salary: £70,000 pa (including total value of £15,000 plus TV and private medical insurance).

*The order of names for the company was based on the toss of a coin. They also agreed on doing away with the commas that usually ran between propriety names: 'Nothing will come between us, not even punctuation ', said Bernbach. Source: page 51, 'The Real Madmen' by Andrew Cracknell.

Book One
The UK

†

*Sadly, this appears all too often throughout my story for people,
and agencies, who have passed away.
I describe my friends and myself as the 'Survivors'.*

I beg forgiveness from all the great Art Directors, Designers and Typographers that I've been lucky enough to work with over the years for my design skills, rusty to say the least. All the typographical sins that follow are entirely my fault.

Also, photographers will appreciate why I never came close to a career in their dark art but why I love what so many of them achieve.

No doubt copywriters will spot a few split infinitives or mistakes in grammar. How many Hail Marys and Our Fathers will I have to say for forgiveness?

Finally, my school motto was 'Veritas', which is Latin for truth. A rule I've done my best to remain true to throughout my life and in this book. Where I've had contact details, such as email addresses, I've sent relevant content to people for them to correct or add any content they feel appropriate.

Contents

Chapter
One

My Mum and 'Swissmass'.

I'd like to pay a special tribute to my wonderful mother[†] who, in Australia, would have been called a "Battler".

Born in 1915 in the city of Limerick in the county of the same name. She grew up in the counties of Galway and Mayo where, as a young girl, she was run over by a pony and cart, leaving her disabled with a curved spine and one leg shorter than the other. In all the photographs of the time you would be convinced that she only had one leg as she would tuck her 'bad' leg behind her good one.

In the late 30s, the family decided to migrate to London. This was after my Grandfather failed in his application for a job on the Irish railway, as the local priest refused to give him a recommendation. The reason being, he was not a regular at church.

They got Mum an apprenticeship as a dressmaker, as they were going to leave her behind to fend for herself; tough parenting you could say. She refused to accept this as her fate and saved the money for her fare.

They couldn't say they were going to London as that was thought of as going to the Devil. They just said that they were moving to Dublin. That was thought to be bad enough back then.

The family arrived one foggy night in Finchley, North London (my Grandfather's brother was already there with his family) and they were greeted by an ad in a newsagent's window saying: 'No dogs or Irish'. Not a pretty welcome, but they did find an Irish landlord who rented them a room.

My Mum quickly found work, and a husband a few years later, but, sadly for her, not for long as I mentioned before. After my Dad's demise, she was now a widow as well as disabled.

Her dream for me was that I go to university. I passed the necessary GCEs but instead took the job as an apprentice compositor.

After becoming a journeyman, I decided to go the London College of Printing (LCP) as a full-time graphic design student. It was her dream fulfilled.

SWISSMASS?

At Christmas a few years later, a friend of mine, Bob Miller, announced that he had a girlfriend in Lucerne who could put us up over the holiday season. (Bob was also in advertising and, as I later discovered, he had been to the same high school as me).

My Mum was now in Barnet General Hospital after a few weeks of illness, but said that she wanted me to take the trip.

So, four of us set off in my VW Beetle that I'd bought off John Hegarty (more about him later). Besides Bob Miller and me, there was Nigel May and my Art Director at PKL, John "Jelly Roll" Horton.

A red light kept on showing on the dashboard and the car crept to a halt on Christmas Eve in a French village called, appropriately, Void. The hotelier put our car's battery on charge overnight and we joined the locals for a celebratory dinner. It included shellfish, which I avoided, being allergic to them.

Christmas morning the village turned out to wave us goodbye. Shortly after, the others begged me to stop and got out of the car to throw up. Yes, the shellfish had their revenge.

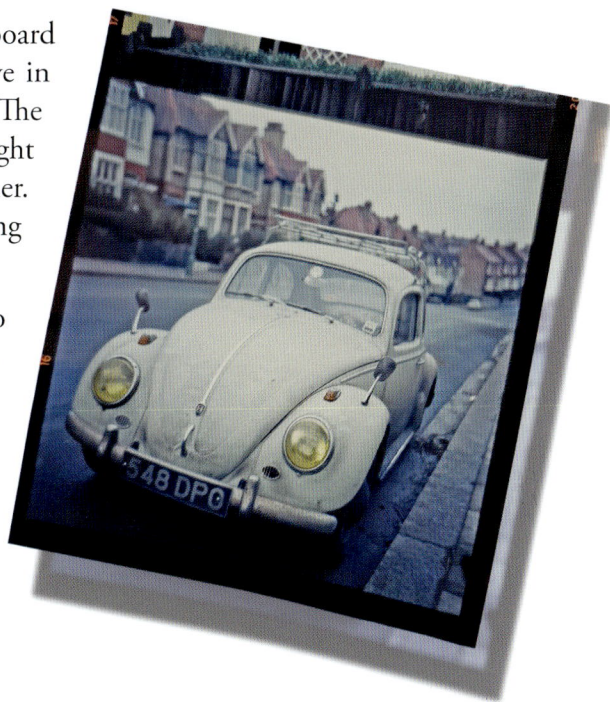

The Guilty Party.

We finally got to Switzerland, but not without taking a wrong turn at a railway crossing and finding ourselves on the railway track.

I managed to find a garage open to replace our battery. And we spent a wonderful few days with trips on the vehicular railway into the mountains.

This proved to be a life saver, as the battery died again, on a mountain pass, when we were heading back home. We 'slept' in the car and shivered all night. I remember my face sticking to the frosty window.

Next morning, Nigel saw that the brushes on the dynamo were but a memory. He used the card of the train tickets to create a temporary brush that miraculously worked and got us closer to the French coast, and home.

The car did come to a halt eventually in a small French town whose name I can't remember. I decided to go to the Gendarme and explain our plight. The others weren't keen as it was the time of student riots in Paris.

The sergeant at the police station was magnificent. I explained that *"Moi voiture c'est Kaput"*. He seemed to understand as he rang the *garage electrique* and ordered them to have our car repaired by the next morning. He then rang the local hotel and got us booked in. By now I had a streaming cold, but the hotel gave me a hot whiskey, water and aspirin that did the repair job.

We finally got home safely only for me to discover that my Mum had been moved from the Barnet Hospital to the Highgate Hospital, and the Neurological ward, where she had slipped into a coma. She stayed in that state for six months before dying of TB and Meningitis.

She was one tough, amazing woman who punctuated my young years with laughter in the house and her singing in the kitchen. Many more tales too numerous to mention here. Mum, I love you and thanks for all your sacrifices.

Mum and I in our local 'greenery', Victoria Park, in Finchley.

Note: for the sake of economy my Mum would roll her own cigarettes and I would be sent across the road to the off licence/bottle shop to buy tobacco for her (you could back then).

She had a device made by Rizla, who made the cigarette papers, and a perfectly rolled cigarette would be the end result, well for those skilled enough, like my Mum.

I liked a Watney Red Barrel beer promotion that was a keyring with the red barrel attached. I would ask for an *"ad-vertise-ment"* with Irish pronunciation and would be corrected by the shop keeper to say *"adver-tis-ement"*.

Whom is to say who was right?

Being "banged out" at the end of my apprenticeship as a compositor, an old printing tradition. I was a slimmer version then. Sorry to have possibly scared all you good people but these photos mark a serious point of transition for me. Transition, not Trannie.

The Accidental Copywriter.

After my years as an apprentice, I became a Journeyman Compositor in 1965.

The day saw my 'Banging Out' ceremony where, at noon, an unholy racket is made by everyone in the company banging whatever came to hand.

Then the other apprentices got their 'revenge' by dressing me in women's clothing (and smothering me in porridge, and anything else that came to hand.

I was then paraded through the local streets, much to the bewilderment of residents. Luckily, the company had a shower so I could get cleaned up ready for the shot with the van.

One of the students in our design class at the LCP, Jim Shurmer, was talent spotted by our design lecturer, as Jim had beautiful cursive handwriting. He was moved out of our class and into one that concentrated on graphic design all day.

I was very jealous and said so at our morning break. Phil Mason[†], who was in my class, agreed with me that this is what we wanted.

I asked the college who was running the course and discovered that it was the wonderful Cal Swann (now living in Perth WA and, before that, Head of Design at the South Australia University).

He was based in another area of London, in Back Hill, where the LCP had its design school. It was quite a walk from Stamford Street in the Elephant & Castle where we were based.

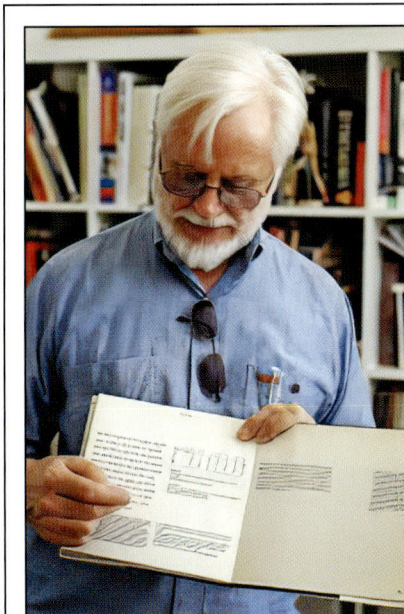

Cal Swan. *He was awarded Honorary Fellowship of ISTD in recognition of his significant and outstanding contribution to graphic design and typography, throughout his long career in industry and design education. During his five-decade career, Cal pioneered typography through practice and teaching – never losing sight of his 'hot-metal' roots.*

Somehow or other I managed to make contact and fix an interview for Phil and myself. Cal agreed to take us both on if our employers agreed. I'm glad to say that they did; in both our cases.

I think they had accepted me as a lost cause to design anyway.

In the class were also Martyn Walsh and Paul Walter (fellow Compositors) who both went on to become award-winning Art Directors and designers. Cal was a great teacher, and, because of him, I wrote a thesis entitled, *The Humanisation of Post-war Swiss typography.*

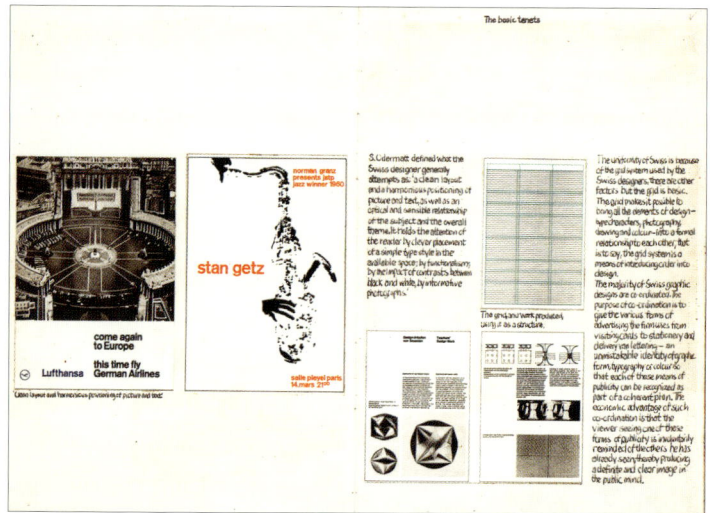

Thanks to Letraset and my best joined up handwriting, to a grid of course.

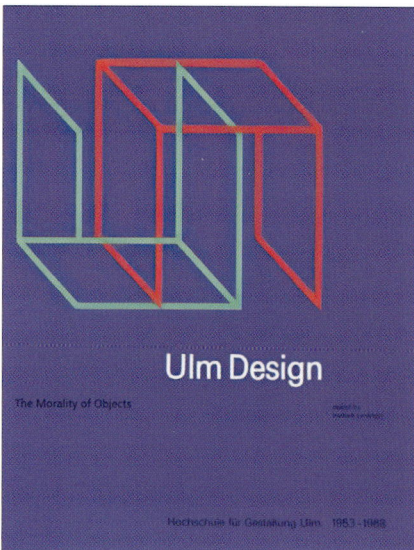

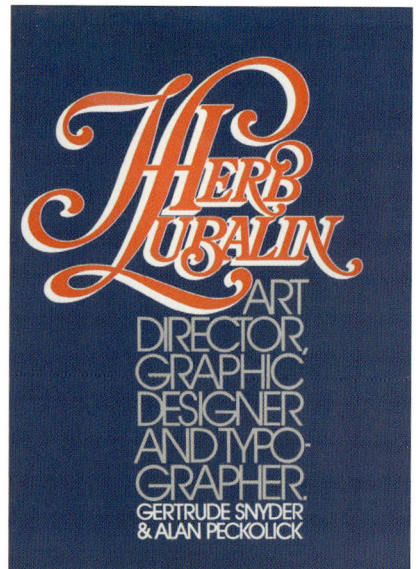

My two sources of inspiration were the Ulm School of Design in Germany and Herb Lubalin in New York. Both were enormously helpful in sending me material I could use to illustrate my thesis. Images: Lubalin: Amazon.com and 'Ulm Design, The Morality of objects' book cover.

The Degree Design course was so impressed that the head of the department, the famous poster designer Tom Eckersley[†], offered me a place on the degree course. I declined as I heard that the graduates from the course couldn't get work and were employed as porters at Harrods. Nevertheless, I realised that design, or something related, was how I wanted to spend my life.

So, after finishing my apprenticeship, I applied for the Vocational Design course at the LCP and was accepted.

Working as a "Comp" for a year and with as much overtime as I could handle, I had managed to stash some money away to fall back on.

Martyn and Paul, as well as Phil, joined me and some other outstanding talents. Geoff Seymour[†], Larry Franklin, Barry Craddock, John Knight[†] to name but a few.

Geoff Seymour was also in my class and was the D'Artagnan to we Three Musketeers; Phil, Martyn and me. Three apprentice Compositors, each with a widowed mother.
He went on to a highly successful career in advertising and was once the most highly paid in the business, with a 'currency' named after him. People would say they were on "half a Seymour" or £50,000. As a forewarning of what was to come, Geoff turned up on our first day wearing a Jaeger Suit with a Pentax slung over his shoulder.

The LCP White City Boys who were in my class. L-R: Larry Franklin, John Knight (then in silk screen printing), David Bouquet and Barry Craddock sporting the pipe.

Location set, courtesy of Adolf Hitler I think. L-R: Paul Walter (not from the White City), Larry Franklin, David Bouquet, Barry Craddock, sadly unknown.

Frederick Charles Herrick (1887–1970)

Was this where the seed was sown for the White City Boys? A bit early, even for me.

Martyn Walsh
My headline for this ad was:
**"Bread and water? Great!
As long as the bread is Hovis."**

Credits: *Location: a bomb site in the Elephant & Castle. Convict outfit made by my Mum.
Pickaxe belonged to my Grandad. Model, a friend.*

*One of **Barry Craddock's** illustrations for the CDP Heineken campaign,*
'Refreshes the parts other beers cannot reach.

*Examples of work by **Larry Franklin**. There was so much talent in our class, we were also lucky as well as being born at the right time.*
Image: Larry Franklin.

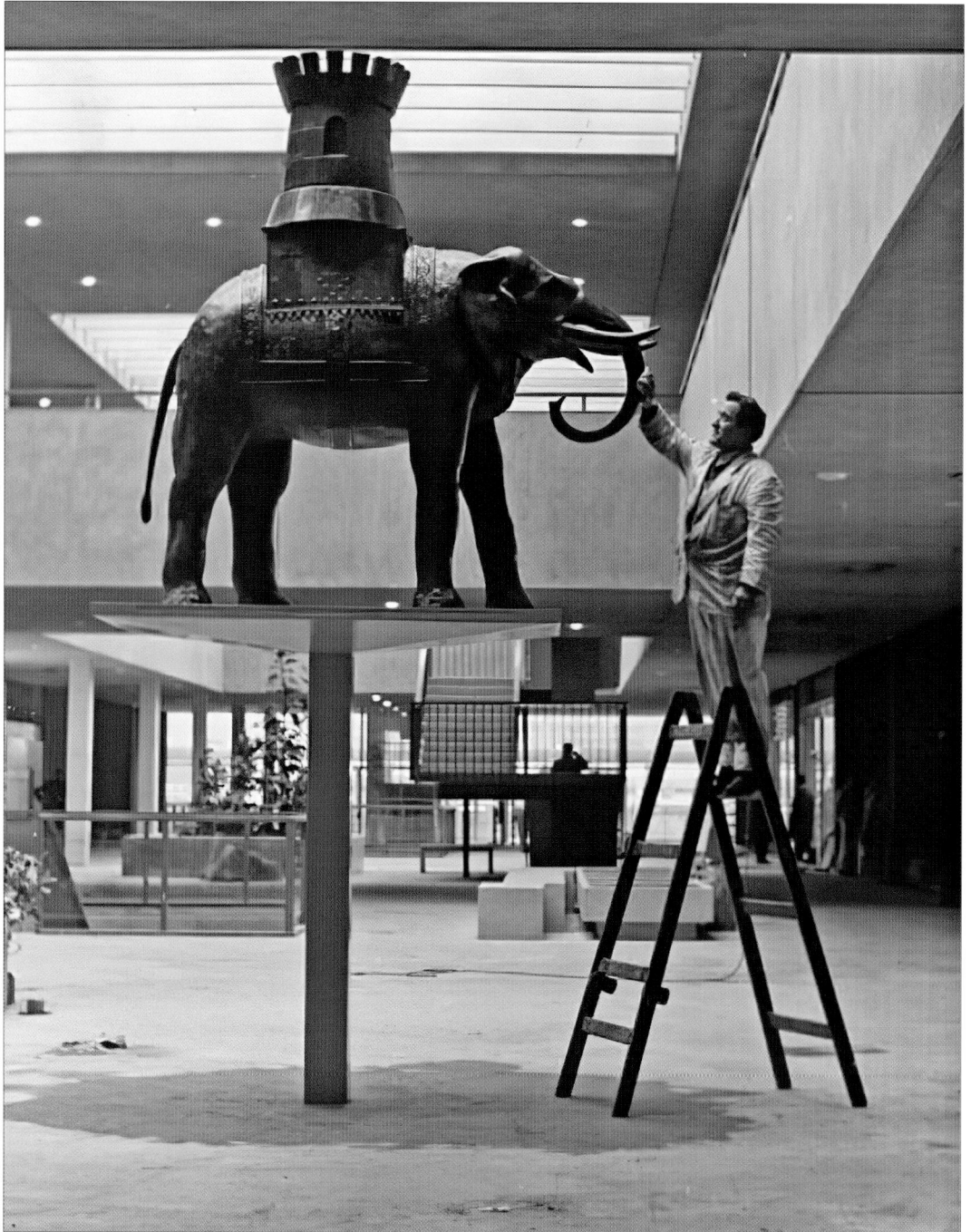

A monument to our college's location.

Other memories from Larry Franklin Tom Eckersley, Freddie lambert Derek Birdsall Michael Forman ,Jim Downey ,Steve Hiett , Rosie de Meric, Carole finer , and many more. We were based in the vinegar factory annex.

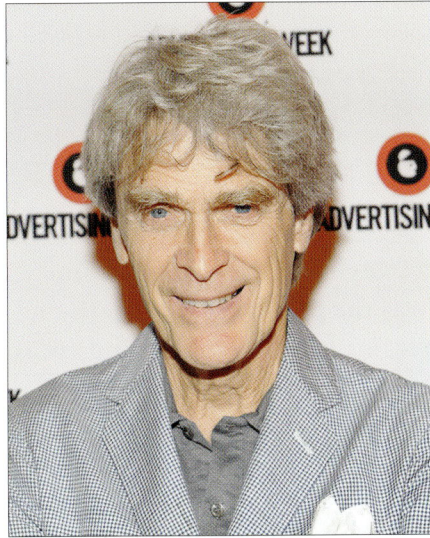

Sir John Hegarty.
Photo of John by Opal Turner,
taken from his book, Hegarty on
Advertising.

Enter "The Heg" into my life.

I'm reminded of the saying, "To succeed in life, it's not what you know but who you know." As an apprentice Compositor at the LCP, I had day release as a student. In those days it was considered cool to wear a college scarf (purple, blue and white stripes). I had noticed this bloke (it was John Hegarty) around Finchley wearing the scarf and then spotted him in the college canteen. Let me make it clear, I was not stalking him, although it may sound like that. This was where John Hegarty (Now Sir John and pictured above) stepped into my life in a major way.

On my first day as a full-time student I'm standing on Finchley Central Tube Station with scarf and portfolio. John walked up to me, introduced himself and asked what I'm up to.

I told him and he advised me that most of the lecturers were rubbish but to contact one called John Gillard [†][*].

Sadly, he has also moved 'upstairs' but this was said about him by John Hegarty in an obituary:

> **"It was John more than anybody else who made me want to do advertising.**
> **He was the Pied Piper of creative talent.**
> **People became better just by being around him."**

For a year I gave the College the benefit of the doubt but came to the conclusion that John was right.

Phil and I had a Christmas gig as interns at a design company run by a man called Frank Overton. He was designing the house style for British Ropes and asked me to create a presentation rough as to how an invoice would look.

I had already failed in lettering at College, providing much chuckling at my poorly formed Trajan Capitals[‡].

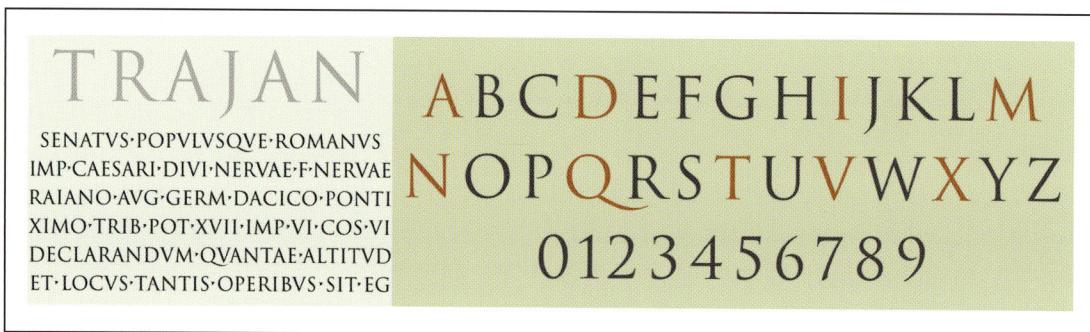

Frank realised that I was not going to be of any help and just indulged me and Phil for a fortnight, but a light was glittering in my brain saying a rethink of my future may be in order.

I made contact with the other John (Gillard) and he accepted Phil and I onto his course. On our first day he dropped the prestigious Design and Art Direction (D&AD) Annual in the wastepaper bin and said, "That's history. The future is with you." Or words to that effect.

*Sadly, I couldn't find a photo of John Gillard anywhere. Many years later I had bought a holiday home in Bishop's Castle, Shropshire where I bumped into John and discovered that he was living there, And, indeed, he was buried with a ceremony at the parish church.

‡ The design is based on the letterforms of capitalis monumentalis or Roman square capitals, as used for the inscription at the base of Trajan's Column in Rome.

The 'Heg' was now a Junior Art Director at the Benton & Bowles agency in Knightsbridge. He invited me over for my first advertising lunch.

There was no alcohol, but it was at the Spaghetti House and I ordered Veal escallop and spaghetti. I had never had anything as exotic as that, let alone learnt how to manage the 'worms'.

John was very patient and non-judgmental as I took forever.

Not the Knightsbridge branch mentioned but the one at Goodge Street, which became a bit of a canteen for me at various times.

Note: another former LCP graduate, Doug Maxwell, who had gone on to be Head of Art at Doyle Dane Bernbach, put on an exhibition of the agency's fabulous work in the College reception. The College put a disclaimer note that the exhibition had nothing to do with them. Talk about the writing being on the wall. The exhibition certainly whetted my appetite. In our classroom I had already put on an exhibition of the inspiring Esquire magazine covers designed by an ex-DDB Art Director, George Lois, the 'Lois' of Papert, Koenig, Lois, later to feature in my career.

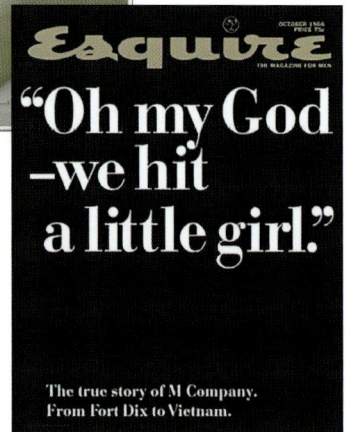

George Lois.
Art Director and one of the Founders of Papert, Koenig, Lois. He has also been described as one of the original Madmen.
Image: 99u.adobe.com

Images for the three covers: theguardian.com. Image for garbage bin: moma.org.

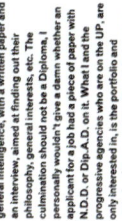

*The article beneath was published in the LCP student magazine, '**Proof**' published June 1965.*

Here it is:

People say the truth hurts. If 'people' are right then quite a lot of you are going to be hurt.

Having left College, with no Diploma and no training some nine months ago, I have come to the conclusion that the present set-up in design education is all wrong. The Old National Diploma of Design was a useless examination and the new Diploma of Art and Design seems equally as bad.
Bad for the following reasons:

1. When students leave college the majority of them will be going into advertising. The Diploma of Art and Design in no way trains them for this 'outside' world. It is not a world of beautiful shapes and textures. That is the painter's world.
It is the world of Visual Communications.
The idea being to help people understand, to persuade and to set the pace in the best possible way.
The Diploma of Art and Design was supposed to be heading in this direction, but when I see students painting and making puppets, I despair.
What the hell has all this got to do with selling by use of image and copy?
2. There is no emphasis or copy(words). Copy is very important, nobody has yet sold anything with just a picture.
3. When the students in the course aren't painting or making puppets, they are dabbling in Graphic Design or Typography. I say dabbling with good reason, because I am sure that most of them would rather be painters anyway.
Go on, go ahead paint. But don't come around to an Ad agency with drawings. We're not interested.
What does a 3 year course in Typography result in? I'll tell you. It means that you will be working as a paste up man and spend many a tedious hour casting type for an Ad or booklet, under the close direction of an Art Director. You'll have very little say. You'll be as frustrated as hell.
Why?
You may think you don't deserve this fate. I'm sorry to say you do! Top ad agencies like mine are looking for creative, provocative and imaginative work. To crystallize this, we want and what the Ad business as a whole needs is men with ideas.
We don't want people with posters for Art Exhibitions, record sleeves, book jackets and pharmaceutical booklets. This is partially the fault of the college principals, the lecturers and the courses they run. It's also YOU the students fault, you sit back and put up with one sided, biased beyond belief teaching.

A word about the Lecturers:
There are far too many second and third rate painters trying to teach visual communication. Designers who have had little experience in the commercial world. Oh yes, they free lance, but they know virtually nothing about the Ad business; handing out the same corny briefs, year after year, after year.
Some colleges employ ex-students almost immediately after they have left. So what they are doing is ploughing the old ideas back in, with no added experience.
The only conclusion that I can come to is that the lecturers and the lecturing is unsatisfactory, to put it mildly.

The colleges are also at fault with:
1. The selection of students. Acceptance is far too easy, the criterion being whether the would be student is a good 'drawer'. You don't have to be able to draw to do an Ad. Don't get me wrong, I don't object to design students who can draw. I object when drawing becomes the be-all and end-all of their philosophy. Because whether they like it or no, after their four years training, most will be going into advertising. It is only fair that I tell you all now that the Fletcher/Forbes/ Gill set-up is on the wane. There are too many small Graphic groups for the market.
The colleges lead the students to believe that this is the ultimate in visual communications —it is not.
2. The colleges do not promote the advertising side of design at all. In many colleges it is regarded as a dirty word. I don't advocate the dissolution of 'Graphic' design (I wouldn't mind if it did come to an end though) but I do feel that the course should be sub-divided into:
(a) Graphics and (b) Advertising.

After 3 months, students should be able to choose which branch they want to specialize in, having been taught both simultaneously during this period. The course will continue shorter.
Here it is:

3 months General advertising and Graphic education.
1 year Choice of advertising—
copywriting, design, photography, economics, business administration and technology of reproductive processes.
9 months Practical application: Visiting agencies, creation of campaigns, specific deadlines for work (unheard of in colleges).

Practising specialists, copywriters, photographers, art directors should be employed all the time to supplement present staff. On student selection, the basis to be general intelligence, with a written paper and an interview, aimed at finding out their philosophy, general interests, etc. The culmination should not be a Diploma. I personally wouldn't give a damn whether an applicant for a job had a piece of paper with N.D.D. or Dip.A.D. on it. What I and the progressive agencies who are on the UP, are only interested in, is the portfolio and attitude of the applicant. Most of the people I've seen have had some sort of certificate, this has usually meant a dull, conservative, non-advertising folio. I know that advertising, if you judge from the majority of ads that appear, do not seem very glamorous, or hold much hope for the creative person. This is the result of years of cockeyed training; training which is not improving. As long as we have bad teachers and inadequately trained students, the business will continue to be the same.

How do you ask, does a good agency work?
Well, I happen to be very lucky, I work for one. A really good one, its called, Doyle, Dane, Bernbach. Its American owned and has won over 500 medals for brilliant creative advertising. Now there aren't many like D.D.B, but there could be.
How do we work? It's simple:—
1. The Art Director and copywriter are left to work out the idea for a campaign, rather cares who has the visual idea or who writes the headlines. The primary concern is a good advertising campaign.
2. We believe in the truth. Whatever we say about our product must be born out when the public buys the product.
3. We go after simplification in our ads.

4. We buy the best photography and art available.
5. The Art Director does his own typography and has complete control over the ad.
6. The Account Executive does not interfere in the creative work and the campaign we give him is 'it'. —no alterations.
7. We have no new business department. We never take up a campaign to woo a client. Clients come to us, which is a nice position to be in.
I doubt if we can change the whole set up overnight, so what advice can I give to you who are stuck with it as it is. Do ads and become a lot more professional with all the elements that go to making an ad. Set and choose your type in the best way you can, cut up the repro pulls, move it around before mounting. Don't treat copy as a grey mass, balancing a picture, treat it as a vital part of the ad. Work with a photographer and get experience in directing photography. Don't be content with the first idea, work round it and see how it stands up after a few days. Don't think about 'layout' until the idea is right otherwise you'll find yourself designing for designs' sake, ugh!

Douglas Maxwell was a student in the Business Administration department at the London College of Printing from 1961-1964, the last three months of this course. During 1963 and '64 he was Editor of Proof, employed in two advertising agencies since leaving college is now an Art Director at Doyle Dane & Bernbach Ltd.

A welcome warning from Doug Maxwell. *The truth about employment in advertising, post College.*

A sobering read for many LCP students. The truth about employment in advertising, post College.

Intern Doyle.
Not the best of starts.

Enter John Hegarty again, and my wanting to get an internship in an advertising agency for the Summer holidays.

John contacted Roy Carruthers[†], an award-winning Art Director at Collett, Dickenson, Pearce (CDP). I heard nothing back so I started to phone Roy every week. Eventually he weakened and agreed for me to come in, unpaid of course, for a few weeks.

Sadly, or luckily, I failed at the first hurdle. He gave me one of his Acrilan ads to mount. In those days they were like a work of art with mounts, masks etc.

Although we were supposed to be being trained for studio work at the LCP, we never had any craft lessons. So, at CDP I was given some card, a scalpel, a tin of 'Cow' gum and a spreader.

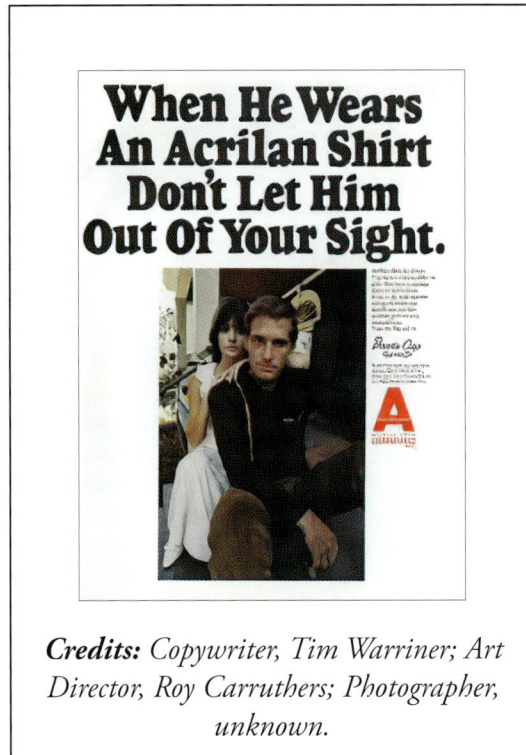

Credits: *Copywriter, Tim Warriner; Art Director, Roy Carruthers; Photographer, unknown.*

To say it was a disaster would be an understatement. Roy was very forgiving and, wisely, gave me no more tasks but did give me career advice as to how I had to be a Creative Director by the time I was 30.

I was in my early 20s so no pressure and, why wasn't he a CD? Wisely, for once, I kept quiet.

Roy Caruthers' artwork.

Dawson Yeoman.
He did help me become a better copywriter

Roy was from South Africa. He had left CDP before I was hired as a copywriter, years later. He had gone to live in America where he built a successful career as an artist. He died in 2013.

I was passed on to another Art Director, the wonderful Alan Brooking, who set me some briefs. So, I started taking my first stab at writing copy. Alan then passed me on to Dawson Yeoman[†] who was working at CDP. Dawson previously had worked at Doyle Dane Bernbach (DDB), and was later to return there, becoming my immediate boss and coaching me in the art and craft of copywriting.

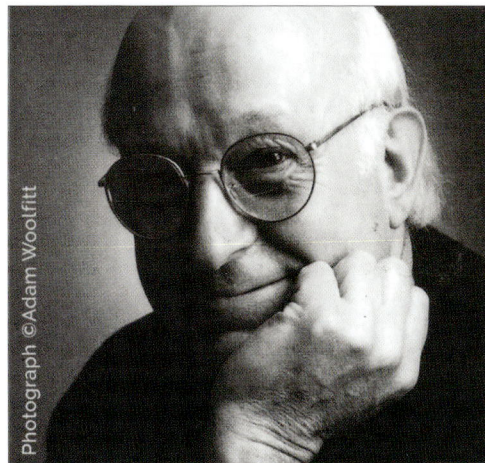

Alan Brooking.
Image taken from his book Who Shot the Pregnant Man?

The Creative Director at CDP, Colin Millward, saw my portfolio and advised me to look for a job as an agency typographer. Perfectly understandable if you looked at the evidence. But my brain was rewiring itself.

Dawson then kindly passed me on to David Abbott[†] who was Creative Director at DDB. David also gave me briefs and critiqued my work. He was amazingly generous with his time in coaching me.

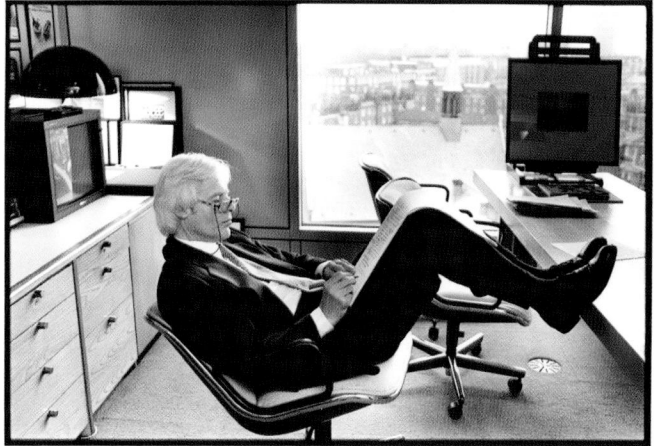

David Abbott.
My memory of David at French, Gold, Abbott was similar to this. He would sit back in his chair and talk his copy out loud to make sure it had the conversational tone that he was looking for.
Image: The oneclub.org.

Meanwhile John Hegarty asked me to help him with writing for a freelance job he had for a New York department store. I don't think I was of any help at all, but John was now at an agency called John Collings in Soho Square.

What is it with all these Johns?

I would visit occasionally and met John O'Driscoll for the first time, lucky old me, and Ruth Franklin; lovely lady and one-time girlfriend.

It was also my first meeting with Lindsay Dale[†] who would later hire me for his group at CDP.

I remember Charles Saatchi also visiting from CDP and his Italian luxury sports car parked outside (it was either a Ferrari or a Maserati). So, this is advertising I thought; I like.

Still at CDP, on my internship, I was moved into the office of Charles Saatchi and Ross Cramer. I was a tad star struck as I loved the ads they were creating for Selfridges.

'Charlie', as he was known at the time, offered me a job as a junior copywriter and I turned him down. I wanted what John H was doing which, in my naivety, looked like he was doing the whole show, copy & art.

Not long after, John had a bad illness, which I seem to recall was because of overwork. So, I decided to concentrate on copy.

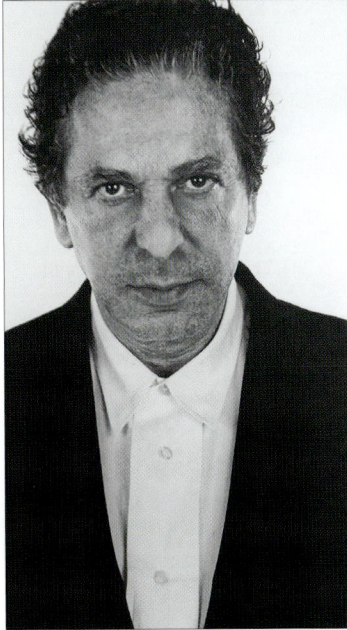

Charles Saatchi.
'Charlie', at a later age, with his gallery and an art collection that's world famous. Doesn't look too happy though. Photo taken from his book Be the Worst You Can Be. *Pre or Post Nigella, I'm not sure.*

Every week, Phil Mason used to come up on the Northern line Tube from Balham in South London to visit me in Finchley, North London to hear my stories about CDP and life in advertising.

I've never lost my love for type and typography.

Postscript from Alan Brooking:
You're so right about our good fortune in being on this earth back in those glorious 60s and 70s. What a magical era that was, certainly compared with the horrors of today. All we had to worry about was getting nuked!

The challenge.

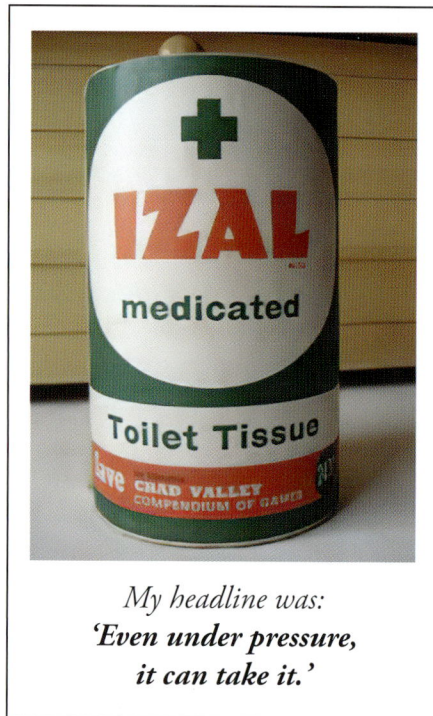

My headline was:
**'Even under pressure,
it can take it.'**

Realizing my passion for advertising, one of our lecturers at the LCP, the acclaimed illustrator Michael Foreman, set me a challenge to create advertising for Izal Medicated Toilet Paper.

Maybe he meant to dampen my enthusiasm.

In my naivety, I decided to do some market research into why people chose their toilet paper.

Many, in those days at the lower end of the social ladder, just used torn up bits of newspaper stuck on a nail in the toilet.

So I set to, initially in well-heeled suburbs like Hampstead and Chelsea.

I remember in Chelsea they preferred pink paper and one that was "soft to the bot".

It was relevant, as Izal was very hard.

I also trod the streets of the Elephant & Castle district, where the college was based, but that was more for users of the newspaper technique.

Look out advertising, here I come!

As I started to look for full-time employment John Hegarty, bless him, again came to my rescue. He rang John Webster[†] who was a group head at Pritchard Wood at the time, suggesting he should see me.

I went for the interview which had Maggie Randall, the TV producer, bopping about to reggae and Brian Mindell, the copy group head, wearing leather trousers.

All very exotic, coming from Finchley. Although my best friend at Saint James' Secondary Modern was Sterling Lee Wo, who was from Trinidad, and whose house was full of this wonderful music.

John Webster immediately went to the Creative Director, Gabe Massimi[†], and I was offered the job on the spot.

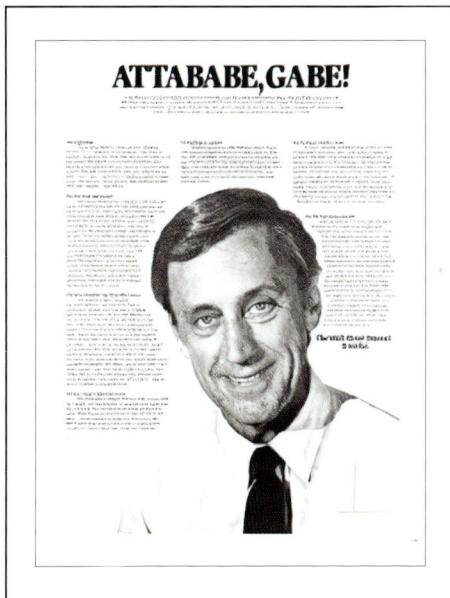

It always puzzled me what part Gabe played in writing the Canada Dry ad. In the New York Art Director's annual where four writers were credited. He was a very nice man though, not a bad epitaph for anyone. Images: Dave Dye.

It seems I was the first student John had seen that actually had ads in his/her portfolio. And more to the point, my research impressed John, given the importance of research/planning at PWP where Stanley Pollitt had pioneered Planning, this unique form for the researching of advertising.

John Webster.
*Said to be the best writer of TV advertising in Britain, if not the world. My first wife, Maggie[†], was hired as his PA and then progressed to be TV Producer. John lived at Hadley, near me in High Barnet.
Image: The Drum.*

Note: John's wife, Maureen (who had been Colin Millward's secretary at CDP) , waved John off to work one morning as a tradesman arrived. He asked what John did for a crust and Maureen told him "advertising". The "Tradie" then rattled off a list of his favourite ads, and they were all by John's fair hand. With a little help from others, of course.

Phil had been hired at CDP by Alan Parker as a Copywriter but after a year resigned to join me at PWP as my Art Director. Colin Millward, bemused, asked him why he was leaving. Phil said, "I'm going to where all the action is Colin". Colin never let him forget that and when Phil returned later to work at CDP, Colin would ask him, "How's the action Philip?"

So, there you have it, my long and winding road to becoming a copywriter. No grammar school, no university but some wonderful and generous people, not the least being the "HEG". God bless him, I say, for a wonderful life and career

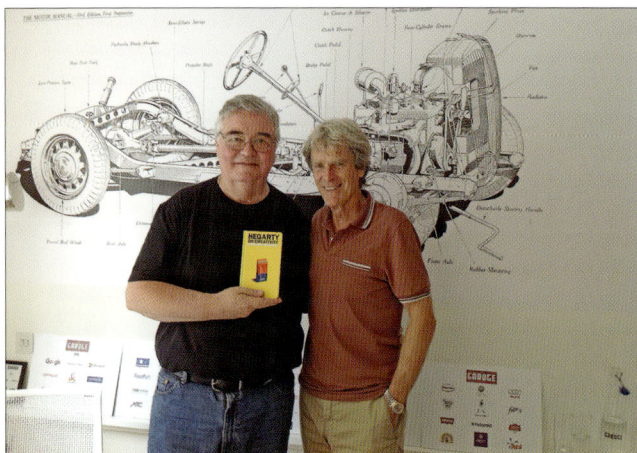

Me with the "Heg".
In 2016 I was able to visit and thank John for all his help at his new agency, 'Garage'.

Some of the cast of other people who would play a part in my life in advertising.

Taken at the Chelsea Arts Club during my first return to the UK in 2011 since leaving for Australia in 1990.
L-R: Jemmy Gray (Illustrator and Master of Fun at BBDO); Bob Miller, (Photographer) who also went to my school; Arthur Robbins (One of the world's great cartoonists/ illustrators); John O'Driscoll, (Art Director), organiser of the lunch and a good friend ever since I first met him at John Collings; Seated: Alan Brooking, (Photographer), one of my first mentors.

The rocky ride starts here.

In 1967 I commenced my career as a copywriter in advertising at Pritchard Wood and Partners (PWP) answering to the legendary John Webster. My career had many highs and lows with me both in and out of work, hence the Rollercoaster image.

Following are my memories and adaptations of a number of posts I made about my career, roughly twice a week online, through Facebook. I hope you enjoy the road/ride/read.

One view of my life in advertising.

Chapter
Two

1967 to 1968 (Under Starter's orders).

Pritchard Wood & Partners (PWP)

✝

My life as a very Junior Copywriter.

After he left LCP, Phil Mason and I ended up working simultaneously at a number of agencies: PKL, BBDO, CDP but we first worked together, as a team, at Pritchard Wood.

Phil Mason.
His balancing act at my wedding reception.

Sadly, I have next to nothing to show for my brief time at PWP. I had to leave Phil, as I received an offer I couldn't refuse from David Abbott to work at Doyle Dane Bernbach. I think Phil did forgive me, eventually.

The photo of Phil's famous balancing act (thanks for this to David Gardner) was taken at my wedding reception with the portrait of Elena Salvoni[†] watching over.

Awash with champagne, the rest of us tried it, without success, as Phil wasn't as hairy as the rest of us.

I met so many great, clever and very funny people in advertising, but Phil will always have a special place in my heart. He would always ask me what weight I was whenever he rang me in Australia. I've no idea why.

Rick Cook[†] used to say while I was in the Northern Hemisphere and Mike Chandler[†], who was of similar (generous) build to me was Downunder, the planet was balanced. The rascal.

> **Note:** One bonus to having been a so-called 'mature' student (I was now in my 20s) was that, although I was a junior, many thought I was more experienced.

Facebook comments regarding Phil Mason & PWP:

Greg Alder He of the rubber chicken feet. I didn't ask where he got them. He went to lunch with human feet and came back with giant chicken feet. A funny man.

Arthur Robins To this day I miss Phil, too young too soon.

Sandra Leamon I started as his copywriter at Pritchard Wood and ended up his best friend until death us did part. Sad but we had some brilliant laughs and the best holidays ever. Dearest Phil. To this day I have a framed photo on the wall of him wearing a bridesmaid's hat and carrying the bouquet!

Jon Parkinson Remembered when all four of you PKL boys arrived at CPV and I was a baby Assistant Art Director. You Phil, John Horton and John Kelley were great inspiration to me even though I then ran off to The London Film School shortly after. So sad Phil passed away so young.

Scott J Graham Great stories Mike.

Max Henry As usual. A great story of so many Gods in advertising brilliantly told. Thanks Mike

First & almost last.

Another first for me was working on the Land-Rover account. The test drive was alarming to say the least, having to drive a Defender down an almost vertical slope, something I would never have asked of my Beetle.

Little did I think that, many moons and half the world away, I would be finally writing ads and material for this client again at the final chapter of my career.

I was 'tickled' to find two of my ads in the 'Classics' section of an American Land-Rover magazine. A small claim to fame. Another ad in the campaign had the headline, *How to go site-seeing in comfort.* While the third showed a line-up of Land-Rovers built as an ambulance, a fire engine and a flatbed with the headline *Please tell us how to build a Land-Rover.* More to come in my second book on my Australian Land-Rover experiences, further down the track.

2 for the price of 1

Is the strategy showing?
I could only get better.

My PWP Generation.

Gabe Massimi (Creative Director), John Webster, Brian Mindel (Group Heads), Vernon Howe, Phil Mason. Apologies to anyone that I've missed.

Fond memories of John Webster. Legend and my first advertising boss.

Brilliantly creative advertising man behind a string of popular commercials.

By Winston Fletcher.

As creative director of the agency Boase Massimi Pollitt (BMP), John Webster, who has died aged 71, was one of advertising creativity's towering figures in the second half of the 20th century. Between 1970 and 2000, he created many of television's most memorable campaigns, loved by the public and garlanded with awards.

Among his figures were the Cadbury's Smash Martians, the Sugar Puffs Honey Monster, the St Ivel Prize Guys and two delightfully different bears for Cresta and Hofmeister, as well as Chas and Dave's 'Gertcha' commercial for Courage beer and the Arkwright dog and Jack Dee campaigns for John Smith's bitter. All won prizes at international festivals.

In a completely different style, he created a Coty L'Aimant campaign which won him one of his two Grand Prix at Cannes, and - for the Guardian itself - the dramatic

Points of View spot which was voted the British best ad of the 1980s. His contribution to the high esteem in which British advertising is held has been inestimable. However, his inventiveness and originality might not have burgeoned so prodigiously but for two other factors - his remarkably resilient and absorbent personality, and the agency in which he worked.

John was an only child, born in Paris, where his father worked for Unilever, and the family did not leave France until the German occupation. He was educated at St Peter's school, York, and Hendon county school. During national service in the RAF, he worked in photography and later, when almost 30, attended Hornsey College of Art. He hoped to become a painter, an ambition to which he returned in the years before he died.

The fact that John entered advertising relatively late in life turned out to serve him well. Commercial television was little more than a decade old, and although he created some fine posters early in his career, an aptitude for TV was John's true metier.

John was the antithesis of the caricature advertising man. Though supremely confident of his own talent, he was never arrogant, did not push himself forward, dressed unexceptionally, threw no tantrums and accepted good ideas from others gracefully, including ideas from clients, something few advertising creative people will countenance. This open-mindedness allowed him to deploy his creativity in an era when focus groups and market research began to play an increasingly intrusive role in advertising.

Just as he was willing to absorb other people's comments, he accepted and exploited the findings of research on his ideas. This is a rare ability. But it was essential at BMP (now DDB London), which he helped to found in 1969, and in which he spent the rest of his career.

Until BMP, British advertising agencies tended to be either creatively-focused or research-focused, and those that were creatively-focused generally sneered at market research, believing creativity to be embedded solely in flair and intuition. But as their clients increasingly employed research to improve the effectiveness of their marketing, for agencies to deride it was ostrich-like. BMP bridged the creativity-research chasm by inventing a system it called "account planning", which is today used by agencies worldwide and provides advertising people with the public's reactions to their ideas while the ideas are still being formulated.

For John, this was perfect. He was a perfectionist who constantly dabbled with, and refined, his own work, sometimes rewriting scripts during a shoot, or even after the shoot had been completed - to the chagrin of colleagues and clients alike. They might not have put up with it had they not liked and admired John so much, and this was another way in which he was different from many creative people.

He was immensely popular and a team player, both literally and metaphorically. He played cricket and golf for his agency - though even he would not have claimed to be great shakes at either - and he was generous to a fault in devoting time to the encouragement and training of young people.

John could not have worked the account planning system so effectively had he not been immensely fecund. Inevitably, the research process kills off some creative ideas, as well as backing and improving others. Only somebody as imaginative as John was could repeatedly come up with fresh ideas, until they find exactly the right one for the job. And only somebody that talented has the modesty and confidence to accept the research's criticisms of their work in progress. For John, the end result was a world-renowned body of original and loved TV advertising.

In the account planning process, the public is quick to damn corny, pushy or dislikeable ideas. This suited John down to the ground. Because he believed they would be more effective, he wanted to create advertisements which people would welcome into their homes. He is survived by his wife Maureen and three children.

John Webster, advertising creative director, born December 17 1934; died January 6 2006.
The Guardian.

Note: It has been said that John had a bit of a mean streak but I encountered nothing but generosity. For example, when my first child was born, as a 'birthday' gift he said we could have the free run of his villa in Provence for as long as we liked. It was a beautiful house with pool, overlooking vineyards and close to the beautiful town of Cotignac. In fact, he was generous enough to let us stay there over a number of years. All I had to do was cut the grass and leave the place as I would wish to find it.

'Under his *(John Webster's)* **influence, British advertising could justly claim to be the best in the world.'**

'Creative Review' quote from the book, John Webster. The Earth People's Ad Man.

A tribute to John from Dave Trott.

One of the legends of British creative advertising, John Webster, the brains behind such creations as the Smash Martians and the Honey Monster, died suddenly earlier this month while out jogging. **Dave Trott** *pays tribute.*

The Independent. Monday 16 January 2006 .

John Webster: Simply the best.

I was the first person John Webster hired when he was made creative director of BMP (Boase Massimi Pollitt). He was the only creative director I ever worked for. I kept trying to leave for better-paid jobs, I even got as far as handing in my notice a few times, but every time, it felt that I'd be wasting a once-in-a-lifetime opportunity to learn from the best there was. And, yes, he was that good.

John won more creative awards than most agencies put together. Everyone knows that. But what you may not know is that he never ever tried to win an award. That was one of the things you learned from John.

Let me try to bring that to life. One year I won a Cannes Gold Lion for a commercial that I'd written. I felt pretty good. The same year John won three Gold Lions for commercials he'd written, another three for commercials he'd art-directed, and another three for commercials he'd actually directed himself. Nine times as many as me. Or, to put it another way, three times as many as anyone else in any field in our business. And that was just one year.

The awards just used to arrive in boxes, stacked up in reception. John didn't go to Cannes to collect the awards, of course. He never did. The people John wanted to impress were not in Cannes - they were in Stoke Newington, Liverpool and Sunderland, on the bus, in the supermarket, in the playground.

The real awards to John were the photographs in the newspaper of milkmen who'd decorated their floats with his characters; or the letters from teachers asking if their class could have a still from his commercial; or hearing people in the street shouting his slogan.

I asked John, as he'd just won three times as many awards as any film director, why he didn't become a film director full time and make shed loads more money. John said he couldn't face directing a script that he knew he could have written better.

That's part of what made John different to everyone else in advertising. It wasn't about the money or the awards or the photograph in Campaign, it was about the work.

He was a typically eccentric Englishman. He approached multimillion-pound campaigns as if he were tending prize leeks in his allotment.

As with an absent-minded professor, everything else disappeared except what he was working on. The work came first, second and third.

Consequently, of all the creative greats in the UK, John was the only one not to have his name above the door of an advertising agency. And yet, at BMP, John was the agency. Every year the competition for D&AD awards would be between CDP and BMP (although everyone knew it was actually between CDP and John Webster). To give you another example: one year at D&AD I sat next to Stanley Pollitt, one of the founding partners of BMP. Stanley was particularly pleased that year because BMP had swept the board with six awards. He saw it as a sign of BMP finally achieving creative maturity. Not because we'd won six awards but because, for once, John had only won half of them. The rest of the creative department had finally managed to get as many as John had got on his own.

So how did John do it? What was he doing that no one else was? Well, precisely that. He was doing what no one else was. Purposely. He looked at what everyone else was doing and said: "Let's do something different."

He didn't see advertising as the whole world. He saw it as a very small part of a much, much larger world. So he wasn't competing with other advertising, he was competing for space in people's lives.

He was competing with films, sitcoms, newspapers, radio, any form of mass media that would cause the public to take something into their lives and talk about it, adapt it or use it. That's why, most evenings, you'd find John in his office discussing the ideas he'd had that day. Not with other advertising luminaries, but with Pat the tea-lady, or Arthur the caretaker.

Which, of course, made John a planner's dream to work with. He wasn't interested in what people in advertising thought about his work. They weren't who he was talking to. The people who watched the commercials and bought the product, they were who he was talking to.

This clarity came out of his passion for what he was doing. To John, his work was more than his job, it was also his hobby. To go into his office was like going into his shed. The walls were full of bits and pieces he'd collected that he thought were far too good to waste, and was sure he'd find a use for one day. During the 10 years I worked with John (several decades ago) among all the other stuff, he always had several photocopies of Saul Steinberg drawings above his desk. Recently, I saw John's Compaq computers ad on TV featuring animated versions of Saul Steinberg's drawings. I knew I'd be seeing them sooner or later.

Before starting to write this, I made a list of all the things I'd learned from John. Each one would take an article the size of this one so, as I can't do them justice here, I haven't started.

But I've been teaching advertising students for the past 30 years, and most of what I teach in those classes I learned from John.

I never told anyone before, but over the years since I left BMP, whenever I've done anything I'm proud of, I like to imagine John at home watching TV, and saying: "Look at this, Maureen, that's wonderful. I wonder who did it."

He was the person I most wanted to impress. Even as I'm writing this, I'm wondering what John would have thought of it ("It's a bit boring, isn't it? Can't you put some jokes in?").

But, as I say, John didn't want to impress anyone. He always told me what we did was trivial compared with important jobs, such as nursing or teaching. That sense of perspective gave him the clarity to be much more powerful and truly effective than the rest of us who take advertising too seriously.

He didn't have the rabbit-caught-in-the-headlights reaction to peer-group approval. The peer group John cared about didn't work in advertising.

This was summed up for me by one of those media or marketing magazine interviews. The question that was put to John was something like "What is your media?"

John replied: "I take MG Owner for its recherché indolence, and Art Weekly for the nudes."

With wit and charm John always kept advertising gently but firmly in its place. Which is, of course, why he was always light years ahead of the rest of us.

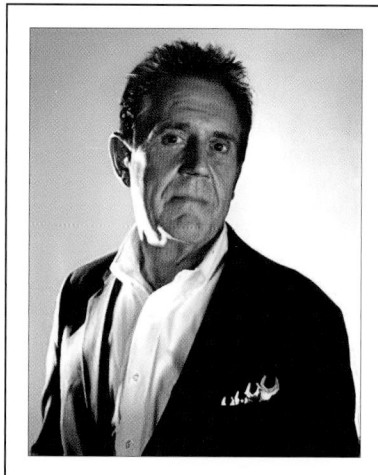

Dave Trott is one of Britain's best-known advertising creatives. He was given the President's Award at the D&AD Awards in 2004.

Chapter
Three

1968 (A busy but very short shelf life).

Doyle Dane Bernbach (DDB)*

A dream fulfilled.

*Now called Adam & Eve DDB after previously merging with BMP.

I owe John O'Driscoll many thanks for finding the snap of me as a very junior, and very wet behind my ears, copywriter at my namesake agency, Doyle Dane Bernbach.

The terrified guy in the Lufthansa ad is yours truly, showing the fear I experienced every time I had to run my copy past my copy chief, Dawson Yeoman.

He had taken me under his wing while I was an intern at Collett, Dickenson, Pearce in the 70s and had then recommended me to David Abbott, the newly appointed Creative Director at DDB.

Dawson was a bit of a bully. Once, while reviewing my copy, probably for this ad, he asked what school I had gone to; talk about a loaded question. I replied, "St James' Secondary Modern, what school did you go to?" He told me, in no uncertain terms, that it was no business of mine.

His secretary was often in tears.

Still on the subject of the copy review, he must have sensed that I was a tad fragile after the 20th rewrite. He told me that that was nothing and that the previous CD, John Withers (He had written the magnificent Chivas Regal Whisky campaign in the US), had made him rewrite his copy 40 times before he was satisfied.

It was a tough schooling and taught me a lot about the craft.

I was briefed to write an ad for a division of Avis that had chauffeur-driven Rolls Royce cars. To get more information about the cars, I went to a local showroom. I clearly did not impress the salesman until, when I gave the office address with my surname on the shingle, everything changed, and he couldn't have been nicer. My revenge was to never own a 'Roller', so there.

Note: While at DDB I got a bill from Claridges Hotel for hundreds of pounds. It turned out that Ned Doyle, a founder of the agency, had stayed there while visiting the UK. Fortunately, the bill was passed on.

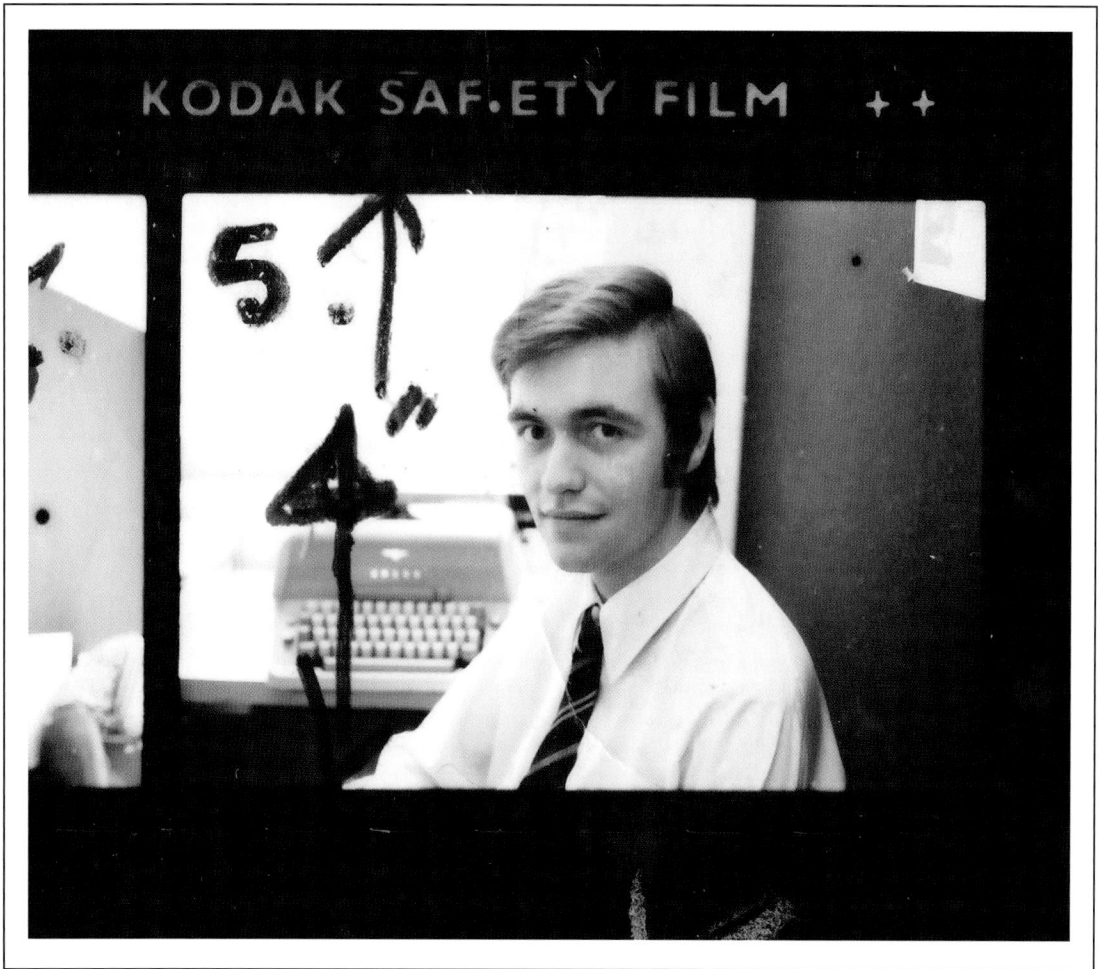

My second job as a Junior Copywriter at DDB London, still wet behind the ears in 1968, in the days of typewriters, pre desktop computers. Image courtesy of John O'Driscoll.

Facebook comment:
Sandra Leamon I remember you when you looked like that! I was an equally terrified junior copywriter at Pritchard Wood . I was John Webster's trainee. Scared? I'll say! Lucky? In spades! Happy days, eh? Xxxxx

Now there's an airline for the young, sick and inexperienced.

When it comes to flying, the fit and well are well fitted to look after themselves.

But people short on years, out of sorts, or just plain green need to be given a hand.

For them we've set up a special ground service. Our hostesses help with all the airport rigmarole. And see them onto their plane, ahead of the hale and hearty.

Once they're aboard, the stewardess takes over. She keeps an eye on the young while they catch forty winks in one of our carry-cots. (It's hung out of harm's way, above the passenger's heads.)

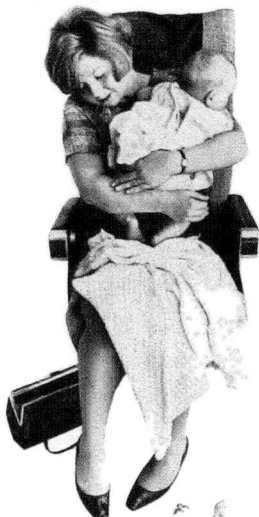

If they're not tucked in there they can tuck into some baby food. We've jars and jars of it, with bottles for the suckers.

Or they can have their nappies off on the new changing table we've set up in one of the loos. (We also lay on spares if mum runs short.)

Then they can get back to playing with the toys.

We've more of these to offer than any other airline. More games, books and puzzles, too.

Which means we've got more peace and quiet to offer the grown ups.

Especially the ones who are sick or infirm.

Besides the welcome hush, they get their own kind of treatment. All of our stewardesses get a nurse's training as a matter of course.

If a wheelchair's their only way of getting around, we see it's ready waiting when they land.

If a passenger's not feeling so hot he can freshen up with a hot towel.

If he feels a cold coming on he can wrap up warm with another blanket. Or bolster himself with another pillow.

And if he's on a special diet we'll see he's catered for. Provided he gives us fair warning when he buys his ticket.

The inexperienced can forget the empty outside by filling their inside. We've a new six-course menu which we serve up on Rosenthal china.

They can down a stiff drink to stiffen that upper lip. Or lose themselves in a game of cards or chess.

When the plane touches down they're all met again by a ground hostess. Who sees them through the customs and crowds.

She'll even fix them up with a car. Or hotel bed.

Just so they can get a good night's sleep. And forget the whole harrowing experience.

Lufthansa International
We'll do all we can.

Credits: Copywriter, Mike Doyle; Art Director, Martyn Walsh; Photographer, I'm guessing Peter Webb or Tony Evans.

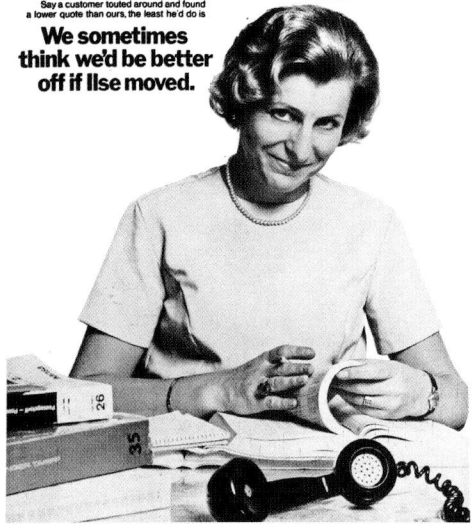

Credits: *Copywriter, Mike Doyle; Art Director, John O'Driscoll; Photographer, Tony Evans.*

Martyn Walsh.
He went on to rebirth the Pirelli Calendar to great success.

One of my favourite ads by Martyn, while he was at DDB, Copywriter was Malcolm Gluck. Photographer, Unknown.

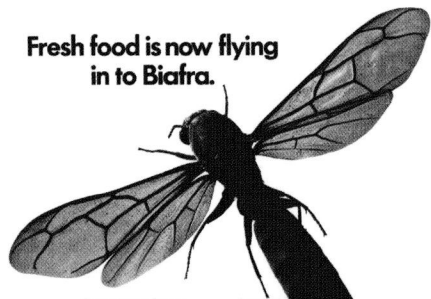

Moral: Always be nice to juniors.

After all, if for nothing else, they might be your boss in the future. While I was a junior copywriter at DDB, I was lucky enough to be answering to, and learning my craft from, the masters such as David Abbott, Dawson Yeoman and Malcolm Gluck. One day Malcolm took down his ads pinned to his office wall, saying, "I don't see why lesser minds should look at these". A fact I reminded him about many years later. To his credit he did blush. Malcolm did go on to be something of a wine expert in the UK. The generation before me at DDB, when John Withers had been CD, all creative staff attended wine appreciation classes. I was sorry to have been late for that particular bus.

One of the world-wide copywriting greats, Bob Levenson[†], paid the agency a visit. He wrote some of the great VW ads such as *Lemon* and *Think small*. He spent a fair bit of time with everyone in the department and even with little old me with 'L' plates showing. He later gave a talk to us all and I remember Tony Brignull (another copy giant) asking him if he knew what the next thing was going to be in advertising. Levenson replied, with a smile, "If I knew that I wouldn't be telling you."

Being nice to Juniors was always a good policy because at some point in your career you may be working for them. And also, they are more likely to be kind to the next generation coming through.

David Abbott would always try and see any aspiring writer if he had the time, and was always very constructive. A fact I can personally vouch for as he spent a lot of time with me while I was a student at the LCP

The studio or 'bull pen' at the agency was packed with talent learning the craft of creating great artwork. I remember John O'Driscoll, Brian Watson, Paul Leeves just to name a few, who all went on to great careers as Art Directors in their own right.

Note: one of my many pleasures ,over the years, was acting as a mentor for the D&AD student scheme as well as being an external tutor for the School of Communication Arts set up by John Gillard.

Bob Levenson.
Image: from his book,
'Bill Bernbach's Book'.

NINE STEPS TO IMPROVE AN AD

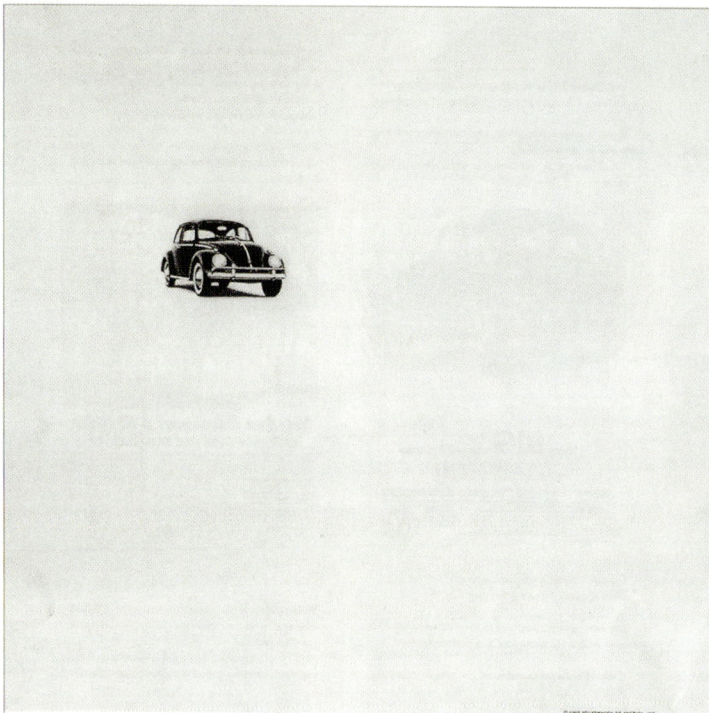

Think small.

Our little car isn't so much of a novelty any more.

A couple of dozen college kids don't try to squeeze inside it.

The guy at the gas station doesn't ask where the gas goes.

Nobody even stares at our shape.

In fact, some people who drive our little flivver don't even think 32 miles to the gallon is going any great guns.

Or using five pints of oil instead of five quarts.

Or never needing anti-freeze.

Or racking up 40,000 miles on a set of tires.

That's because once you get used to some of our economies, you don't even think about them any more.

Except when you squeeze into a small parking spot. Or renew your small insurance. Or pay a small repair bill. Or trade in your old VW for a new one.

Think it over.

In 1963, Fred Manley, who was, at the time, creative director of BBDO San Francisco, gave a presentation to his advertising peers. With a little artistic help from Hal Riney, he pulled apart DDB's famous 'Think Small' ad for VW and put it together the way some 'ad people' believe it should have been in the first place

I'M SURE YOU'VE SEEN A CERTAIN AD for the Volkswagen car, and heard it praised, and watched it pick up prizes the length and breadth of the land.

I believe this ad is one of the most inept, most ineffectual, most misguided efforts of recent years.

Why? Because it's a perfect example of the disease that has spread throughout our business. A disease called 'cleverness'. Today, in some advertising quarters, cleverness is all that matters. You no longer have to have the selling idea. You no longer have to communicate that idea in clear, understandable terms. All you have to do is be witty. And amusing. And sophisticated. In short, 'clever'. And the more sane, sensible, tried-and-true rules you break along the way, the better.

The result, of course, is advertising like this. Advertising that titillates the precious few who work along Madison Avenue. That wins awards from ingrown groups of art directors. That makes conversation pieces at cocktail parties in Westport, Connecticut. Advertising that utterly fails to communicate with anyone who lives anywhere west of the Hudson River.

These are serious charges, I know - but I'm prepared to prove them. With your permission, I'd like to show you what this ad could have been - if only it hadn't worshiped at the shrine of cleverness. With the sensitive aid of art director Hal Riney, I'll reconstruct it step by step, following the sensible rules that guide so much advertising today.

I first saw this exercise in how to ruin a great ad in Communication Arts *magazine way back when. It happens all too often in advertising when the client doesn't trust the agency. Or simply doesn't have the good taste to let the agency do its job. Note the irony in the headline.*

Rule: Show the product.
Don't turn it into a postage stamp or a test of failing eyesight. Show it. Boldly. Dramatically. Excitingly. Like this:

Think small.

There. See the difference already? Now, I'll admit the headline no longer makes complete sense - but that brings us to another obvious improvement.

Rule: Don't use negative headlines.
'Think Small' may be very clever, very witty... but what an idea to leave in the minds of everyday readers.

Think BIG!

'Think BIG!' Now I ask you - isn't that better? Isn't it more positive, more direct? Note, too, the interesting use of type to punch home the excitement of the idea.

Well that brings us to still another improvement - and one of the most important rules in all advertising.

Rule: Mention your product name in the headline.
Which the people who thought up this ad could have done so very, very easily.

Think BIG and you'll choose VOLKSWAGEN!

See how this ad is beginning to jell?
How it's starting to come alive?

Let's see another way we can breath some life into it - with a warming touch of humanity.

Rule: When possible, show people enjoying your product.

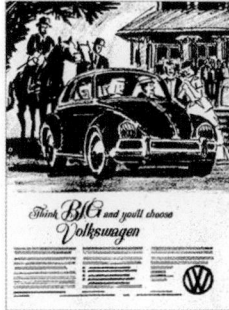

Think BIG and you'll choose Volkswagen

That's more like it. A gracious mansion. A carefree band of dancers. And a proud pair of thoroughbreds.

Now for an improvement to correct a fault in the product itself. You'll note that the Volkswagen, unfortunately, is totally lacking in news.
From year to year, while other cars bring out a host of exciting changes - it stays its own dowdy self.

Rule: Always feature news in your advertisement.
And if you have no news, invent it. Like this:

New from Volkswagen! A '63 sizzler with new sass and skeedaddle!

How's that for news?

Rule: Always give prominent display to the logo.
And I don't mean an arty jumble of initials no one can read. I mean a proud unashamed logo like this:

New from Volkswagen! A '63 sizzler with new sass and skeedaddle!

Rule: Avoid unpleasant product connotations.
Which brings us to a somewhat delicate area: the country of origin of the Volkswagen car. I don't have to dwell on the subject of World War 2 and its attendant unpleasantness for you to grasp my meaning. Let's simply say it may be wise to 'domesticate' the car, so to speak.

Think BIG and you'll choose Volkswagen

New from Volkswagen! A '63 sizzler with new sass and skeedaddle!

VOLKS WAGEN THE ALL-AMERICAN CAR!

VOLKSWAGEN: THE ALL-AMERICAN CAR!
In a flash, apple strudel turns into good 'ol apple pie!

Rule: Always tell the reader where to buy.

New from Volkswagen! A '63 sizzler with new sass and skeedaddle!

"At your friendly authorized Volkswagen dealer". Note the warmth of words like "friendly". And the use of "Authorized" to make sure that prospects don't stumble into places that are unauthorized.

Rule: Always localize your ads.

NEW! from Volkswagen! A '63 SIZZLER with new sass and skee-daddle!

And mind the way you spell the dealer's names.

There you have it. No clever, precious, self conscious waste of space like the ad we started with; but an honest, hard-hitting, two-fisted ad like this that really sells. I said "sells".

Image: Campaign Brief Special Supplement, Caxton 2005.

My first advertising Antipodean.

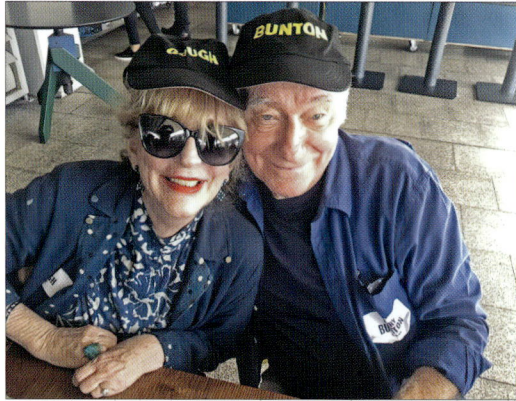

Terry Bunton.
Terry's on the right, just so you know.
Image: Campaign Brief 'Legends' lunch in 2019.

Terry Bunton, was working as a copywriter across the department from me. Two Americans were also there. Patrick Kelly, whom one could hear having a nervous breakdown as paper went into his typewriter, clatter of the keys, paper ripped out and that repeated endlessly. He recovered and went on to write the wonderful campaign for Federal Express with the line *'When it positively, absolutely has to be there overnight'.* His Art Director, Art (appropriate?) Taylor destroyed the lift doors one Christmas party doing a Samson impression.

Postscript about, and from, Terry Bunton.

Terry, after working at DDB, and then BBDO, returned to Australia where he set up a film production company and had a successful career directing commercials.

As an investment in his Pension Plan he bought a boarding house, overlooking the ocean and turned it into a wonderful boutique hotel called 'Dive'.

The Dive hotel's wonderful sign, as seen from the street.

Here are Terry's comments on what I had written:

"Without the benefit of Dawson's forensic eye, I can't find any fault with your description of my time at DDB:

Antipodean, true. Terry, true. Bunton, true. Copywriter, true. So you're in the clear.

50 years on, we have sold the Dive. (26 years was about all I could take of bell-boy duties.)

Admittedly, I do miss the interaction with our wonderful variety of guests, and I think we were truly blessed in that regard."

The man from Jamaica.

John Pringle.
Image: Jamaica Tourist Board.

Our very fine Managing Director, John Pringle[†], was from Jamaica and had chosen the New York office for the Jamaican Tourist campaign. He did this by looking at all the ads published that week, and finding out the agency responsible for his favourites. A man of excellent taste in advertising and much else. And the rest was history as they say.

Fear and loathing.

Sorry for lowering the tone, but every so often someone in the agency's Creative Department would find one of these sitting and gleaming on their desk to welcome them in the morning.

But it wasn't a cute cartoon version. No, some person in the studio had created a facsimile of a human turd out of Cow Gum fixed to a board and it was known as the *"Turd Ad of the Month Award"*. This was given, as the name suggests, for the ad judged by the lads in the Studio (Judge and Jury: John O'Driscoll, Paul Leeves, Brian Watson et al) as the worst. Luckily, I never got one but I do remember the headlines of a couple of candidates: 'Out of the flying plane *(corrected thanks to Sandra Leamon)* and into the foyer.' for a trade ad for Forte and 'A greasy offer from Forte', I presume for holidays in Greece.

Facebook comments about DDB:

John O'Driscoll Only winners, if my memory serves me right, were esteemed members of the creative department. There was also the Golden Magic Marker for the best. Ronnie Turner and Terry Bunton won it on more than one occasion. Idea was Paul Leeves.

Sandra Leamon forgive me Mike, I never worked at DDB so why I should think I've got any knowledge of what went on there I really don't know. But, I always thought the headline you reference was 'Out of the flying plane into the foyer'. I also thought it was one of the finest puns of our wonderful, witty generation. Wasn't it Gray Jolliffe? Have I got the whole thing wrong? Oh well, if I have, too bloody bad!

My reply: I have a hatred of puns, Ed McCabe, one of the world's finest copywriters, called it the English disease. The punning headlines were by Gray Jolliffe who Colin Millward said to him in a corridor conversation at CDP, "You only seem to be able to write puns Gray." To which he is said to have replied, "What would you prefer Colin, old or current puns?", which did make me smile.

If any of your customers feel fruity, recommend the Williams pear.

This sweet and juicy pear is certain to satisfy your customer's desire.

It's a triumph in Anglo-French relations.

Years ago this fine fruit left our shores and was adopted with great success by French growers.

Now it returns to grace your table, courtesy of Elibel.

This label is your guarantee that the fruit will be in perfect condition, free from blemishes and of a standard size (each pear must have a diameter of 60-70mm).

They come packaged in wooden boxes, net weight 13 kilos, clearly marked with quality and size.

If by now you're feeling fruity get in touch with one of these suppliers. Like our pears they're to be recommended.

Scanno Ltd, 53 London Fruit Exchange, London E1. Tel 01-247 8787

Formosa Monro Ltd, 272 Flower Market, New Covent Garden, London SW8. Tel 01-720 8566. Telex 919219

Tom Conaty Ltd, 422 London Fruit Exchange, Spitalfields, London E1. Tel 01-247 4767.

Consumer Fruiterers (UK) Ltd, 408-413 Market Towers, New Covent Garden Market, London SW8. Tel 01-720 7766. Telex 919759 (Fruiblen London)

Meldrust Ltd, 0805 109 Fruit and Vegetable Market, New Covent Garden, London SW8 9LL. Tel 01-620 7111/5. Telex 917992/3

Jacques Dorna & Co Ltd, 10 London Fruit Exchange, London E1. Tel 01-247 7101/7925. Telex 886063/888900

Rowe & Co, Cardrew, Redruth, Cornwall. Tel Redruth 5681

Giga Glover & Co Ltd, 9-11 Langley Court London WC2E 9JY. Tel 01-836 5961/7. Telex 21308

Now's the time to tell your customers that you've got a fine pear.

September and October are the prime months for Beurré Hardy, that excellent dessert pear from France.

If the skin is greenish yellow, tinged with reddish brown in places.

If the pear is full bellied.

If the flesh is crisp and white, with a good sweet 'nose'.

And if it sports an Elibel label then you know you've chosen the perfect Beurré Hardy.

The Elibel label guarantees that you'll receive them strongly packed in wooden boxes, as firm and unblemished as the day they left the tree.

Now you know how to pick the perfect pear, perhaps you'd like to order. The time is ripe, as they say.

Scanno Ltd, 53 London Fruit Exchange, London E1. Tel 01-247 8787

Formosa Monro Ltd, 272 Flower Market, New Covent Garden, London SW8. Tel 01-720 8566. Telex 919219

Tom Conaty Ltd, 422 London Fruit Exchange, Spitalfields, London E1. Tel 01-247 4767.

Rowe & Co, Cardrew, Redruth, Cornwall. Tel Redruth 5681

For my sins, I did weaken once into punster land while at French, Gold, Abbott. These ads ran in the trade magazine, The Grocer. *This publication was a great opportunity for fledgling creatives to strut their stuff. Credits: Copywriter, Mike Doyle; Art Director, Rob Tomnay; Photographer/illustrator, sadly unknown.*

DDB New York had a dark side.

Every month we would be sent a roll of proofs of current ads being produced out of the New York office.

These were not the Great and Godly ads for the likes of VW, Avis, Mobil, El Al etc but clients who knew nothing about creativity. And they were awful.

The PA who wouldn't leave.

The PA in question had a partner, John Kent, who was an Art Director/cartoonist at FCB (a.k.a. Foot, Sore & Bleeding) a few doors up from us in Baker Street. He was the creator of a famous cartoon strip (Varoomshka)in the Guardian newspaper.

She had been fired but refused to go, and they had her doing menial tasks but with no effect, so she was reinstated.

I did go to their flat one night for a dinner that included oysters. That's when I discovered I was allergic as I decorated their bathroom walls in a manner you would not wish for. Funnily enough, I was never invited back but my shame lives on today, as does my allergy.

So much creative talent in one agency.

Hilary Fletcher and me in Paris where, after DDB, she was living and working as a Suit..

Hilary's father was a highly intelligent, Russian 'bear' of a man and her mother was a classic 'English Rose'.

They sent her to the Sorbonne in Paris and she then studied copywriting at Watford College of Art before becoming our copy typist at DDB. After that she worked as a cook on narrow boats on the French canals before becoming an Account Executive or 'Suit' for a Paris agency specialising in advertising to women. Sadly, we lost contact many moons ago. I used to go the ballet with her and it was one of those rare, but true, cases where she was a girl 'friend' in the true, old-fashioned (or new?) sense of the word. She also lived near me for a while in Holland Park and liked to borrow my Aretha Franklin LPs.

DDB did 'let me go' a year later but I must have kept my nose clean as David Abbott later hired me at his new agency, French, Gold, Abbott.

The quality control stamp.

Every decent agency had a strict quality control. No concept would be allowed to be presented to a client until it had been signed off by the Group Head, the Creative Director and the Account Director. That way the client knew the concept and copy had been through a rigorous process. It had to be part of why British advertising could be counted amongst the world's best.

One of my pet hates in advertising: 'brainstorming'.

In my experience, nothing good ever came out of this process. It was usually taken by desperate people in a panic. Not the best mind set and, like the illustration, usually ended up under a black cloud.

I remember a documentary filmed at DDB and broadcast on TV where they had David, Dawson and others sitting in a small room and trying to come up with a solution to some problem, which I've forgotten.

But even those inspired minds couldn't crack it. The camera crews being there may not have helped.

Another pet hate was Creative Directors saying, "have fun with it" as they set us off on the path to creativity. These people were usually in the 'bad' agencies.

Timekeeping.
Not one of my strengths.

As the man who slept through the hurricane that devastated the south-east of England in the 1980s, I can lay claim to the above.

October 16th 1987　　　*'In the Wake of the Hurricane'*　　　*Bob Ogley*

I was often so late for my job at the printers, my Mum persuaded our elderly neighbour to knock on my bedroom wall (from her side) to get me up in time. She wouldn't stop until I had knocked back.

Even at CDP I was known to be a tad late at times. The funny thing was my Group Head, Lindsay Dale, would take me to lunch at a fine restaurant to take me to task. It was more like a reward. And he could claim it on expenses.

Legend has it that the Art Director, Ron Collins, was confronted in the Creative department corridor on morning by Colin Millward, "You should have been here at 9 Ron." He replied, "Why? What did I miss?"

At DDB I was briefed to write an ad for the part Bulova were playing in timing Mexico City but not the Olympics, hence this ad. The photo was stock and, sadly, I can't remember who the Art Director was. Apologies to him or her.

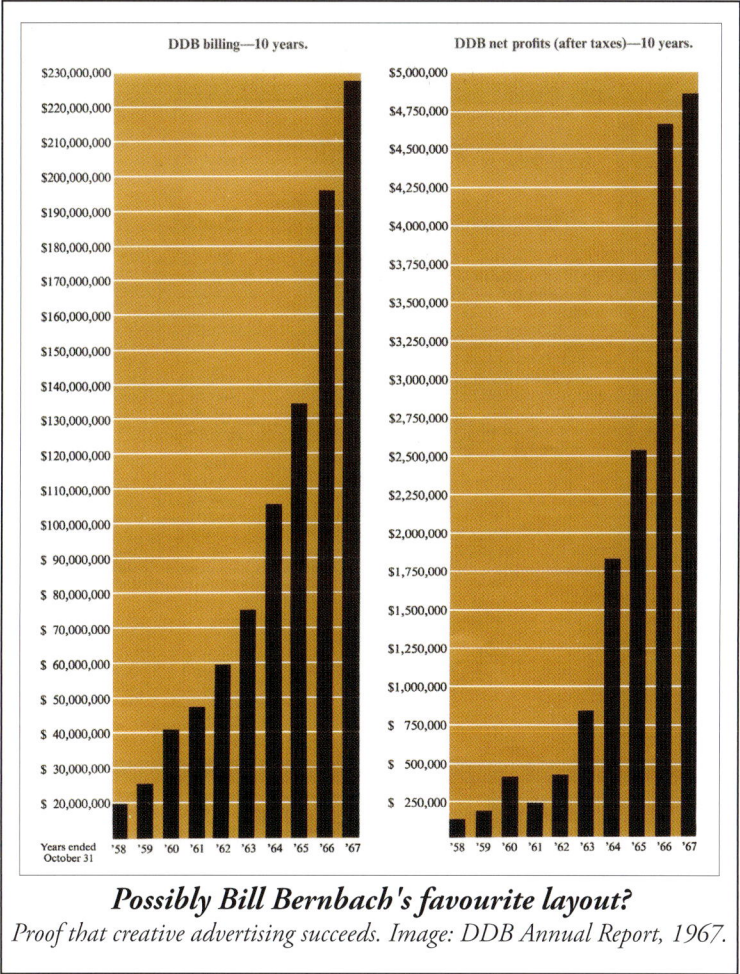

Possibly Bill Bernbach's favourite layout?

Proof that creative advertising succeeds. Image: DDB Annual Report, 1967.

Note: One year, while at DDB, I had a holiday on the island of Hvar in what was then Yugoslavia. One night at the hotel bar I got chatting to a couple of young Americans from New York. I was amazed that they knew my agency and could even quote some of the Volkswagen headlines. Fame indeed.

My DDB generation.

David Abbott (Creative Director), Dawson Yeoman (head of Copy), Malcolm Gluck, Tony Brignull, Terry Bunton, Patrick Kelly, Art Taylor, John O'Driscoll, Brian Watson, Paul Leeves, Hilary Fletcher.
Apologies to anyone that I've missed.

Chapter
Four

1968 — 1969 (all too short).

Papert, Koenig, Lois (PKL)

✝

From council house to Harrods.

Having a mother who was disabled, and a widow, meant that money was always a tad scarce. But our humble home was near the very rich. To be precise, Bishops Avenue in East Finchley, which was also known as 'Millionaire's Row', leading up to 'happy Hampstead'.

Like most teenagers, I needed to earn money, at least to be able to meet girls.

So, every weekend I'd get on my trusty bike and pedal off to Hampstead Garden Suburb (more rich people) and offer to wash cars or weed gardens. They seldom said "No" and I often got an afternoon treat for tea into the bargain.

After Doyle Dane Bernbach "let me go" (to this day, I don't know why) my confidence was shattered. My Mum wanted me to return to the relative safety of printing, but I had been bitten by the advertising bug.

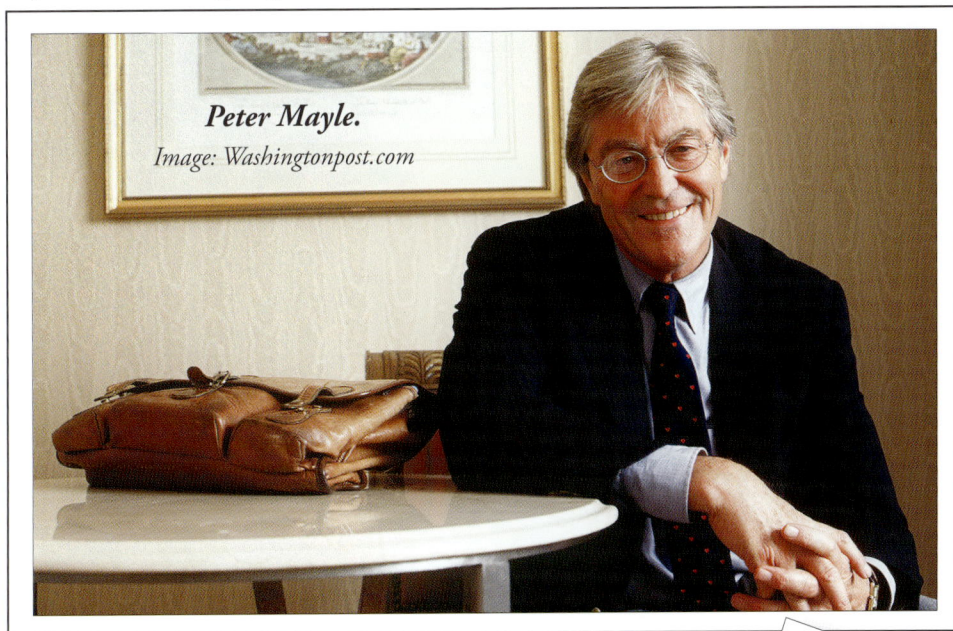

Peter Mayle.
Image: Washingtonpost.com

Luckily, the wonderful Peter Mayle[†] Creative Director at Papert, Koenig, Lois, hired me and put me back together again. No Humpty Dumpty comments, if you don't mind.

After Advertising, Peter went on to write best-selling books such as *Where did I come from? A year in Provence, Rude Food, Up the Agency* and many more.

Paul Walter. *Another LCP friend who did great work at PKL and afterwards, and who designed Peter's best-selling book, 'Where did I come from?'. Paul also lived in Melbourne for many years.*
Image: Paul Walter.

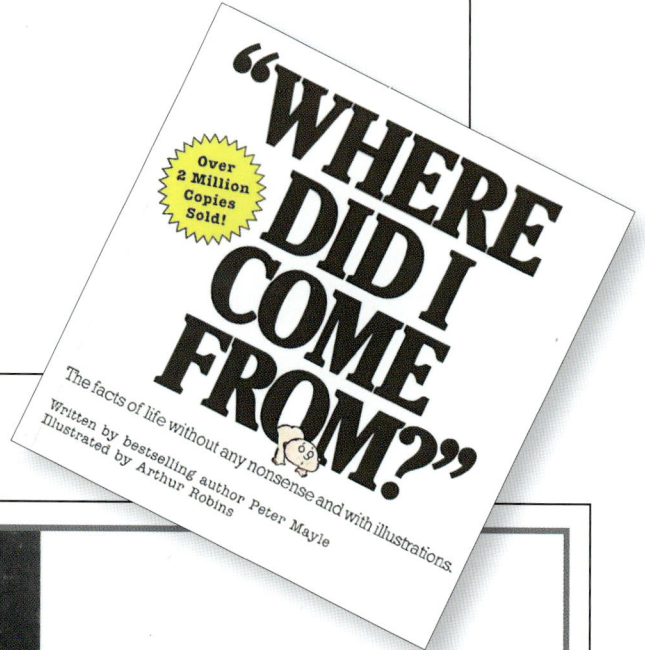

Over 2 Million Copies Sold!

"WHERE DID I COME FROM?"

The facts of life without any nonsense and with illustrations.
Written by bestselling author Peter Mayle
Illustrated by Arthur Robins

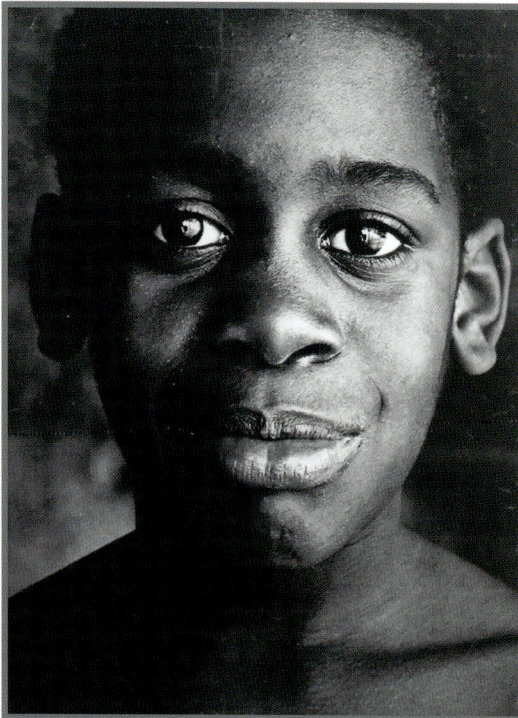

This time next year, we'll be struggling to grasp something he's been doing since he went to school.

When he started school in Accra, one of the first things he learned was that 1 cedi equals 100 pesewa. Ever since then, he's been doing his money sums in decimals.

From February next year, we'll all be doing the same.

Not just the simple business of adding and subtracting. But pricing. Invoicing. Marking-up. Calculating. Estimating. Discounting. Percentaging.

If it involves money, it's going to involve decimals.

Which means we shall have to alter the business habits of a lifetime.

You can look at it two ways. As a damned nuisance. Or as a step that will simplify our business methods, and bring them into line with the rest of the world.

However you feel about it, it's going to mean extra work. But it needn't mean chaos.

Olivetti have people, machines and systems that have been dealing with decimals for 30 years in 136 different countries.

If you run a restaurant, and need a decimal adding machine, Olivetti can offer you a choice of five models.

If you have a flourishing stockbroking firm with an antique accounting system, Olivetti men can re-design the system. And Olivetti accounting machines can make the system work.

If you're an engineer, we can show you an electronic calculating machine that does a job in ten minutes where a slide rule takes three hours.

If you need something more complex, we have a desk-top computer. For bigger computers, we have a vast supply of terminals.

It's our business to anticipate the problems of your business. Decimalisation is just one of them, and it's one you'll have to face soon.

What you don't have to do is face it alone.

olivetti

For advice about decimalisation, and the machines that can make it a painless process, write to Mr. P. Pearson, Olivetti, 30 Berkeley Square, London, W.1.

Credits: (Olivetti) *Copywriter, Peter Mayle; Art Director, Paul Walter; Photographer, Peter Webb.*

Where the Queen shops.

Sir Nigel Seeley[†], was not only the Managing Director at PKL but also Account Director on Harrods. And being a Knight of the Realm didn't hurt when dealing with the 'Royal' Department store; who were great clients I must say.

We were based in Sloane Street, Knightsbridge, almost above the store.

Nigel would pop over with our concept roughs and be back the same day with approval.

Note: As an aside, and continuing the 'posh' theme, my good friend from the London College of Printing days, Geoff Seymour, invited me to his 21st birthday dinner at his parents' hotel in the town of Woodstock, next to Blenheim Palace. Naturally, we had pheasant and other fine things.

Geoff's girlfriend at the time was Anne Leworthy who was an Art Director at J. Walter Thompson and her Dad was Equerry to the Queen. I did go to their house in Kent, but only the once. Was it something I did or said?

Harrods. From Milkman to Sandman.

Some customers crawl to us for service.

Credits: Copywriter, Mike Doyle; Art Director, John Horton; Photographer/illustrator, Sadly unknown to me.

The location for 'Room Service' was the newly bought home of Neil Godfrey (Legendary and described as the UK's most-awarded Art Director) and the house was said to be haunted by the previous owner, an elderly lady. OOOer!

One Drunken Night.

OK, OK, we had more than one in advertising way back then, not to overlook long, liquid lunches but, in this instance, it coincided with Papert, Koenig, Lois in London being appointed to the London Hilton account.

The night in question was when a team of us went on a fact-finding tour of the hotel. During the evening we visited every restaurant and bar, sampling the wares.

At the end of the evening, as we saw our office manager staggering down the escalator and out into the night, my Managing Director, Sir Nigel Seeley, without any sense of irony, turned to the Banqueting Manager and said, "You wouldn't believe that man was an alcoholic a year ago."

The London Hilton.
Image: Wikipedia, Sabrina756

If one of us had to work late, or weekends, to make up for lost time over lunches, we would come in on a Saturday. The Office Manager's drinking buddies would crawl out from under the boardroom table and scuttle off into Sloane Street and Knightsbridge. No doubt stopping for a 'livener' somewhere along the way.

How my internal organs are still functioning is quite remarkable, considering my 'naughty' years. The work still won awards despite some naysayers.

24 hour eating.

Anytime you feel peckish, drop into the London Hilton.

Breakfast: For a hearty start to the day, try the London Tavern. You'll find it in the lobby. Open 7-11.30 a.m. 12-5 p.m., 6-11 p.m.

Afternoon Tea: Sit, sip and watch the world go by amidst the potted palms of the Hilton Patio on the second floor. 24 hour service.

Elevenses: When the shopping's getting on top of you have a quick 45-snack in the Scandinavian Sandwich Shop. It's in the shopping Arcade. Open 8 a.m.-7 p.m., Sun. 10 a.m.-7 p.m.

Dinner: Take your sweetheart up in the sky to the Roof Restaurant. Where you can wine, dine and dance to romantic rhythms. Open Mon. to Sat.12.30-3p.m., 7.30 p.m.- 1 a.m.

Lunch: The International Restaurant on the second floor takes you round the world in 70 courses. Garnished with a view of Hyde Park. Open 12.30-3 p.m., 6-11.30 p.m.

Supper: Try the 007 Night Spot for size. A nice up and light snack go down well before hitting the sack. To find the spot go to the second floor. Open Mon. to Sat. 6.30 p.m.-2 a.m., Dancing 9 p.m.-2 a.m.

London Hilton
5 bars 5 restaurants
Park Lane, London, W1 01-493 8000

The Hilton Lunchtime Variety Show.

Waiter, when hunger strikes, make for Park Lane.

There, under the Hilton roof, you'll find enough bars and restaurants to satisfy any gastronomic pangs.

If your taste is tropical, there's Trader Vic's on the lower ground floor. This Polynesian restaurant serves Tahitian recipes like Paauau Ota. An fish soup served with coconut cream and chopped shallots.

Closer to home, there's the London Tavern in the lobby. Two of you can polish of a spit-roasted Aylesbury duckling, costing 96.

While liquid luncheons are for George's Bar in the lobby. With London's of Britannia Bitter, the world's strongest beer.

Across the lobby, in the Shopping Arcade, there's the Scandinavian Sandwich Shop. Lunchtime they serve delicacies like Danish canape at 64b. Or Norwegian sardines and tomatoes at 5l.

But if that's not your cup of tea, take the lift to the second floor. Here, in the Patio, there are rich sandwiches to tackle and cocktails to swallow.

For the more sophisticated taste

there's the International Restaurant across the way. Try the lamb, salmon and shrimp. It's a 70th treasure from the Caribbean.

And finally, for our Grand Finale, consider the Roof Restaurant. With London at your feet, you can enjoy an aperitif. Followed perhaps by an entrecote steak with Sauternes sauce. Bring £50 for this.

On that note and three more lines, we bid you adieu.

We trust it's helped our in throwing a lunch matinee banzai.

And that all our much loved restaurants put together will be well visited.

London Hilton
5 bars 5 restaurants
Park Lane, London, W1 01-493 8000

Credits: *Copywriter, Mike Doyle; Art Director, John Horton; Photographer/illustrator, sadly unknown.*

Fond memories of Sir Nigel Seeley, PKL MD and genuine 'gent'.

Sir Nigel Seely, 5th Bt, who has died aged 95, was a leading player in the fast-moving London advertising scene of the 1960s and 1970s after a first career as a theatrical agent.

Photo of Nigel and his friend 'Henry', taken from Daily Telegraph online obituary.

Seely's entrée into the ad business came in 1964 when he was asked to open a London branch of Papert, Koenig, Lois, one of a thrusting new breed of Madison Avenue creative agencies that would later inspire the Mad Men television series.

"First horrified then intrigued" by the invitation – his only prior experience of the sector having been as a client – Seely accepted and became PKL's managing director. Assisted by a brilliant young copywriter called Peter Mayle† (author of *A Year in Provence*), he steered the new venture through teething troubles which included vastly over-optimistic estimates of its potential billing income.

Patrician manners, titled connections and hints of hush-hush wartime work for Winston Churchill marked Seely apart from other admen of the era. "We all thought he was a toff because he took snuff," recalled Mayle, who claimed always to wear brown trousers when travelling on aeroplanes with Seely for fear of arriving sprayed with scented tobacco.

One historian of advertising wrote that PKL's eponymous founders had opened the London office "for no better reason than that, according to Lois, Papert was an Anglophile who wanted someone to book his West End theatre tickets".

The film director Sir Alan Parker, who also worked briefly at PKL, recalled that the third partner, Koenig, preferred Ascot and Newmarket and "never came near" the

Sloane Street office, where the atmosphere was dominated by a brace of aggressive New Yorkers sent over by the founders to represent them.

One Yuletide, just before the staff party, one of these Americans stormed into Seely's office – "and it wasn't to wish him a Merry Christmas", as Mayle recalled. Fisticuffs and a broken champagne glass were followed, according to ad-world legend, by a dash to Middlesex Hospital with the American bleeding from a cut throat.

Despite such ructions, the firm won work from Granada Television, John Player and Perfectos Finos cigarettes and Auto Union, the maker of Audi cars, for which PKL ran a promotion giving ignition keys – and if the key fitted, a free car – to Diners Club cardholders. Later clients included Harrods, Sony, Watneys and Gillette.

But in 1969, when the New York parent agency suffered a dramatic loss of billings, Seely and Mayle took the opportunity to buy a controlling interest in the London arm and make it independent. "It's hard to find that through no fault of your own, you might fail to get new business because of events 3,500 miles away," Mayle explained.

Two years later, they sold the business to another US firm, BBDO, for which Seely briefly became UK chairman. He went on to be managing director of James Garrett's ground-breaking advertising film production company – where the young freelance directors he worked with included Ridley Scott – before moving again in 1973 to be deputy chairman and international head of the Dorland agency, which became part of Saatchi & Saatchi.

Eventually Nigel Seely was forced out of Dorland. The executive tasked with breaking the news was invited for drinks at Seely's Bayswater home, presided over by a parrot called Henry – who took an evident dislike to the guest, flew across the room to perch on the edge of his glass, flicked his tail feathers and dropped a deposit into it.

His life before PKL. Nigel Edward Seely was born on July 28 1923, the only child of Sir Victor Seely, 4th baronet, by his marriage to Sibyl (Nancy) Gibbons, who had previously been married to another baronet, Sir John Shiffner.

Victor and Nancy were divorced in 1931 and Nancy took as her third husband the Labour politician Reggie Paget, later Lord Paget of Northampton and master of the Pytchley Hunt; Nigel's childhood was divided between the Seely family seat on the Isle of Wight and his stepfather's home in Leicestershire. Victor Seely married twice more during the 1930s, had three more children, and was a PoW during the Second World War.

Nigel was educated at Stowe and also served in the Army – details of his secret work remain hazy – before embarking on a theatrical management career which first found him stage-managing a show called *Residents Only* at the St James's Theatre, of which

The Stage noted: "On opening night a cry of 'Rubbish' was heard."

He went on to work for Gordon Harbord, a grand theatrical and literary agent in St Martin's Lane, on whose behalf he talent-spotted the young Roger Moore[†] and a voluptuous teenage drama student, Diana Fluck, whom the agency renamed Diana Dors[†].

Harbord himself was credited with finding a new name for a handsome Lithuanian-born actor, Laruschka Skikne – but it was actually Seely (by his own account) who suggested Laurence Harvey[†], the surname borrowed from the Knightsbridge department store, Harvey Nichols.

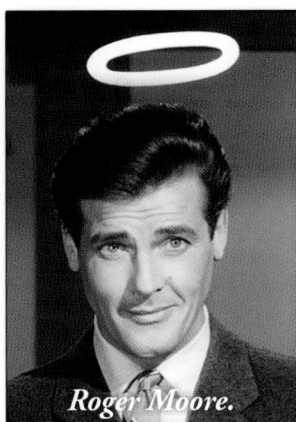
Roger Moore.

Diana Dors.

Laurence Harvey.

In the 1950s, Seely worked as a cinema manager in Baker Street; later he was international sales director for a colourful Czech entrepreneur, Baron Rolf Beck, whose company manufactured a gearbox lubricant called Molyslip. Its US advertising was handled by PKL, which in due course poached Seely for its London opening.

In retirement, Seely stayed largely in London but maintained the style of a country gentleman. He was chairman of Buck's Club in Mayfair, where he enjoyed organising backgammon.

On his father's death in 1980 he inherited the baronetcy created in 1896 for his great-grandfather Charles, a long-serving Liberal MP for Nottingham. Nigel Seely's first marriage, to Loraine Lindley-Travis in 1949, was dissolved; he married secondly, in 1984, Trudi Pacter, who survives him with three daughters of his first marriage. The baronetcy passes to his nephew William Seely, born in 1983.

Sir Nigel Seely, 5th Bt, born July 28 1923, died April 25 2019.

Daily Telegraph **obituary.**

Note: *One day Phil Mason and I were invited in to Nigel's office for a "chat". We had no idea what it was about. He said he found out that we both had widowed mothers and should provide for both them and our financial futures.*
He advised us to invest in Tyndale Unit Trusts and would put part of our salary into the Trust in our name each month. We had no idea of the significance of this but remembered our good manners and thanked him. For me it meant that my fund had accumulated enough money to put down a deposit on my first home, a newly built flat in High Barnet. Thanks again Nigel. If anyone is 'upstairs' it must be him.

A country boy called 'Doyley'?

While I was at PKL I was assigned to the ICI Agricultural account. Was it my Irish ancestry? It was good to work on. The team, besides me, consisted of my Art Director, John "Jelly Roll" Horton, the Suit, Stephen Bull (How appropriate was he with that surname?) and the wonderful, freelance photographer John Claridge.

We would spend a day on the nominated farm where I would interview the farmers while the two Johns set up and then took the photographs. There was usually great hospitality from our hosts into the bargain.

Stephen went on to run a very fine restaurant, beef was served.

Credits: Copywriter, Mike Doyle; Art Director, John Horton; Photographer, John Claridge.

Mighty Mike.[†] My double?

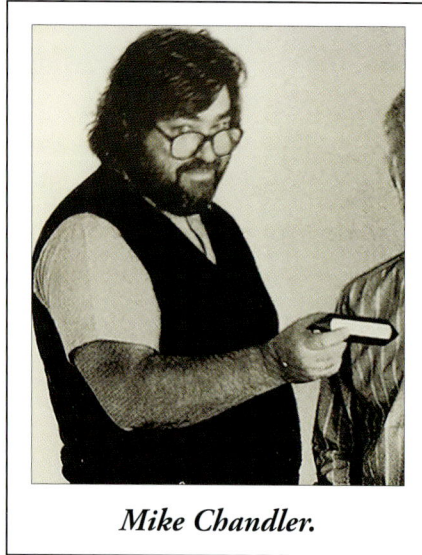

Mike Chandler.

"The Australian ad industry will be saddened to hear of the passing of Australia's greatest typographer Mike Chandler. He was inducted into the CB Hall of Fame in 2004, helped improve the work of every single great writer and art director in Australian advertising throughout the 70s, 80s and 90s."
Campaign Brief.

I first met Mike when he was hired as Traffic Manager at PKL in London.

Allegedly, Dave Ashwell, our Head of Art at the time, met Mike in a pub and discovered that he had been managing truck drivers and felt Mike met the brief of what the agency needed.

We didn't know what had hit us as we had carried merrily along at the time unaware of timelines for jobs. Talk about a rude awakening. And Mike could be rude at times.

Mike eventually left us to be part of the Ronchetti and Day Studio, producing artwork.

And he later moved to Australia, setting up the hugely successful, and influential, Face Studio, let alone playing a large part in my life and it's travels. He acted as my 'champion' with agencies before and during my job hunting in Australia many moons later.

Mr Ivy League.

The man who used to be responsible for creating our artwork at PKL was an American called Phil Meyer[†] for whom I can find no image.

To Phil Mason and me, he was our style role model with his button-down shirts, Ivy league Suits and Burberry mac' with Prussian collar. The only place we knew where you could get the Arrow brand of button-down shirts at the time was sold exclusively at Austin Reed's in Regent Street.

We then discovered a shop in Richmond called The Ivy Shop, which had everything we could wish for including Bass-Wejun, Penny and Tassel Loafers. We offered to help them with their publicity and window displays for free clothes, but they declined our generous offer.

We were chosen by the police on that day for a line-up identity parade in the local "Cop Shop". We were not found guilty.

My love affair with all things American continued with a diet of authors such as Fitzgerald, Hemingway and Saul Bellow, to name but a few.

At the LCP, Phil and I read every copy of the New York Art Director's Annual that we could get our hands on. After seeing the credits with, to us, very exotic names, Phil felt his was too 'white bread' and considered changing it to Karman Hammerschlog, not entirely seriously.

Phil had known me as "Mick" from LCP, which my Mum hated with its derogatory associations. So I chose to be called "Mike". If ever I was called Michael I knew I was in trouble. Maybe I should simply have changed it to "John" given that name came up so often in my career.

Not actually Phil Meyer,
but could be a lookalike.

PKL resigns £1m

'We want more time to concentrate on fewer accounts. We would rather get the structure right now even if we lose immediate profits'

PKL, the London agency that is buying control from its American owners, has resigned £1 million worth of business.

It is giving up nine accounts —including Hotpoint, worth £400,000, Potterton central heating £150,000, and ICI Fertilisers £130,000.

The reason: the agency wants "more time to concentrate on fewer accounts". All the resigned accounts were profitable, says PKL, and had caused no "difficulties, dislikes or disagreements".

Peter Mayle, 30, deputy chairman and creative director, said yesterday: "We want to stay a small agency where we can be personally involved in doing work for a few clients. There is no limit to billings— up £5m would be possible provided we can handle them.

as a small agency with greater potential to do good work. For by 1975, it says, "it is likely that there will be only two kinds of agency: the giant American-owned operation, turning out indifferent work for international clients; and the small agency, which will survive because it produces interesting and effective advertising for a small number of accounts."

It sees no future for the conventional medium-sized agency "which will eventually be swallowed up by purchase or merger."

This year the agency expects to make a pre-tax profit of around £75,000—compared to £62,000 last year. Next year, with half its billings gone, it faces a projected loss of £25,000. But, says Nigel Seely, 46, chairman, "we do not intend losing any

The sad end of an era.

This came about partly because the agency resigned almost half of its billing, a revolutionary move at the time.

After an all staff meeting at the Turk's Head pub, where we discussed the clients who were proving difficult to work with, we did not think that the sacking of clients would be the outcome.

Four of us were asked to keep our evening free and went over to Nigel's town house in Onslow Square, where we were informed of the forthcoming event and that, sadly, we would no longer be working for the agency. The four, besides myself, were John Horton, John Kelley and Phil Mason.

Peter said he would hire us all back as soon as the business allowed, which proved to be true to his word, with me being a later 'return'.

Phil Mason got so drunk that night, he almost wrote off his car but survived to tell the tale.

Note: PKL and another agency, Geers Gross, were said to be the two most profitable agencies in their day.

Later, CDP resigned Ford and Nestle many years later because they asked for more than one concept for a campaign.

Both now gone, but not forgotten.

L-R John Sherfield[†] and Peter Mayle.
*John's studio created all our artwork at BBDO. He cheekily
ran an ad in Campaign with the headline.*

Artwork at popular prices. Well I like them.

*I was told, true or not, that because his prices were so high,
the agency lost the Zanussi and Toyota brochure print business
and that was part of the reason for me losing my job. I suspect
it was more about my evident frustration.*

My PKL generation.

Peter Mayle, David Ashwell, Paul Walter, Bob Wilson, Peter Little, John 'Jelly Roll' Horton, John Kelley, Phil Mason, Mike Chandler, Vick Waterhouse. Apologies to anyone I've missed.

A tribute to Peter Mayle,
a great mentor and boss.

His early life. Born in Brighton, Sussex, the youngest of three children, Mayle and his parents moved to Barbados in the aftermath of World War II, where his father was transferred as a Colonial Office employee. Mayle returned to England after leaving school at 16 in Barbados.

Peter's advertising career. His first job in 1957 was as a trainee at Shell Oil, based in its London office. It was there that he discovered that he was more interested in advertising than oil and he wrote to David Ogilvy, the head of the advertising agency that had the Shell account at that time, asking for a job. Ogilvy offered him a job as a junior account executive, but Mayle's interest was more on the creative side of the business and he subsequently became a copywriter in 1961 based in its New York City office.

In due course another agency, Papert, Koenig, Lois poached him from Ogilvy and sent him back to London to head up the creative team in its UK office, where one of his colleagues was Alan Parker. When the US parent hit trouble in the mid-1960s, he and a colleague bought the London operation. They developed the business with accounts that included Watneys, Olivetti, and Sony and after five years, it was bought by BBDO, one of the top American agencies. He then commuted between the U.S. and the UK as its creative director.

A 1972 advertising slogan written by Mayle for Wonderloaf Bread was used as a football chant by supporters of Tottenham Hotspur, and became the basis of the song "Nice One Cyril".

By 1974, Mayle had had enough of advertising and transatlantic commuting, and quit the business to write full-time.

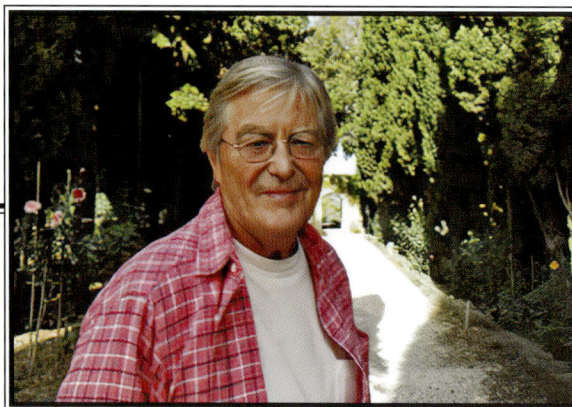

Peter as Author.

Mayle started off by writing educational books, including a series on sex education for children and young people. He also penned, in collaboration with illustrator Gray Jolliffe, a series of humorous books about the character Wicked Willie, based upon a personification of the male organ. He relocated from Devon to the Luberon, southern France, in the late 80s but his plans to write a novel were overtaken by an account of life in his new environment. This resulted in his 1989 book *A Year in Provence* which became an international bestseller, chronicling his first year as a British expatriate in Ménerbes, a village in the southern département Vaucluse.

Several more books followed, which have been translated in more than twenty languages. He also wrote for magazines and newspapers. *A Year in Provence* was subsequently produced as a TV series starring John Thaw and screened in 1993. The novel *A Good Year* was the basis for the 2006 film of the same name directed by Ridley Scott and starring actors Russell Crowe and Marion Cotillard.

Mayle relocated to Amagansett on Long Island, New York, to get away from fans and sightseers at his home in Provence. He subsequently returned to France and at the time of his death in 2018 resided in Vaugines, also situated in the Luberon, in Provence. He died in hospital near his home in January 2018.

His awards.

British Book Awards named *A Year in Provence* Best Travel Book of the Year (1989) and him Author of the Year (1992). The French government made him a Chevalier de la Légion d'honneur (Knight of the Legion of Honour) in 2002, for coopération et francophonie. *Wikipedia*.

Chapter Five

1969 — 1970, blink and you'd have missed it.

Colman, Prentis & Varley (CPV)

✝

My time in the 'Wilderness'.

After the exit from PKL the four of us resolved to stay together as a group, if possible.

The following months were slightly surreal. We had an interview with the writer of the PG Tips Tea 'Chimp' campaign, Tony Toller, in a hospital where he was a patient.

His proposal was for us all to set up a new agency as he could raise the money. He was good friends with the owner of National Car Parks, who was looking for a means of reducing his tax bill.

Three of us were willing but I felt in my waters that it was not a trustworthy idea.

As luck would have it (or so it seemed at the time) we ended up being hired, as a group by CPV, with Tony Beerbohm as Creative Director.

John Horton and I did OK with campaigns for Corfam directed by Terence Donovan[†] and another for Teflon, directed by Alan Parker (now Sir), who had left CDP and was starting to build a career directing commercials. CDP had created a studio in its basement where Alan could film the pilot commercial and then, once approved, a professional would make the finished article. Only Alan's products were better. Sadly, I don't have copies of either commercial.

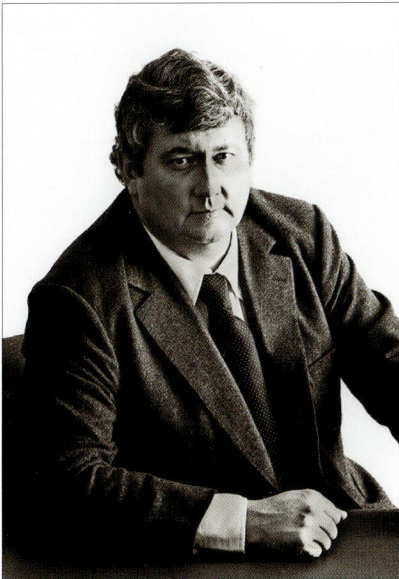

Terence Donovan[†]. He was one of the three great UK photographers known just by their surnames: Donovan, Duffy and Bailey.
Image by Darren S Feist.

Sir Alan Parker[†].
He had worked as a copywriter at PKL before CDP, where he had hired Phil Mason. He went on to direct some outstanding movies such as Bugsy Malone, Midnight Express, Mississippi Burning, Evita, The Commitments, Angela's Ashes *to name a few.*
Image by filmdirectors.eu.

John Kelley and Phil Mason did great work, but it never saw the light of day.

The final straw for me was when a commercial John Horton and I had made for the launch of the tabloid form of the *Evening Standard* newspaper had its end title changed by the Suit, without consulting us.

When Lindsay Dale rang (he knew me through John Hegarty at John Collings) and offered me the job at CDP, there was no hesitating, but I did feel as if I had left the others in the lurch and the brown smelly stuff.

Note: John had been a musician before joining PKL and had been part of a band called 'The End'. The band was managed by Bill Wyman of The Rolling Stones and, while living in Barcelona, had been *Top of the Pops* in Europe.

During the music recording session for the Teflon commercial John went into the recording studio with the musicians and briefed them on the music that he wanted. A Renaissance man?

My CPV generation.

Tony Beerbohm (Creative Director), John Horton, John Kelley, Phil Mason, Jon Parkinson and a scary looking Scot, Randy MacDonald, who had worked in Mexico but proved to be a pussy cat in real life; but not with Suits.
Apologies to anyone I've missed.

Chapter
Six

1970 to 1973 (a glorious time).

Collett, Dickenson, Pearce (CDP)

✝

One of my two 'universities'.

The two universities?

One: Advertising said to be the 'University of Life' as we covered such a wide spectrum of life's needs and events.

Two: Collett, Dickenson, Pearce has been described as the University of advertising with 'graduates working all over the planet'.

The Post Office appointed us, it was said, because of the modest, civil-service nature of the offices. Ryman desks and white Formica walls. Not very glamorous at all. The Directors had offices on the ground floor and that was known as 'Soft Furnishings' as they had fitted carpet.

Sir Frank Lowe.
Image: Campaign' online.

I had first worked with Frank (now Sir Frank) Lowe at Pritchard Wood on National Provincial Bank (it later became NatWest), where he was seen as a rising star. He was the perfect example of acting the part as he would 'patrol' the Creative Department each day as if he were Managing Director. Who better to fit the roll when it became vacant? When the tax crisis hit CDP, Frank left with many of the accounts and some of the staff to form Lowe, Howard-Spink (now Lowe & Partners Worldwide) and great success.

After Frank became 'King' of the agency, following management changes, he brought in a set designer, David Bill, to redesign our modest foyer.

A team came in and fitted marble walls. The next day they were found smashed on the floor as the set builders, it seems, weren't used to the concept of longevity.

One of the extra incentives for me to accept Sir Nigel Seeley's generous offer to move to Dorland was that CDP had four Creative Directors, or so it seemed to me at the time.

There was the overall and original one, the wonderful Colin Millward[†], the daily version, John Salmon[†], an outstanding copywriter; the Managing Director, Frank Lowe, and then out of the woodwork came Geoff Seymour.

Yes, it may be sour grapes with me, but I had a script approved by John Salmon who then went on leave and Geoff told me, in a corridor discussion, that he didn't like the idea and that it wasn't to go ahead. I was about to leave for a meeting with the chosen production company.

Colin Millward was reported to have said to John who was complaining about Geoff, in a Board Meeting "You created the monster, you handle him."

However, at Dorland I quickly realised that I had made a huge mistake in leaving CDP and those problems were minor.

Nevertheless, I doubt whether they would have had me back as I had said to John, that I resigned because I couldn't cope with three CDs.

I had been spoilt by working for David Abbott at DDB and Peter Mayle at PKL. One voice, one agency.

Note: when showing John Salmon my copy he would occasionally delete a phrase I had loved. His comment was "Sometimes you have to kill the little darlings."

Colin Millward, arguably the 'father' of Britain's 'Golden Ad Age'.

Colin Millward was the most influential creative figure in post-war British advertising.

Colin Charters Millward, advertising executive: born Hull, Yorkshire 29 August 1924; creative director, Collett Dickenson Pearce 1960-79; married 1953 Felicity Brown (two daughters); died London 5 May 2004.

Colin Millward.
Image: Festival of British Advertising.

It wasn't just the quality of the work that emerged from the benign dictatorship he ran from the fourth floor of Collett Dickenson Pearce throughout the Sixties and Seventies as the agency's creative director, although this included acclaimed advertisements for Heineken, Harvey's Bristol Cream, Bird's Eye, Hovis, Benson & Hedges and Hamlet cigars.

His most lasting contribution was the ethos he created at CDP and the confidence he inspired in those he allowed to share it with him. I'm pretty sure I speak for Alan Parker, Frank Lowe, Brian Duffy, Ridley Scott, Charles Saatchi and many, many more when I say that Colin Millward taught me more than anyone I ever met. More about myself, and more about my potential; and he did it in a most unusual way.

When I was a very young account executive at CDP, a "suit", on most days I would be required to take a piece of work into his office for approval. He'd sit nibbling his nails for a while and then, in his broad Yorkshire accent he'd say, "It's not very good, is it?" And I'd say "Isn't it?" and he'd say, "No, it's not very good at all." And I'd ask "What don't you like about it?"

"You work it out, son. Take it away. Do it again. See you tomorrow."

For what felt like years, I was terrified of him. I'd leave his office and just stare at the bloody ad. Then I'd go and talk it over with a copywriter, or one of the art directors, and we'd sit and curse Millward. But 99 times out of 100 he was right, and we would come back the next day, invariably with something far better. Years later I said to him, "You know, you were a real bastard to work for. You were always hyper-critical, and I never remember you steering us in any particularly useful direction."

"No," he said. "I did something much more valuable, I taught you to bloody well think. At the same time he had taught all of us at CDP another incredibly important lesson; one that I have never forgotten; that what is "competent", or even what's "good", can only ever be a point of departure, never a satisfactory point of arrival.

Colin Charters Millward was born in Sculcoates, on the outskirts of Hull, in 1924, and was educated at Hull Grammar School and Leeds College of Art. After Second World War service, he won a scholarship to the Ecole des Beaux-Arts in Paris, where he remained for a year before returning to London. He joined the creative department of the advertising firm Mather & Crowther, then moved to Coleman Prentis & Varley, where he met John Pearce, who went on to co-found Collett Dickenson Pearce.

Millward joined the firm in 1960 as creative director. He drove home his commitment to talent by spending several hours every week looking at the work of young people; photographers, typographers, artists of every kind had their work assessed and criticised, and very few left without a clearer sense of the direction their work should be taking.

The standards I and everyone else at CDP set for ourselves were Colin Millward's standards. Our expectations were his expectations. What looked like our successes were, in reality, his successes, for as Frank Lowe once succinctly put it, "Colin's achievement was in putting all of our rubbish where it belonged - in the bin!"

think for yourself." And he had.

At the same time he had taught all of us at CDP another incredibly important lesson; one that I have never forgotten; that what is "competent", or even what's "good", can only ever be a point of departure, never a satisfactory point of arrival.

Colin's own career began and ended as a painter, and a very fine one. Hopefully, the totality of his creative contribution will eventually be celebrated with a retrospective that will include a selection of his paintings, something he could never be persuaded to do in his lifetime.

Lord David Puttnam, *The Independent*.

A happy choice of music.

Music may be the food of love but it was the lifeblood of Hamlet commercials.

By Mike Everett.

Posted in an-at-om-ised on: January 30th, 2017.

In the advertising website, *More About Advertising*, editor Stephen Foster reprinted an article that had been written by the late John Webster for a magazine called *Commercials*. Stephen published John Webster's article as part of his *Desert Island Ads* series. John Webster very gamely chose ten commercials from an agency that was Boase, Massimi, Pollitt's (the agency where Webster was the creative director) greatest rival, Collett, Dickenson and Pearce. Not only that, but all 10 commercials were part of one campaign, for Hamlet Cigars.

Of course, as John Webster points out, the Bach music is crucial to the Hamlet campaign, and we have Colin Millward to thank for that. Colin was CDP's first creative director and had served in the Royal Air Force. Shortly after the end of the Second World War, he was posted to India where he lived in a hut for six months. The previous occupant had left Colin a gramophone, but only one record. On one side of this disc was Debussy's 'Clair de Lune'. On the other, Bach's 'Air on the G String'. Colin remembered the Bach music and suggested to its creators, Tim Warriner and Roy Carruthers that it should provide the soundtrack to their Hamlet campaign.

In 1959, a French Jazz Musician called Jacques Loussier had formed the 'Play Bach Trio'. They released a series of albums under this name, featuring the simple combination of piano, bass and drums performing improvised versions of Bach. Amongst these was a jazz version of 'Air on a G String'.

John Ritchie, who at that time was the account handler on Hamlet, was duly despatched to Paris to persuade Jacques Loussier and his trio to record a 30-second version for use in the commercials. Ritchie tracked down Loussier to his apartment on the outskirts of Paris. Loussier wasn't home so Ritchie camped outside for three days until the musician turned up. To keep himself going, Ritchie had been popping uppers, so when he finally met Loussier he was hyper, unable to sit still, and conducted the negotiation with Loussier while running around the room. Nevertheless, he was successful and Loussier agreed on a £1,000 fee.

While I was researching a book that I have written that describes the conception and execution of many of CDP's greatest ads, I sought the help of a musician who is a friend of mine, Mike Townend to explain why the music is so apt. Mike has worked with people like Smokey Robinson and Burt Bacharach, so he knows what he's talking about. As well as pointing out that the correct title of the piece is 'Air from Suite No 3 in D Major', he told me to study Bach's original version. He said it is typical of Bach's early work in as much as it builds tension, then moves towards a release, or 'climax'. When I heard this, it sounded just like the structure of a Hamlet commercial – tension in the form of an unfortunate event or situation, followed by release as the protagonist smokes the Hamlet – so that may be why the music is so appropriate. That, plus the fact that it's a damned good tune, of course.

As Hans Christian Anderson said, 'where words fail, music speaks'. There are few words in Hamlet commercials, but each commercial speaks volumes – in emotion, storytelling and humour. To a large extent, that's thanks to the music and, of course, Colin Millward who had the prescience to choose it. I would also like to offer posthumous thanks to John Webster for acknowledging the Hamlet campaign as probably the greatest TV campaign ever to be created in the British Isles. Thank you, John.

A tribute to John Salmon. Another creative 'giant' and a true gentleman.

John Salmon was born in Highgate, London, on 18 January 1931 to Thomas and Amelia Rose Salmon. In 1953 he married a Frenchwoman, Suzanne Jouvray, who later became a painter.

Known as "Smokey" Salmon, (18 January 1931 – 7 April 2017), he was also known for his role at Collett Dickenson Pearce (CDP) and for "firing" the Ford Motor Company as a client after their public relations department attempted to interfere with his agency's creative process.

John Salmon.
Image John Claridge, another John.

His career. After service in the Royal Air Force, where Salmon became close friends with the writer Len Deighton, he worked as a typographer and copywriter in advertising. He got a job at the American agency Doyle Dane Bernbach and in 1967 at Collett, Dickenson, Pearce (now Dentsu) in London where he rose from copywriter to creative director and later chairman, being known as "Smokey" Salmon, The agency has been described by Mark Whelan as being, in its heyday, "Mad Men personified".

At CDP, Salmon worked with Charles Saatchi and Alan Parker. He mentored Alan Waldie who developed the Benson & Hedges "Gold" cigarette campaign. He recruited Omar Sharif to appear in advertising for Olympus cameras and Alan Whicker to promote Barclaycard.He developed memorable print advertising for the British Army and the Metropolitan Police. He "fired" the Ford Motor Company after their PR department attempted to interfere with his agency's creative process.

When Frank Lowe, later Sir Frank Lowe, left CDP to form Lowe Howard-Spink, Salmon declined an invitation to join them.He was described by Lowe as "one of the three greatest copywriters of the late 20th century" along with Tony Brignull and David Abbott.Jim Aitchison has written that as creative director of CDP, Salmon "presided over that agency's golden years of creativity".

John's later life. After retirement in 1994, Salmon studied art history and obtained two degrees from the Open University. He and Suzanne indulged their interest in contemporary art and cookery. Salmon was an enthusiastic follower of American baseball. He died on 7 April 2017 and was survived by his wife and three children.

Wikipedia.

ADVERTISING'S OSCAR WILDE.

An appreciation of the work of Geoffrey Seymour.

By **Mike Everett.** *An-at-om-sed, July 17, 2019.*

Geoff Seymour in the 70s. *Image: FM Seymour.*

It is one of the great ironies of the advertising business that one of its most talented writers is better remembered for his salary than his work. When he joined Saatchi & Saatchi in 1982, Geoff Seymour was paid £100,000 a year, a sum of money that soon became known in advertising circles as a 'Seymour'. It may have been as an eye-watering amount at the time but, to pinch L'Oreal's famous end line, he was worth it. In the 14 years leading up to 1982 he had been responsible for some of the most ground breaking and original work ever seen on the TV screens of Britain.

As Sir Alan Parker has said, "Geoff was quite brilliant. He was one of the best thinkers of his generation of ad men and responsible for some seminal work, which helped revolutionise British and world advertising. I have to say my memories of working with him were completely pleasurable – invigorating, anarchic and fun". If that endorsement wasn't enough, what about this from Sir Ridley Scott: "Anything that Geoff Seymour wrote I very much paid attention to because he was kind of special. The main draw to direct Hovis was working with Seymour". So what was this work?

In the beginning. Let's start by going back to 1968. A twenty-one year old Geoff Seymour is handed a brief to write a TV campaign for Bird's Eye Dinners for One by Frank Lowe. 'Let's do some famous work' Frank tells Geoff. Frank remembers that Geoff was unfazed by this exaltation and soon did something that Frank clearly remembers about Geoff. "He had a great facility for writing good lines, which I often thought of as based on the strategy we agreed, before he wrote the actual commercial".

In the case of Dinners for One, Geoff fretted that the product name would work to its disadvantage; that the name might suggest that it was a product for sad bastards, who live alone with no mates. Geoff got round this by writing the line 'especially good for those who aren't used to being on their own'. He brought the line to life with scripts that spoofed two feature films, Desert Song and Brief Encounter. Alan Parker shot them in glorious black and white. If you were to ask Alan Parker today which of the many commercials he directed is his favourite he would tell you Brief Encounter.

Another irony that concerns Geoff Seymour is that he is credited with writing many commercials that he didn't. In his obituary in the Guardian, for example, he is cited as the author of the famous Hovis Bike Ride commercial. He is not. David Brown wrote the script for that commercial. However, Geoff did write the end line 'As good for you today as it's always been' and wrote two commercials that preceded the Bike Ride commercial, Seaside and Northern. In other words, he wrote the campaign, a far harder task than the writing follow on commercials, no matter how good they might be, as David Brown would surely concede.

The Guardian also credits Geoff with writing 'It makes a dishonest woman of you' for Bird's Eye pies. Not so. Tony Kenrick and Vernon Howe wrote that campaign. Likewise, 'When you've got to make it something fast' for Bird's Eye Beef Burgers was also written by Tony Kenrick and Vernon Howe, not Geoff. Not only are these credits inaccurate, they belie the vast amount of work that Geoff actually did for Bird's Eye.

After his success on Dinners for One, Frank Lowe kept feeding Geoff Bird's Eye briefs. A couple of notable examples are More for Bird's Eye Deserts, an Oliver Twist spoof, and Princess for another range of Bird's Eye deserts known as Hidden Centres. There were many more.

Geoff also wrote the campaign line for Nescafé, 'If you're serving coffee, better make sure it's Nescafé', together with a number of commercials to accompany it. In 1972 he was asked to create a campaign for an ersatz sports car that Ford was launching, the Capri. His slogan for this campaign 'The car you always promised yourself' was far more elegant than the car it advertised.

Talking of elegance, there is one commercial that Geoff wrote that illustrates his apparently effortless ability to parody the British class system, Lifeboat, for Cockburn's Port. This sixty-second one act play was shot by Alan Parker in Malta using the tank that had been constructed for the sea sequences in Ben- Hur. To sublime comedic effect it shows the survivors of a shipwreck being more concerned with their after dinner drink and the pronunciation of its name than their immediate and highly inconvenient plight.

He was no slouch when it came to writing print advertising, either. An early example of Geoff's prowess in print is an ad for the Ronson electric toothbrush. It shows a set of dentures in a glass of water with the headline 'How long will you be able to call your teeth your own?' He also wrote ads and posters for Whitbread Tankard beer using the line 'Tankard helps you excel, after one you'll do anything well'. The posters were in the style of circus advertising, as were the commercials that Geoff wrote to promote Whitbread Trophy.

All this work, of course, was done at Collett, Dickenson and Pearce, just as it was entering its creative heyday. Geoff was a significant contributor to CDP's creative success – and boy, did he know it. He was often to be seen flouncing around the corridors of the agency with an insouciant swagger, his flowing locks leading him to look like a latter day Oscar Wilde.

Under Frank Lowe's patronage he was made deputy-creative director, a promotion that before long led to trouble. He mounted an unsuccessful bid to usurp John Salmon from the role of overall creative director. This move and Geoff's increasingly errant behaviour started to disrupt the smooth running of the agency. So Frank Lowe convened a board meeting to discuss how to deal with Geoff. Colin Millward, CDP's original creative director was present at this meeting. After listening to Frank talk for a while about the difficulties Geoff was causing, Colin spoke. "Well as far as I can see, Frank, he's your monster. You created him so you have to destroy him". That was the end of Geoff Seymour at CDP.

Well, if he couldn't run the creative department of one agency, he could jolly well run the creative department of another. Thus, Geoff moved to Royds as creative director, charged with re-invigorating the agency's staid creative product. Looked at whichever way, this was a mistake, both for Royds and for Geoff. He soon went elsewhere.

In partnership with art director Peter Cherry (also ex-CDP) and account man, Dick Hedger, Geoff set up Cherry, Hedger, Seymour. This proved to be a more productive time for Geoff. He resumed his practice of formulating the strategy by writing the strapline first. For Morland's Sheepskin Coats he coined 'When luxury becomes a necessity' and under the banner 'Allow us to spoil you', he created a campaign for Air India. Another end line written by Geoff at Cherry, Hedger, Seymour was one that later survived transition through several other ad agencies: 'Made in Scotland from girders' for Irn Bru, a fizzy drink enjoyed north of the border.

But perhaps the best regarded of his straplines is 'Temptation beyond endurance' for

Planter's Peanuts. In combination with art director Glen Clarke, and using illustrator Patrick Hughes, Geoff created a poster showing a huge shadow reaching out to steal a peanut from the man whose shadow it was. This poster went on to win the 1982 D&AD Silver Award for a 4-sheet.

A further notable campaign that Geoff created during this period was for Foster's Lager, featuring Paul Hogan reprising his Crocodile Dundee character as a galumphing, unsophisticated Aussie trampling over British traditions. These extremely funny commercials were signed off with a devilishly simple but clever strapline, 'Foster's, the Australian for lager'.

Time moved on and so did Geoff. His old boss from CDP days, Frank Lowe asked him to join the agency he'd just set up with Geoff Howard-Spink. It was while he was here that Geoff came up with the end line for the Stella Artois campaign, 'Reassuringly expensive', although at first he didn't know that he'd come up with it. Frank Lowe fished the line out of piece of body copy that Geoff had crafted for a Stella print ad. Unfortunately, this serendipitous discovery has given rise to another misattribution concerning Geoff Seymour. He did not originate the Stella Artois campaign, only the end line. The credit for creating the campaign and its strategy falls to David Watkinson and Bob Isherwood at Collett, Dickenson and Pearce eight years earlier.

As well as gifting the Stella Artois end line to Frank's agency, Geoff Seymour did a memorable Heineken commercial with Alan Waldie, Windermere based on Wordsworth's famous Daffodil poem. Despite these successes, his time at Lowe Howard-Spink was far from turbulence-free. Many members of the creative department resented the way Geoff had been parachuted in by Frank Lowe. This caused tensions, that along with other matters related to the share allocation at LHS, eventually led to the resignation of the founding creative directors, John Kelley and John O'Driscoll. Not surprisingly therefore, Geoff's tenure at LHS was short-lived. He moved to Saatchi & Saatchi and the famous £100,000 a year salary.

When he joined Saatchi, Geoff stipulated in his contract that he would never work on the agency's Procter and Gamble business. He feared that working on such a client would contaminate his creative flair. Instead he was put to work on Saatchi's British Airways account. Geoff's method of working – writing the strapline to inform the strategy – once again came into play. Buried in some research that he was given to read was the fact that British Airways carried a greater number of passengers than any other airline on earth. Geoff took this fact and turned it into a phrase that has since passed into common memory, 'The world's favourite airline'. That line alone probably went a long way to paying Geoff's salary for the first year.

But before long, Geoff's feet began to itch again. He decided to become a commercials director, setting up Geoffrey Seymour Films. This was never entirely successful. Some might say that this was due to the fact that Geoff had upset so many of his potential clients that they were unlikely to favour him with work. It's true to say that Geoff could be acerbic and had got on the wrong side of quite a number of people. However, it's also a fact that Geoff had entered a crowded and competitive market. There were plenty of more accomplished directors around. Geoff was a long way down the pecking order, so he ended up doing most of his film work abroad, far from the plum London scripts. Increasingly, though, Geoff was falling victim to ill health.

In 1997 he was diagnosed with a non-Hodgkin's lymphoma and later was discovered to have a brain tumor. This led to his untimely death in December 2009 at the age of 61. It is a final irony in his story that it was his brain, one of advertising's finest and most original, that ended up killing him.

Geoffrey Seymour,

advertising copywriter, born 15 January 1947; died 19 December 2008.

Alan Waldie†, a most unusual but inspiring, Art Group Head.

Alan Waldie
Image: Campaign online.

Alan Waldie (pictured above) was my Art Group Head along with Lindsay Dale†, who was my Copy Group Head. I called Lindsay the "Welsh Dresser", but not to his face. Sadly, I couldn't find a good photo of him.

Lindsay Dale.

As Alan is now "upstairs" I think he will forgive me if I break the rule of "What happens on tour, stays on tour". Alan went with me on my 'research' trip to Ireland, which I describe on the next page.

Alan has been described as one of Britain's best Art Directors and had fantastic taste in photographers.

He was a bit of a wild man and one Saint Patrick's night he asked to come along with me to celebrate.

He steered me to a French restaurant, L'Caveau in Soho , the French singer there on the night, (think Francois Hardy with a guitar and sitting on a stool singing French songs)was most upset as he took over the piano and started crashing out Jerry Lee Lewis rock and roll numbers, at which he was brilliant, but it was inappropriate and we were asked to leave.

Credits: *Copywriter, Mike Doyle; Art Director, Alan Waldie; Photographer, sadly unknown. The ads barely do Alan justice as he was one of Britain's finest art directors.*

On Tour with Waldie.

Ballymaloe
Image: Ballymaloe

The Tour was to Ireland back in the dim and distant 70s when I was working on the Aer Lingus account. The agency Head of Art, Arthur Parsons[†], Waldie and myself were packed off for a month to help with the creation of a new campaign.

We arrived at Swansea docks for the ferry to Cork. Arthur had packed a Gladstone bag with bottles of gin, tonic water and glasses and we whet our whistles, sitting in Arthur's Ford Zephyr while waiting for the ferry. Remember those? Massive Mafia-looking type cars.

We arrived in the Emerald Isle and went straight to the wonderful Ballymaloe House. Owned by an Irish Quaker whose wife, Myrtle Allen, loved to cook. The place had become a magnet for Dubliners and people from advertising.

The food was magnificent and almost all locally grown.

One day we went out on the hotel's fishing boat, a Galway Hooker. No, she's not a lady of easy virtue, it had bulbous bows to withstand the huge waves coming in off the Atlantic into Galway Bay. Waldie, in hiking boots, gave us cause for concern as he shimmied up and down the mast. Having said how great the food was, this day differed. Some of the fish caught was boiled in a bucket with potatoes and was awful, but we had to put on a brave face. We then moved on to fresh pastures and stayed in a hotel where the brother of the

A Galway Hooker.
Image:
galwaycitymuseum.ie

117

actor, Richard Harris, was holding 'court' and being patronising to the wait staff.

Next morning, we discovered that Alan had dunked him in the hotel swimming pool. Alan also couldn't remember what he had done with his jacket which had his money and ferry ticket in the pocket.

We hunted high and low and eventually discovered that he had given it to the barman in his drunken state, after the barman had admired it.

We next headed off to Galway (not for the Hookers) to fly out to the Aran Islands in Galway Bay where they still speak Gaelic. Our pilot, funnily enough, was an Australian dressed in an Aran sweater and an Aussie Akubra hat.

The departure lounge was in the Galway Hotel. A small bus took us out to a field outside the city where donkeys and cows were grazing, but it had a windsock and milk crates marking the landing strip.

The pilot told us if the engines failed, we could still glide to the island. Alan had been taking on board Dutch courage but still looked very nervous. One guy chased the animals away before we took off.

We met a wonderful woman, Maggie Dirrane[†], who starred in the movie *Man of Aran* made in 1934 by Robert Flaherty. She had been to New York and London for the documentary's premiers but had always returned to her island on the wild edge of Europe.

She had arranged for a ceilidh in our honour that night, but Arthur said we had a schedule to keep. I will go to my grave regretting we didn't have that experience.

We then went up to Donegal and met local weavers working on hand looms to make

Maggie Dirrane.

Photo by Arthur Parsons. ▶

Image from Man of Aran ▼

Note: *while writing this book I discovered that Maggie had passed away at the ripe old age of 109 years, a great testimonial to the simple life on the Aran islands.*

tweed, and crossed the border, in and out, without any troops to be seen.

On another day, we sailed up the Shannon. We then drove down to the Wicklow mountains.

One night, Alan and I got into an argument, (probably about Irish politics. I can't remember) but he was banging on my door at 2am clad only in his saggy y-fronts trying to continue the 'discussion'. He was later found wandering on the road to Dublin and brought back to the hotel, mercifully in one piece.

When we finally got back to the agency, the then Executive Creative Director, Colin Millward, summoned the team and John Salmon to explain why so many of us had been gone for such a long time. I can't remember how it was explained but I lived to tell the tales.

Arthur took some great photographs, many of which were used in the campaign. My favourite was of a lone fisherman in a rowboat on a magnificent lake, surrounded by mountains with the headline: *Fishermen in Ireland have a saying: One man, one lake.*

The ads never ran in the UK because the 'Troubles' had taken off, but they did run in Europe. The French won an award for that ad and only credited themselves. Perfidious French?

There is one story, to finish, that Rick Cook† told about visiting Alan at his home one weekend and suggesting that they take his kids to the local zoo. The kids didn't seem keen, which puzzled Rick.

He understood why, however, when they got to the Zoo and Waldie started tormenting the apes or monkeys by offering a banana and then snatching it away when they reached for it. They were escorted out of the zoo.

Having said all that, Alan was usually taken for an English gentleman and had fantastic taste in photographers, buying books on emergent American photographers of whom I had never heard.

I just hope they like Jerry Lee Lewis music in Heaven. Although with 'Great Balls of Fire' he may be performing downstairs.

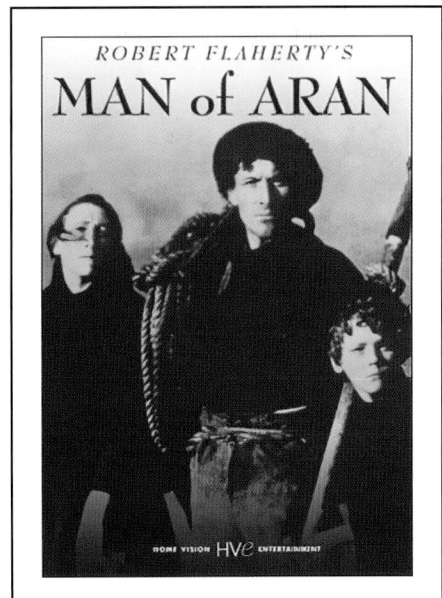

A celebration of Alan's career.

by **Mike Everett**

an-at-om-ised, Posted on: November 6th, 2015.

The other day I was privileged to experience something that one person who was present described as 'magical'. It was a specially-convened event to celebrate the remarkable career of Alan Waldie. Alan is noted for many great pieces of work but most famously for the Benson & Hedges 'Swimming Pool' commercial which won a coveted D&AD Black Pencil in the late seventies. Last Tuesday, Alan was presented with another Black Pencil, to mark his extraordinary career. But rather than describing the event in detail, I can do no better than to publish below a press release prepared by Tim Lindsay, CEO of D&AD. Here it is.

Legendary art director Alan Waldie fêted by D&AD and colleagues from CDP and Lowe Howard-Spink.

At Chelsea's Sloane Club yesterday, industry legend Alan Waldie was presented by D&AD's chief executive Tim Lindsay with a special Pencil "in recognition of an extraordinary career in advertising". Present at the event were many of Alan's colleagues from CDP and Lowe Howard-Spink days.

Adrian Holmes, in a warm tribute to his old partner, described Alan as 'an art director who came from another era: the era when craft in advertising actually mattered'. He also acknowledged that 'with Alan's magic came its constant companion: mischief', and proceeded to share some of the more notable 'Waldie stories' with his audience.

Alan is probably best known for his work on the ground-breaking Benson & Hedges 'surreal' campaign. This included the famous 'Iguana' cinema commercial directed by Hugh Hudson, itself a recipient of a D&AD Black pencil in 1979 and often cited as one of the most influential commercials ever made.

Alan was also involved in the early days of the Heineken 'Refreshes the Parts' campaign, and was art director on many of the award-winning commercials including 'Water in Majorca' and 'Blues Singer'.

As Alan, now 75, left the room, a chorus of 'Waldie, Waldie' was taken up by all present – an echo of the same chant which filled the Grosvenor House at the D&AD awards night 36 years ago.

Note: *I was sorry to have missed it.*

More memories of Waldie by the other Mike.

More than his work though, Waldie was a creative achievement in his own right. Here colleague **Mike Everett**, *now of anatomised, remembers Alan Waldie.*

Alan Waldie was unforgettable for me long before I ever met him. My first creative boss, Ron Brown, told me stories about Alan from his time working with Alan at, I think, the Roger Pryor advertising agency. My first full time art director, Phillip Eldridge, also regaled me with the antics of Waldie, gleaned from the time when he was Alan's assistant. That was in 1969.

In early 1970, I moved to Charles Barker advertising, to work with John Sherfield. John had been at Allen, Brady and Marsh with Alan, and John, too, was a compendium of 'Waldie Stories.'. So, too, was the creative secretary at Charles Barker, Maureen. She also described dozens of adventures she'd had in the company of Alan Waldie when she worked with him. I couldn't help thinking, who was this amazing character who led such a colourful life?

I finally met him in 1973, when I joined Collett, Dickenson and Pearce. He looked the very opposite of the person I imagined. There he was, the absolute epitome of the English country gentleman: tweed jacket, tightly knotted tie, Tattersall check shirt, V-neck cashmere sweater and corduroy trousers. He couldn't have appeared more conservative if he'd tried. But when he spoke, he was more unforgettable than ever. That conservative exterior belied an anarchic interior. This was a man who was either barking mad or a genius. Or both. At times it was hard to tell. I was soon able to form my own opinion, though.

Almost a week into my sojourn at CDP I was invited by Terry Lovelock to join him, Phil Mason and Alan for drinks at the Caveau Club*, a terrible dive in a basement somewhere in Soho. As I descended the steps to the front door I saw the headwaiter spot Waldie, and hastily lock up the club's upright piano. We entered, and Waldie, undeterred, made a beeline for the cutlery tray. He took a knife, prised open the piano and proceeded to play the opening bars of Jerry Lee Lewis's 'Great Balls of Fire'. That was my induction – first hand – into the wonderful world of the unforgettable Alan Waldie. It's a world that my life would have been all the poorer, all the duller, and all the less entertaining, if I hadn't become one of its inhabitants.

I guess the inhabitants of Heaven are now undergoing a similar experience to mine – and if anybody can manage to play Great Balls of Fire on a harp, it will be Waldie – assuming God doesn't lock the harp up first.

Alan Waldie, *advertising art director, June 12, 1940 – December 9, 2016.*

✳Scene of St Patrick's Night incident where we were asked to leave.

Discovering my Irish roots.

Growing up in London, we kept very quiet about being Irish. My Mum was often taken for being a Canadian, but working on Aer Lingus made me very proud of my ancestry and started an interest in Irish history, which I still enjoy today.

This is a tribute to London's Creative 'Murphia' of which I consider myself to be a fortunate part, and additional notes on that trip as a unique experience.

London's Creatives in Advertising and the 'Murphia'.

There was also the 'Kosher Noshstra', the 'Taffia', you get the idea.

Members include those I knew and worked with Hegarty, Delaney(s), Dempsey, Donovan. Duffy, Flemming(s), Kelley(s), O'Driscoll, Walsh, Morrow et al. Apologies to anyone who I missed.

Tom Moult Here's a picture of me great-grand-daddy outside his store in Longford. Am I entitled to a Murphia passport too Mike?

Note: The first time I met Tom (son of Ted Moult, farmer, radio and TV personality in the UK), before he headed to Oz, was at a St Patrick's Night dinner at Sandra Leamon's place, where we had green potatoes but not green meat, if my memory serves me well. There was an Irish copywriter from JWT also there (sadly his name escapes me) who introduced me to the wonderful Irish traditional musicians, The Wolftones.

My reply The O'Moults no doubt Tom; I bet he served a 'terrific draught'. The passport is in the post.

These photos come from the *'Tour'*. As with the campaign for SAS, by Carl Ally in the US that promoted Scandinavia (one of my favourite campaigns), we promoted Ireland. I had only been there to visit Grandma Doyle when I was around eight years old. She had returned from London to live in Wicklow Town.

The perfect spot for a 'Wake' was taken by me in the Town and shows why I respect photographers so much. The pub in Wicklow with my name on it proved to be a magnetic spot for yours truly.

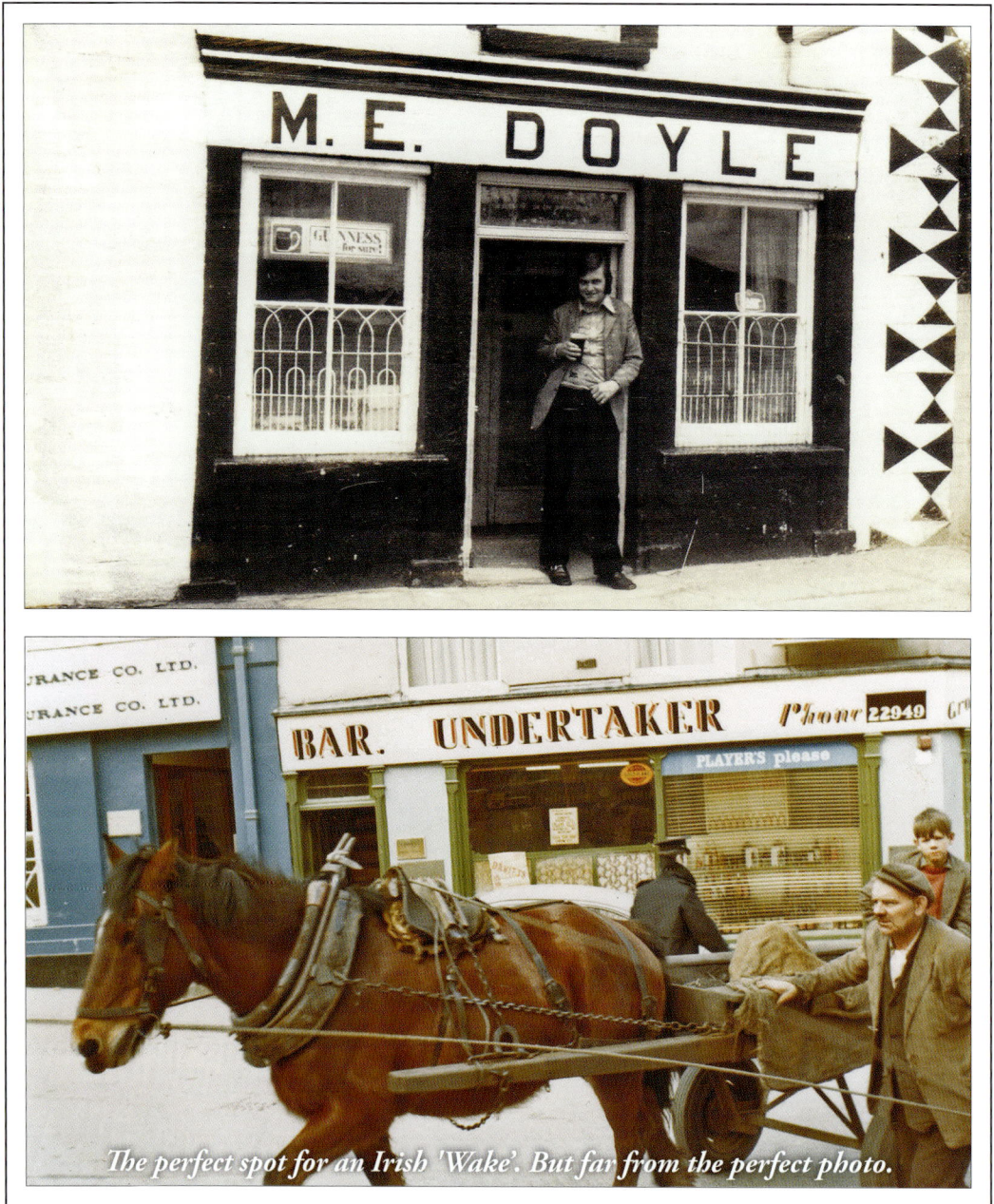

The perfect spot for an Irish 'Wake'. But far from the perfect photo.

That's me in 2016 outside the ancestral home in Claremorris, Mayo, Ireland. In 2020 it will have been 100 years since my grandmother had her photo taken in the same doorway. A rare example of me being good at maths.

Getting technical.

While at CDP I was briefed to write an ad for the new National Panasonic (as it was called then) TV.

Unlike with Sony at BBDO (more later), there was no client product briefing, so I took myself down to the local dealer and discovered that the set had a unique selling point; that meant I had something to work with and compete with the great Sony ads coming out of DDB US and BBDO London. They also renamed their hi-fi range as Technics and I was briefed to create the ads for their new range. Again, lots of store visits.

This, believe it or not, is the perfect picture.

There's one good reason for this apparent paradox.

It's our exclusive Magic Line tuner.

This, briefly, is how it works.

By pressing a button you get a broad green line on your screen. Turn the button until the line gets as narrow as possible. Push the button again so the line disappears and hey presto, you have the perfectly tuned picture.

With this perfection in mind we also produce our own tubes. (Many other manufacturers, in contrast, settle for someone else's).

The picture on a colour TV is made up of red, green and blue phosphorous dots.

We surround each dot with black to give you sharper, more vivid colours. Other manufacturers surround their dots with white and suffer the consequences.

We could have used the same mechanical controls you'll find on other TV's. But they're vague and imprecise compared with the electronic controls we use.

For instance, a mere touch on our channel selector and you're there, no twiddling of dials.

We also saw fit to give you an instant 'on' button which does just what it says. And an hermetically sealed flyback transformer so that no dust or damp can interfere with your viewing.

Furthermore, we use all solid state circuits instead of the cheaper and more vulnerable valves.

Not every manufacturer sees the need for these refinements.

But then not every manufacturer can offer you the perfect picture.

"Just slightly ahead of our time."

NATIONAL PANASONIC

Accepted for D&AD annual 1974.

Credits: *National Panasonic/Technics Copywriter, Mike Doyle; Art Director, Ted Ekman; Photographer, Adrian Flowers. Tony Brignull, a legendary copywriter popped his head into my office one day to compliment me on the ad. It was an intensely competitive agency and that was praise indeed from him. For the following ads I would visit local dealers to get the sales benefits from them as I knew nothing about hi-fi.*

Proof, if you needed it, that one turntable is not like another.

Judging by the graphs things look pretty black for our belt-driven competitors. Consider the facts.

1. Frequency spectrum of Rumble.

The Technics direct-drive motor has none of the belts and idlers which aggravate the problem of rumble.

Hence our remarkable showing above of 65dB.

2. Wow & Flutter.

Now as every audiophile knows, an AC motor rotates thousands of times a minute. As it does so it not only suffers wear but also causes wow and flutter.

Since our DC motor rotates at the same speed as the record and needs no speed reduction mechanism . . . well the graph speaks for itself.

3. Turntable speed constancy.

We resorted to a number of devices to achieve the above beeline. One of which is our 13" dynamically balanced turntable. This is balanced by a computer to reduce the wobble created by excess weight. A problem many of us are familiar with.

Then there's our strobe light which interprets the dots around the edge of the platter and helps monitor the speed. (This is coupled to a variable pitch control which increases or decreases the rpm.)

Another of our monitoring devices has the engaging title of analog feedback control.

En masse, they produce the result in graph 3.

One other relevant point is that we operate on a mere 20v DC.

So our performance never varies, even when the mains supply veers between 200-240v AC. (A conversion circuit translates AC to DC.)

In addition . . .

The sound absorbing legs on the turntable enable you to dance in hobnail boots, should you so wish, with no audible effect.

Gold-plated cartridge contacts on our S-shaped tone arm silence any inherent noise.

And the arm comes complete with an anti-skating device, balance and pressure control together with a viscous-damped cueing device.

Finally, with Quadrasonics looming on the horizon, we included low-loss leads for later conversion.

As you may have guessed such overall quality doesn't come cheap.

But at £134.95 you can console yourself with the fact that the SL-1200 is still the least expensive direct-drive system in the UK.

Technics

Quadraphonics Simplified.

The subject of quadraphonics is wrapped in confusion. Why, the jargon alone is enough to put one off: Matrix, QS, SQ, Discrete, CD4.

Our unique SA-8000X receiver is designed to simplify the whole affair.

How?

By being totally compatible to all matrix discs, all stereo discs and tapes, CD4 discs and quadraphonic tapes.

Courtesy of the ingenious "AFD" device we can decode any system in use now, or indeed in the future.

Our biased opinion.

Admittedly we have a preference for CD4. After all, the combined strength of Technics, JVC and RCA helped develop it.

Rather than compromise, as with matrix systems, we insisted on a system whereby all four channels were entirely separate. With minimal cross talk or signal loss (the bane of matrix systems).

The truth of our labour you see below you. It differs from most CD4 receivers in that the necessary demodulator fits neatly inside, not alongside the set.

Faint hearts.

Many people choose to meet "quad" half way by investing in the quadraphonic amp or receiver but continuing to use it in "stereo".

Our receiver is designed in such a way that even in stereo you use all four amps in the set, rather than letting two lie fallow.

A simple tune.

The four pole MOS-FET, used and developed by us is actually superior to the conventional but renowned FET.

We can boast of 1.5uv which is so sensitive it almost hurts.

Both FM and AM tuning capacitors are designed for even dial spacing without bunching and confusion of stations.

In simple terms, this all boils down to precise and effortless tuning.

What is more.

Provision has been made for the use of two tape decks so you can record and dub from any sound source.

Each speaker is monitored by one of four large Vu meters. And each channel has a separate volume control.

Then there's an MPX socket ready for the day when discrete 4-channel broadcasting takes to the air.

As we said earlier, with CD4 there's just no compromise, so we'll wind up with the uncompromising price of £319.95 including V.A.T.

Technics

Quadraphonics doesn't mean you've heard the last of your stereo collection.

People are still tending to fight shy of quadraphonics.

After investing in a fortune in their stereo collection they fear it will all be so much useless plastic if they change over.

They're sadly mistaken.

There is sufficient information on a stereo disc to produce a synthesised four channel sound.

All that is needed is a four channel amplifier that can interpret it.

Hence the Technics SA-5400X Receiver below.

You can of course happily continue in stereo without going the whole 'quad' hog, unlike other 4-channel receivers, ours allows you to use the full power capacity in stereo.

In fact, ours is one of but ingenious devices, enable us to cross-together two pairs of amps. Thus giving you a stereo out put of 25 watts RMS per channel.

When there's enough in the kitty you can then buy the necessary speakers and demodulator for CD4. Understandably this is our personal preference in quadraphonics. After all, together with JVC and RCA we helped develop it.

The beauty of this system is that there's no compromise. Each channel is separate without the intrusion of cross talk and, signal loss, the bane of matrix systems.

However, should you prefer matrix for economic reasons say, the receiver is perfectly compatible.

Whichever system you choose to play there are independent volume controls for each channel.

We've also made provision for the use of two pairs of stereophones (one quad).

And we've incorporated an AM/FM linear disc scale for easier and more precise tuning. Plus an FM MPX Output for whenever 4-channel broadcasts take to the air.

Just think for £174.95 you can buy a decent stereo receiver.

For the same price you can buy the SA-5400X and get the best of both worlds.

Technics

The corridor auction.

At the end of the working day, if there was an emergency ad that was needed for the next day, the Suit would walk down the corridor of the Creative Department offering payment to anyone willing to turn around the ad that night.

The fee would increase until someone bit the bullet.

I bit one night, and this ad ran with queues of drivers lining up the day the ad ran.

I can't remember what the fee was, but we weren't paid a lot for the privilege of working at CDP, so any financial help was appreciated.

What petrol station in its right mind would offer free petrol?

Answer: the Woodville Service Station, Whinmoor.

Tomorrow, at 7am, we open our grand, brand new Texaco self-service petrol station.

As a welcoming gesture to you, our motoring public, we're giving, on our first day, the first gallon away free when you have four or more. Plus a free badge of a Great British Regiment.

We're also giving quad stamps with every gallon bought for cash.

As if all that wasn't enough, our Texaco girls will be handing out such bonus perks as free felt tip pens, pencils, balloons and lollipops.

And if you buy a gallon of Havoline Multigrade Oil you get a free picnic flask along with 500 stamps.

(You'd best be early for all these, as we're not sure how long our stocks will last.)

While you're visiting look in on the sales shop, our station manager Mr. Blackman, will be pleased to show you the special bargains. An example being beach balls at only 10p.

How do we follow that?

Well, for the next four days (20th-23rd July) there'll be 5p off every gallon together with quad stamps. And a free regimental badge with every four gallons bought.

Then, for the following ten days (24th July-2nd Aug.), there'll be 10p off every four gallons, again with quad stamps and free badge.

From the 24th of July and for the next four weeks you can also have a free car wash with every four gallons.

The station will be open seven days a week: 7am-11pm weekdays, 8am-10pm Sundays.

We look forward to your company. **TEXACO**

**Woodville Service Station, York Road, Whinmoor, Leeds LS14 2AA.
Grand Opening, Thursday, 19th July, 7am.**

Credits: Copywriter, Mike Doyle; Art Director, Ted Ekman.

A charitable view of advertising.

The brief for Oxfam was their campaign theme of the time: *The Quiet Revolutionaries*.

There were to be no photos either of suffering children in the third world.

The outcome you see here.

It did mean that one of my ideas never saw the light of day. It featured the photo of the face of a starving child and the headline, 'The unacceptable face of capitalism'. You win some and you lose some, but I imagine it was just too political for them, and off-brief. Sadly, although the ads had coupons, I never heard how they had performed.

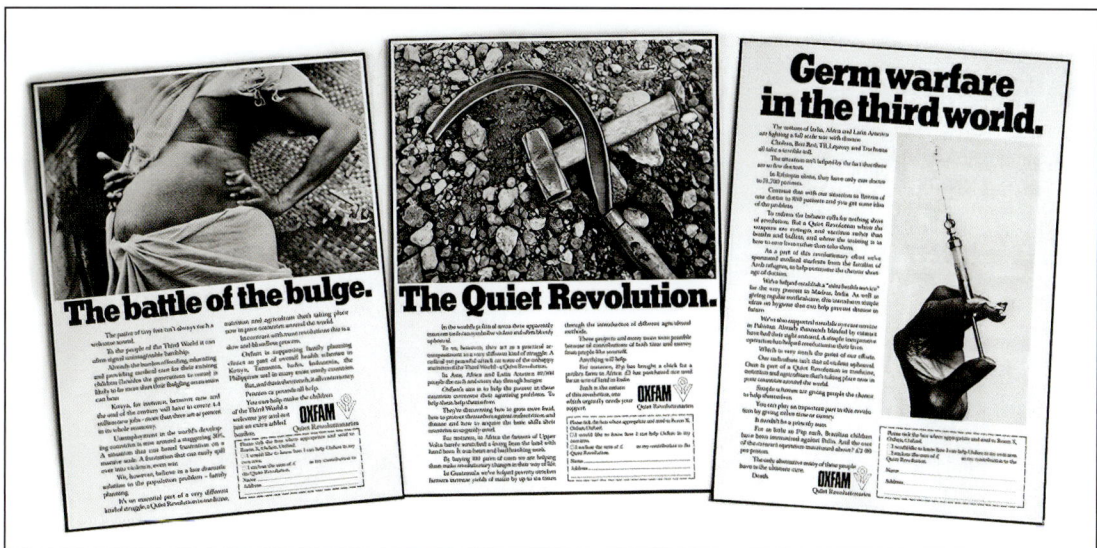

Credits: Copywriter, Mike Doyle; Art Director, Ted Ekman; Photographer, sadly, unknown.

Note: while on the subject of charity, David Abbott was a champion in this regard. There was an Art Director at French, Gold, Abbott who had a nervous breakdown. David informed her family and ex-husband that she needed help. The agency paid for her to go to a Harley Street psychiatrist and for her, and a friend, to have a holiday in a country of her choice. She chose Israel. The treatment worked.
Years later, one of London's finest copywriters and storytellers died owing sizeable debts and without sufficient funds to settle his debts. David, together with Alan Thomas (Creative Director at JWT, where this writer had also worked) generously helped to 'clean the slate'.

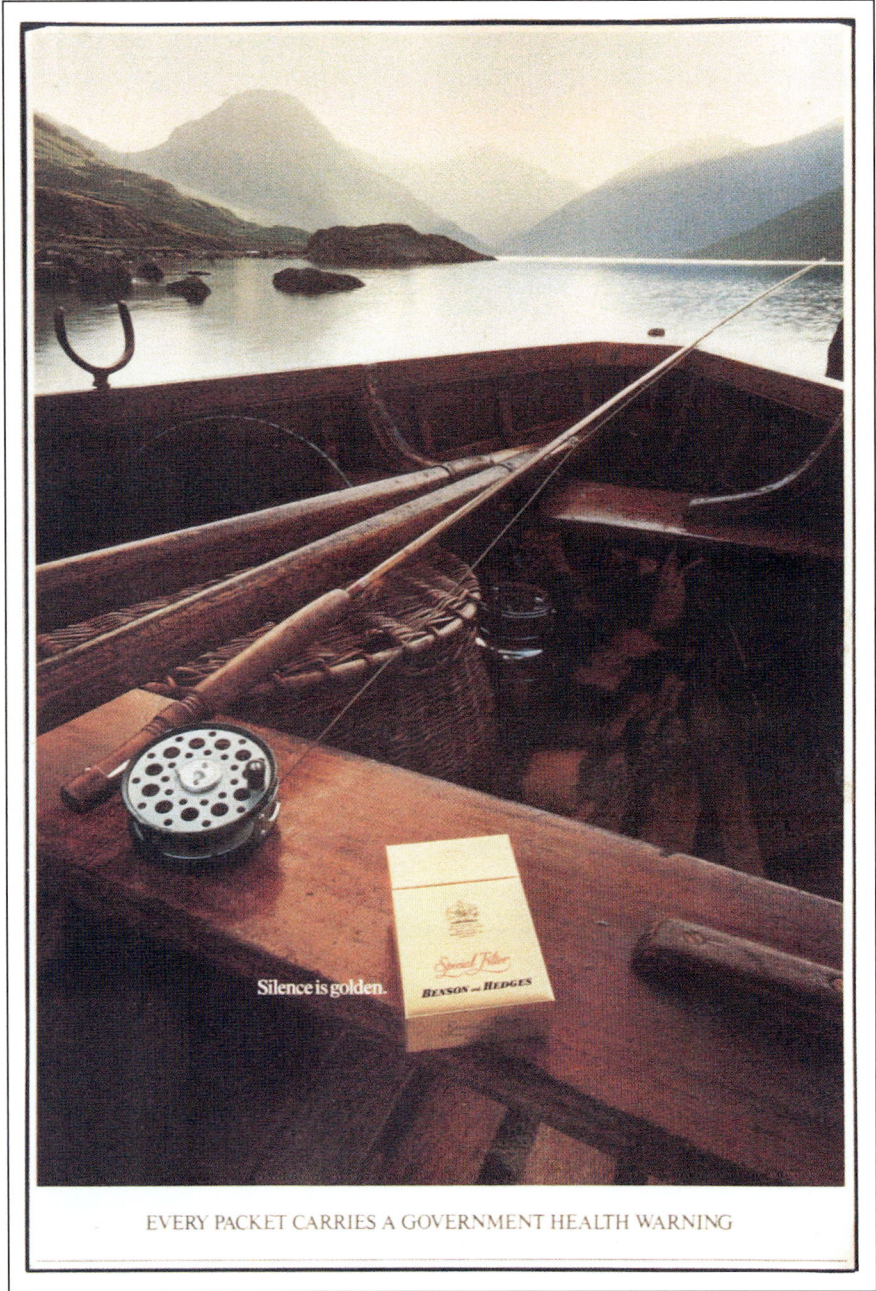

This won a silver in D&AD 1973, Maybe it should have been a gold?

Credits: Copywriter, Mike Doyle; Art Director: Pete Cherry, Photographers: Bruce Brown.

The 'Silence' is broken.

Pete Cherry originally chose an American Photographer, Richard Noble, to take the shot. The location was in Ireland. We landed at Belfast airport with the photographer's freelance assistant. Noble met us and drove us to the chosen location. It turned out to be a lake at the end of the garden of the house he was renting.

We rejected that and spent the next few days touring around until we found something we liked. We found a rowboat but had to spend days sanding it down and applying varnish.

The day of the shoot came. Noble threw into the boat, the beautiful fishing tackle we had been loaned by Laurie Petch, the CDP Office manager (he had only just bought it and gave it on trust). He then casually put the cigarette pack on the seat.

A group of his mates had turned up to watch. Crime of crimes, he only had a 35mm camera. Pete had been specific about requiring a 10 x 8 plate camera. You could cut the atmosphere with a knife.

I retired to the car and remember Noble towering over the small in stature, but large in ego, Pete as he fired the photographer. At dinner that night we tried to explain the B&H values, but he never understood.

Pete persuaded the assistant to drive us down from Donegal to Killarney the next day for a test shot.

Pete was so sick we stopped at a chemist and he bought a bottle of Kaolin & Morphine and drank the lot. Not surprisingly, he slept the entire journey.

At the Killarney hotel we asked for a dawn call. We woke at 10am the next day. The receptionist said we looked so tired they thought we needed a lie in.

We managed to get a shot that evening with the pack on a rock and repeated that the next morning. The shots were enough to convince Colin Millward, our Creative Director, that it was worth a reshoot back in the UK.

Pete went off to the Lake District with Bruce Brown as photographer and nothing was heard for a week. It turned out that it had bucketed rain for a week (well it is the Lake District). On the Friday, the sun came out and they got the shot. It went on to win a silver 'gong' at D&AD awards.

PS: there was a shoot in Paris at Maxims restaurant. I went on the photographic shoot as in those days you could only take a small amount of currency out of the country and the restaurant wanted cash in hand, so yours truly got to see Paris. Pete Cherry was the Art Director and Len Fulford was the Photographer. We thought we'd get a slap-up meal on the day. All we got was a bottle of beer and a boiled egg each, skinflints. Sadly, I have nothing to show for the ad as it must have got lost in the journey down south. It did amuse me that Len, that night at another restaurant, treated the bread crumbs on the table like a still life, arranging them into a better shape.

Down 'Tobacco Road', again.

I was briefed to write a cinema commercial for Benson & Hedges Small Cigars. (Tobacco brands were banned from TV advertising by then).

There had been a very successful series of commercials based on stealing valuable items, including the 'Gold Box'.

So, I wrote one that featured a beautiful oil painting in close-up as it was ripped into around the edges by a Stanley Knife. The owners returned and looked shocked at the empty frame over the baronial fireplace and cutting away to a puff of cigarette smoke emerging from the closed door of a cupboard.

The client gave approval and we were discussing production with companies when the Creative Director, the legendary Colin Millward, came into my office (yes, we had our own office in those days) and asked me to write a new script that broke the mould and might even win a few awards. So, I wrote 'Spy Exchange'.

The client/s, bless them, (we never met the clients at CDP) gave approval. So, I lobbied for Ridley Scott to shoot it, as I admired his work and he had made my first ever commercial for Hotpoint while I was at PKL.

Alan Parker, who was virtually 'house' commercials director was less than pleased about this, but I was convinced that Ridley would give us a cinematic approach. I was dispatched with Geoff Kirkland, Ridley's Production Manager, to Austria to find locations and props.

Our local 'finder' was a Jewish gentleman who had fled Austria for England in the 1930s (a wise move) and our driver was tall and blonde and had fought for the Hitler Youth. An interesting mix.

After much searching for locations, right up to the Hungarian Border, we found a place called 'Hell's Valley' and for cars at the border exchange, we found the only Tatraplan in Vienna together with a Rover 3 Series.

We only wrote scripts at CDP, no storyboards, which meant I had the treat of sitting in Ridley's hotel Suite in Vienna while he sketched out for me how he saw the commercial. I wish I had had the nous to keep it as it was beautiful.

The KGB HQ we set in a royal hunting lodge in the woods outside Vienna. On the day of the shoot we had police to close the road to the bridge where the exchange was taking place, with the locals getting anxious as they thought the Russians were back, having occupied Austria at the end of WW2.

Some wonderful footage ended up on the cutting room floor, in particular, footage of Ridley shot with a hand-held camera from the back seat of a motorbike, approaching the 'KGB' HQ.

The Head of TV, Ray Barker, rushed back to the office ahead of the rest of us, rumour had it that it was so that he could claim full credit.

It did go on to win awards at D&AD as well as the British TV Advertising Awards in 1972. Not a bad career move, although the D&AD writing credit went to my group head, Lindsay Dale. He gave me the award after, but I couldn't get the record corrected unfortunately. It still hurts.

Credits: *Copywriter/s Mike Doyle and my Copy Group Head, Lindsay Dale (who suggested the false bottom in the returning spy's Suitcase revealing Das Kapital and then a copy of Playboy with a final reveal of the golden spread of packs.) Director, Ridley Scott. The music was a jazz version of a piece by Bach recorded by the French jazz pianist, Jacques Loussier. Happy days.*

Facebook comments on 'Spy Exchange':

Rudi Vranken I think one of the spies is Vladek Sheybal, a relative of my wife. He was often called upon to do Vincent Price voiceover rip-offs when the budget wouldn't stretch to the real thing earning him the nickname the 'Cut-price Vincent'.

Alan Orpin Dear Boy, I had no idea that this was an O' Doyle Magnificence. Bravo, Sir - a classic. I can just hear you suggesting to Ridley that using a 600mm might generally be a nice idea for the future.

Hilary O'Driscoll Brilliant film Mike. Brilliant. We forget that no one was making films look like that at the time.

Iwona Krol Wow Mike!! Love this!

Gail Shaw Fabulous Mike. Love your work! (I was just over the road at McCann's at the time - thinking up ways for British American Tobacco to get around the ban).

Note: During a visit back to the UK, a few years ago, I had a reunion with the TV Producer, Sandy Watson (Scott), who worked with me at PKL on the Hotpoint commercial. She told me that I was her cupid between her and Ridley as they were soon to be married. Sadly, I've lost my cupid looks but you can't have everything in this life.

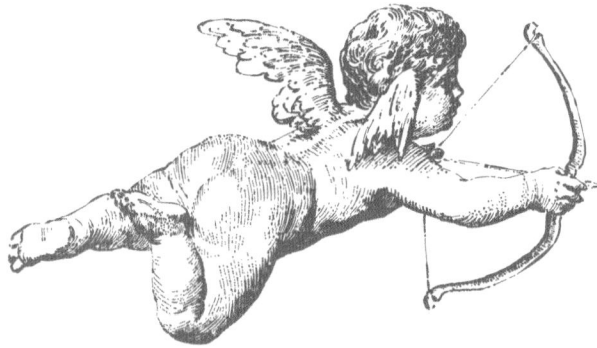

Brexit, foreshadowed?

Is this any way to enter Europe?

There seems to be an attitude abroad in the nation that if one ignores the Common Market for long enough it'll go away.

How wrong can you be?

For better or worse (according to your views) we will become part and parcel of the European Community on January 1st 1973.

Bar Britain sinking beneath the waves before then, or some cosmic disaster, we're going to need to know just what we're letting ourselves in for. And how we can best shape our country's future.

The European Movement was founded for this very purpose.

Some of you may shy away, suspicious that we're some kind of lay arm of the government.

Your suspicions are totally unfounded.

We're an independent movement with just the one ambition, namely that of making sure that the entire European venture is a success.

If you decide to join us you will automatically get a free subscription to 'New Europe', the monthly magazine written by leading authorities, on European affairs both in this country and across the Channel.

You'll also receive all the publications, pamphlets and leaflets issued by our various affiliated groups and committees.

There are lectures and seminars for you to attend all over Britain and on the continent.

The seminars will give you the opportunity for informed discussion.

You'll find it a refreshing change from the prejudice and jingoism so common on the European issue.

If you have the time and inclination, we'll also help you set up a local branch of the Movement.

For more detailed information drop us a line at the address below.

Nothing ventured, nothing gained as they say.

The European Movement, Europe House, 1a Whitehall Place, London, sw1.

I was briefed to write a campaign for The European Movement back in the 1970s, just before we entered 'The Common Market' as we knew it then.

Ignorance was not assumed to be bliss and the Movement meant to correct matters.

My first visual for the ad had a cartoon of a blindfolded John Bull stepping over the English Channel into France.

This was felt to be too much to swallow by the client so I came up with this visual as an alternative.

With the fiasco of the Brexit event in 2019, nothing much seems to have changed.

The headline would need to change to: 'Is this any way to exit Europe?

Adland's 'Toy' story.

The release in Australia of the movie *Toy Story 4* in 2019 reminded me of the magnificent 'toys' or talents we were allowed to play with way back when. No offence meant if the use of the term 'toy' upsets any of you, but we were blessed with some true masters of their particular art to help us make our work stand out.

While at Collets I remember the Art Director, Ted Ekman, being sent off to New York to oversee the photography for Silk Cut cigarettes.

Only the best would do. Photographic legends such as Elliott Erwitt, Bailey, Duffy and Donovan were regulars. And then a whole new batch of photographers doing great work came on the scene. Some of whose work appears in this book.

We also had outstanding illustrators and animators such as Oscar Grillo and Richard Williams. Pride of place for me was working with not only Sir Alan Parker† but also Sir Ridley Scott (so many knights now, enough for an Arthurian, Advertising Round Table?).

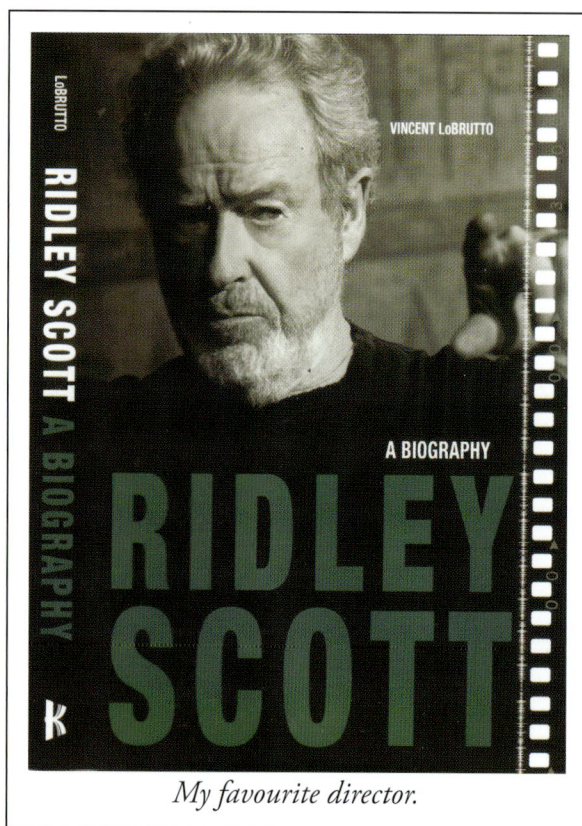

My favourite director.

Ridley shot my first commercial for Hotpoint while I was at PKL, but it never saw the light of day. The agency resigned Hotpoint, as they were felt to be incompatible as a client.

Ridley directed my Benson and Hedges 'Spy' commercial while I was at CDP, which meant

I spent weeks in Austria looking for locations and props. We never created storyboards at CDP for commercials, just a script was enough to sell the idea. But I wish I had kept the 'Ridleygrams' that he drew in his hotel room before the shoot. They were beautifully drawn and detailed.

Then, I made the great mistake of following the money, when I doubled my salary by moving to Dorlands.

At Dorlands I pitched for Tennents Lager, Scotland's biggest beer account and won it with a commercial directed by Ridley. *The Evening Standard* newspaper reported it as being the most expensive commercial to be made at the time. He went on to direct another five commercials in the series.

We were like kids with the most wonderful toys in art, photography and music. It doesn't get much better than that.

Note: Tribute should be paid here to **John Goss** who had been an Art Director at CDP but, like Alan Brooking, had gone on to a career as a photographer.
John would often be brought in to 'rescue' jobs where the famous photographer had failed to deliver the goods.
Later, when I was at Dorland, John worked with Roger Cazemage and me on a shoot for Dows Port at Oxford University. He was also very generous in paying for us to join him at Ronnie Scott's Jazz Club in Soho.

*I should also say a big "thanks" to **David Taylor**[†] of Studio 10 who created the artwork for CDP press ads, particularly B&H, and had a number of photographers under his "wing". He often acted as an unofficial headhunter for me over the years, letting agencies know when I was available for hire, which could be said to be often.*

Mrs Doyle Mk #1. In memoriam.

I met my first wife, Maggie Fuller[†]/Doyle/Campbell when she was the Receptionist for the Creative Department at CDP.

From there she was 'poached' to run the office of Tony May, the photographer.

Her next port of call was Sydney, Australia, which she hated.

She then came back to the UK to marry me, the poor thing.

She went for an interview at the agency Boase, Massimi, Pollitt to be John Webster's PA but he was nervous about "pillow talk" knowing she was married to me. Martin Bose, the MD of the agency said not to worry and she was hired.

I did sometimes get to see John's scripts and he was always keen to share his latest ideas with me when we went to his house in Hadley. What impressed me was how a sometimes ordinary idea could be lifted to brilliance with the choice of the right director, casting and music.

Maggie then became an agency producer, producing most of John's commercials.

The agency did pay for us to go to Nashville so Maggie could negotiate to get the rights to us the song 'Big John' for a John Smith's beer commercial. She was successful and they gave us tickets to the Grand Old Opry TV show where we saw Jerry Lee Lewis perform, amongst others. It was the day Reagan first got elected as President and there were men walking around the hotel sporting ridiculous, twenty-gallon polystyrene hats whooping and celebrating.

She and I parted company after ten years. She married Joe Campbell, musician and composer, and lived a happy life by all accounts. As did I.

She then became a freelance producer working for various agencies and also succeeded in getting a university degree in the bargain.

She passed away a few years ago leaving Joe and a daughter.

My film school.

Finchley was well served with cinemas. Well, when I was young, few people had TVs, so for popular movies there would be huge queues.

We had the Gaumont and the Odeon in North Finchley, the New Bohemia in Finchley Central (Bohemians were arty types before the days of Hippies) and the Rex cinema in East Finchley. But my favourites were the Everyman Cinema in Hampstead and the Prince Charles Cinema in Soho. There I was introduced to the wonderful world of French cinema with movies by Godard, Truffaut, Tati and Italian movies by Fellini. Later came the wonderful wave of Australian films such as *Picnic at Hanging Rock, My Brilliant Career* and *Gallipoli*. I also saw the Barry Humphries films at the Prince Charles and couldn't understand why the

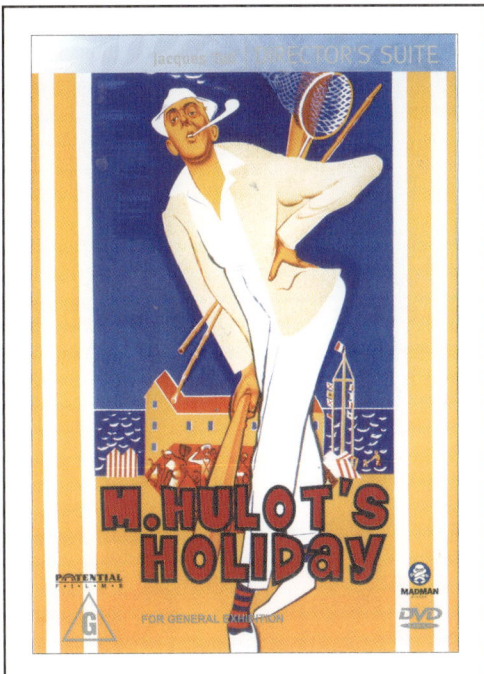

audience (mostly Australians) were laughing at certain references. It also introduced me to the innovative films of Jacques Tati and Ingmar Bergman.

And let's not forget the amazing films directed by the advertising fraternity; *Alien, Bladerunner, Thelma & Louise* and *Gladiator* by Ridley, and a raft by Alan Parker, which I mention elsewhere.

Credit must also go, however, to the nuns at St James who regularly had us in the school hall to watch films by David Lean such as *Great Expectations*.

My Aussie Hat Trick and first steps on the rocky road to Australia.

If the road to Dublin is a rocky one (or so the song goes), my road to Sydney (where my family and I now live.) has had a number of twists and turns. Many, however, have been positive encounters with Australian Art Directors in London and Downunder.

Ever since I was a child, Australia featured in my life. Every Christmas my grandparents would play the 78rpm record of *The Wild Colonial Boy.* My Grandfather would 'feed' his pipe with *Digger** Tobacco. I remember it as a vivid yellow pack with a man wearing a strange hat.

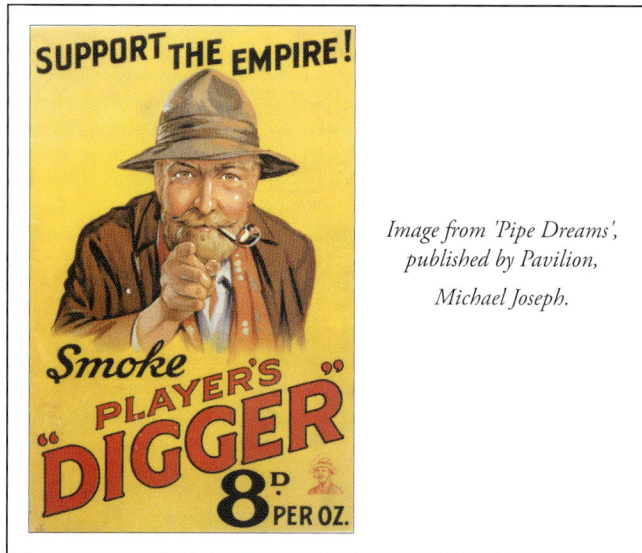

Image from 'Pipe Dreams',
published by Pavilion,

Michael Joseph.

An Uncle, and twin, red-haired cousins, visited my Grandparents from Sydney when I was aged about seven and tried to persuade my mum to move to Australia with the "Ten-pound POM" scheme. She declined.

Later in my advertising career I was out of work, and while at a friend's house for lunch with Mrs Doyle Mk 1, they asked me what my plans were. I replied that I was thinking of looking for work in Australia. My then wife said "Over my dead body" as she had lived in Sydney for a year and hated it. Her remark was greeted by a deadly silence, or so it seemed at the time.

The upside was that I had a great working relationship with three Aussie Art Directors in London; Rob Henderson and Pete Cherry at Collett, Dickenson, Pearce and Rob Tomnay at French, Gold, Abbott (FGA).

*The term 'digger' is generally accepted as slang for an Australian soldier, and the myth is that it came from Australians digging trenches at Gallipoli in WW1.

Rob Henderson.
See examples of Rob's great photography at:
www.robhenderson.net
Sadly, no images of Pete Cherry seem to be available. A man of mystery.

◀ ***Rob Tomnay and I*** *enjoying(?) the weather on the Truman shoot. Were anoraks really ever fashionable?*

With Rob Tomnay, at FGA, I worked on Hepworth's and Ben Truman beers.

The beer's strapline was, *There are more hops in Ben Truman*, with a Long John Silver character as brand image. I wrote a press campaign about hop picking.

We had an appointment at the brewery in the afternoon. No client was anywhere to be seen. No message. We sat for an hour and I suggested we go back to the office and fix another appointment. The Suit said we should wait.

The client eventually turned up six sheets to the wind having had a very liquid lunch, and rejected the ads.

We lost credibility and the client didn't even have the good manners to apologise.

However, we did make a commercial about hop picking.

Our TV campaign recreated the harvesting of hops in the early years of the previous century, where poor Londoners would flock to the hop fields for a paid holiday helping the farmers.

Sadly, I have no copies of the commercials, nor do I recall the Director's name. I used to keep all my crew Call Sheets but they went elsewhere in our many moves. Shame on me, it was a great shoot as well.

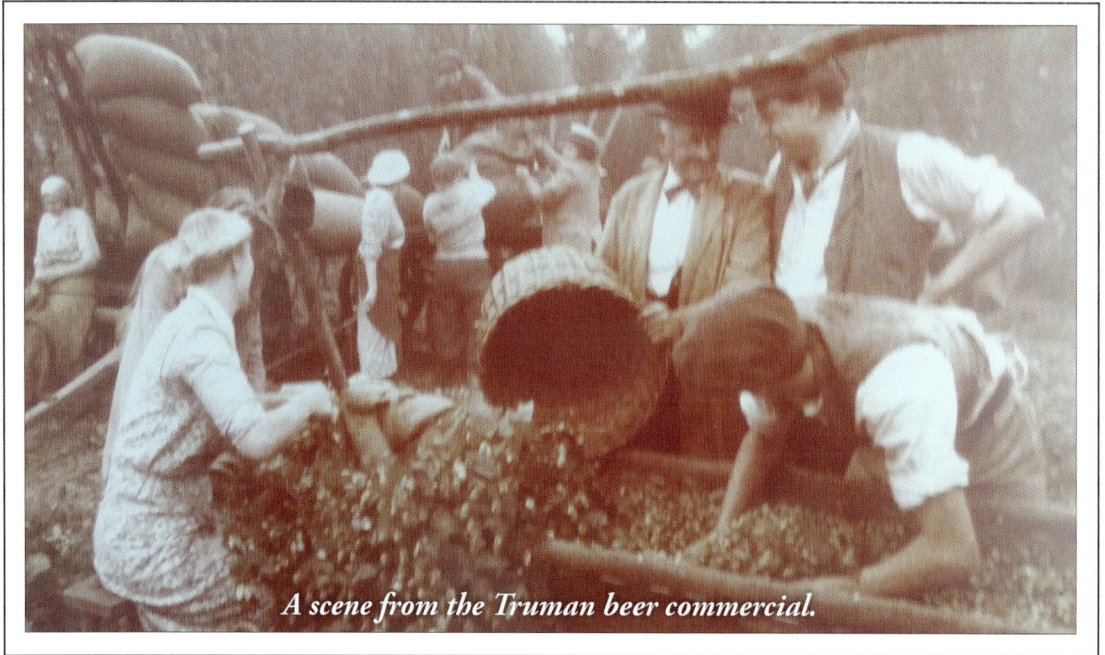

A scene from the Truman beer commercial.

Note: CDP had a very funny Suit who was from Australia, Ray Abraham. When we heard a police siren in the street he would say, "Hullo, sounds like McCann Erickson had another idea." Bitchy, but funny.

They were a big American agency who had offices on the opposite corner to us.

Another of his sayings when the client had given quick approval to a concept was "It went through like a Bondi tram."

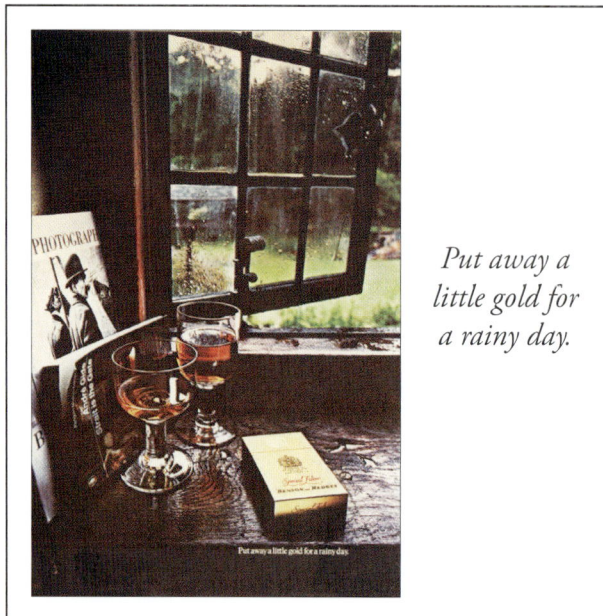

Put away a little gold for a rainy day.

142

THANKS TO HARDY AMIES, THE SHRINKING POUND NEEDN'T CRAMP YOUR STYLE.

If you're feeling the pinch these days it may not be just the economy. It could be your suits saying "enough".

Help is at hand though.

True to his fashion, Hardy Amies has again designed for Hepworths a range of exclusive, classic styles.

One of which is illustrated here. And none of which will break the bank.

Prices for one of our suits in a top quality cloth start from as little as £50.

Rest assured, we don't cut any corners on the tailoring. Each suit is hand-cut and made to your measure.

To take your measure each of Hepworths' 350 branches has skilled and experienced fitters.

They'll also help you decide on lapel widths, number of vents, pocket styles etc., and guide you through our wide range of cloths.

You'll be agreeably surprised how far we can stretch your pound.

Hardy Amies

At Hepworths.

Credit facilities available. Ask for details.

OUR SUITS HAVE BEEN DESIGNED BY HARDY AMIES TO ACCOMMODATE TODAY'S SLIMMER WALLETS.

Are your suits, like the economy, a little worse for wear?

If so, you may well be interested in our proposition.

True to his fashion, Hardy Amies has again designed for Hepworths a range of exclusive, classic styles.

One of which is illustrated here. And none of which will break the bank.

Prices for one of our suits in a top quality cloth start from as little as £50.

Rest assured, we don't cut any corners on the tailoring. Each suit is hand-cut and made to your measure.

To take your measure each of Hepworths' 350 branches has skilled and experienced fitters.

They'll also help you decide on lapel widths, number of vents, pocket styles etc., and guide you through our wide range of cloths.

How your cloth is cut now has a lot less to do with your means.

Hardy Amies

At Hepworths.

Credit facilities available. Ask for details.

Credits B&H: Agency CDP
Rainy Day: Copywriter, Mike Doyle; Art Director, Rob Henderson;
Photographer, Julian Cotrell.

Hepworths: Agency FGA.
Copywriter, Mike Doyle; Art Director, Rob Tomnay; illustrator, sadly unknown.

More of my B&H work, for my sins.

In the search for gold, leave no stone unturned.

This year, I promise to be as good as gold.

Pocket a little gold.

"Turn again Whittington."

Accepted for D&AD annuals 1973, 74.

B&H Credits: It's worth a mention that Pete Cherry would often have two or three photographers briefed on a shot and the best one won, with a fee for the runners-up.
(Leave no stone unturned) Copywriter, Mike Doyle; Art Director, Ted Ekman; Photographer, Adrian Flowers who was worried that the legendary 'curse' might affect him as the facsimile was so real. (The ad coincided with the hugely popular exhibition at the British Museum.)
(Pocket) Copywriter, Mike Doyle; Art Director, Peter Cherry; Photographer, Tony May.
(This year) Copywriter, Mike Doyle; Art Director, Pete Cherry; Photographer, Ray Rathborne.
(Whittington) Copywriter, Mike Doyle; Art Director, Pete Cherry; Photographer, Tony May.

Facebook comments on the B&H press ads:

Alan Orpin Wonderful stuff!!👍 ♥

Max Henry Thanks Mike. So refreshing.

Max Henry If I didn't know you better, I would say you're just a names dropper. HA.

Jimbo Downie The Doyle Years.

Pete Matthews Very nostalgic. I think we shared an office while you were doing the B&H stuff. Flossie bringing the tea round. Goodness, tea ladies - I guess they're an extinct species now.

Bob Miller Great visuals joy to see again.

Kevin Kneale What about the account men who had to explain such expensive meanderings? (Me, for example!) And convince them that transparencies really would reproduce in print while they're sizzling like a toasted cheese sandwich on the light box. Fine days.

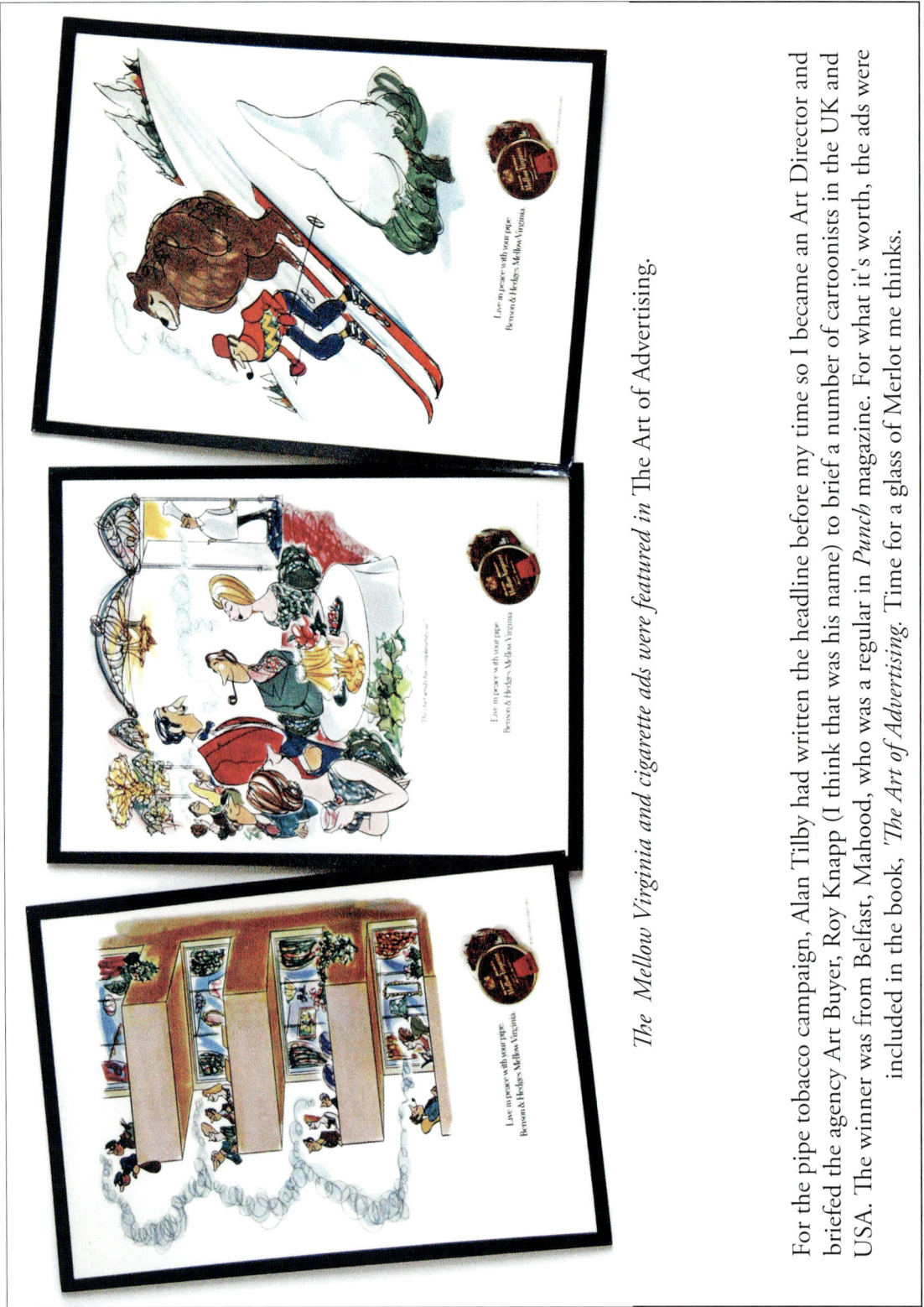

The Mellow Virginia and cigarette ads were featured in The Art of Advertising.

For the pipe tobacco campaign, Alan Tilby had written the headline before my time so I became an Art Director and briefed the agency Art Buyer, Roy Knapp (I think that was his name) to brief a number of cartoonists in the UK and USA. The winner was from Belfast, Mahood, who was a regular in *Punch* magazine. For what it's worth, the ads were included in the book, *The Art of Advertising.* Time for a glass of Merlot me thinks.

A footnote to B&H and CDP.

My Best Man at my first wedding was the Suit on Benson & Hedges, Graeme Robertson (pictured below, I'm not pulling strings or tickling him), who was also Second-Best Man, after Richard Kelley as Best Man, at my second wedding. His family remain great friends and are much loved. Apropos of nothing, Graeme has one of the most complete collections of 'Eagle' comics and original artwork I have ever seen. He kindly gave me this copy, knowing the pleasure I got from the comics as a kid, and even now as a Big Kid.

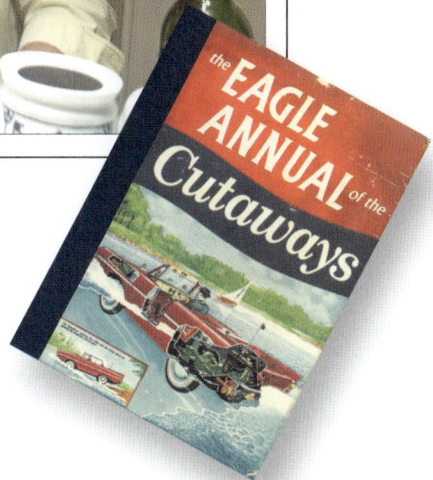

Graeme later became MD of a division of Ogilvy handling accounts such as Barclays Bank and Heathrow Airport. Alan Lofthouse ('Lofty') worked for him then as a copywriter. Lofty had previously been working at Dorland, and before that, with me at BBDO. See page 179.

Postscript from Graeme: "Lofty mostly worked with me, copywriting very successful appeals for TV and other fundraising channels for the biggest UK dog rescue charity - Dogs Trust. The client adored Lofty's quiet Yorkshire accent, and frequently asked him to do voiceovers - but always the most modest of men, Lofty declined."

'Tobacco Road' and an uncomfortable choice.

While at CDP, in the 1970s, as you now know, one of my main accounts was Benson & Hedges. An interesting choice as I was a non-smoker but then I had seldom shopped at Harrods, and still wrote a number of ads for the store.

One day I found my then wife, Mrs Doyle Mk 1, smoking. I told her that she was crazy, as an asthmatic, to be endangering her health. She replied, "Well you advertise them." I said if I stopped would she, and she agreed.

The account was arguably the agency's most profitable, with a figure of 15 million pounds sterling buried at the back of my cobwebbed brain. And me on a humble £3,500 per annum.

I went to see the Creative Director, John Salmon, with the news. He was none too thrilled and said advertising booze could lead to liver disease. But they respected my decision.

It helped when I resigned to go to Dorland, after Nigel Seeley had made me an offer I couldn't refuse.

The upside was it left the way free for my art Group Head, Alan Waldie, to create the award-winning 'surreal' B&H cigarette campaign.

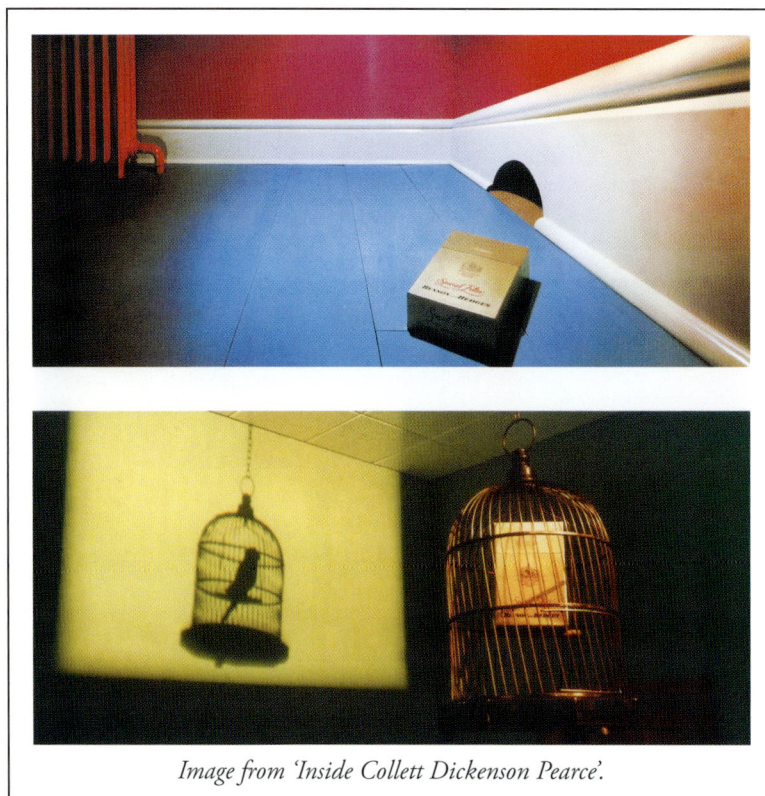

Image from 'Inside Collett Dickenson Pearce'.

Credits: *Art Director, Alan Waldie; Copywriter, Mike Cozens; Photographer, Brian Duffy.*

Later, when I was working at French, Gold, Abbott, the Creative Director, David Abbott said he would like to team me up with David Harrison to work on the British Army recruitment campaign. I apologised and said I couldn't as the Irish were being killed by British soldiers at the time. Before you jump down my throat, I know the Irish were doing the same. But maybe because David had an Irish wife, he was sympathetic and didn't hold it against me.

Wearing of the green, well a suit anyway, while at CDP.

My CDP generation.

I would also like to include (in no particular order) some of the very talented people in the Creative Department at the time not mentioned elsewhere: Pete Cherry, Arthur Parsons, Pete Mathews, Paul Fonteyn, Richard "Dickie" Dearing, Bob Byrne, Tony Brignull, Terry Lovelock, Neil Godfrey, Tony Whetton, Bob Isherwood, Phil Cherrington, Alan Raddon, Bob Wilson, Kevin Kneale, Tony Bodinetz, David Metcalf, Geoffrey Seymour, John Bacon, Judy Smith, Joanne Mond, Doris Dibley, Dave Horry, Bob Miller, Carole Nelson, Clive Holmes, Mike Everett, Ian Macarthur, Barry Mathews, Ray Barker, Paul Briginshaw, Rita Dempsey, Brian Duffy, Paul Fishlock, Graham Watson, Gray Jolliffe, Alec Wignall, Anne Winterflood, David Watkinson, David Brown, Angela Cherry (who became Angela Bray in Oz when she remarried down here).
Apologies to anyone I have left out.

Illustration by Bob Wilson who, wisely, escaped the Dorland experience. Bob had first started copying the cartoonist Calman but was threatened with legal action. I remember him at PKL, in the evenings, on the Grant projector, developing his Saxon style, which has since made him a decent living.
This was for a Heineken ad. Proof, again, that great work sells.
Image from 'Thirsty Work'.

Chapter
Seven

1973 to 1975. (Well, we all make mistakes.)

Dorland Advertising

†

Have you ever seen a Suit cry?

Having accepted the offer from Nigel Seeley, I arrived at the Paddington offices of Dorland. New pastures indeed, but not so fresh smelling as I quickly found out.

In my defence the financial demands of being newly married, and the agency having won awards for its Dubonnet and Heinz campaigns (the latter written by Alan Parker, freelancing unbeknown to me)made the move seem very attractive.

An Art Director at CDP, Bob Wilson, had agreed to move there with me so I felt it was a safe bet. But he pulled out at the eleventh hour and I couldn't go back as I had already resigned.

One of my first briefs was for the stable-mate of Old Spice, Oriental Spice, which was on its last legs in the market.

I came up with the idea of Confucius-type sayings (sexist? Yes). There was a battle over the ethnicity of the models, but we did have research on our side, albeit Eurasian models were acceptable.

The Account Executive had not allowed me in the client meeting, I think he was worried that I may have been a tad too honest about the client's prejudice.

The Suit won the day and cried in the corridor after the meeting having won the argument. The campaign ran at Christmas time and cleared the shelves and then the product disappeared. I would have thought it was an argument to keep it but that was Shulton for you.

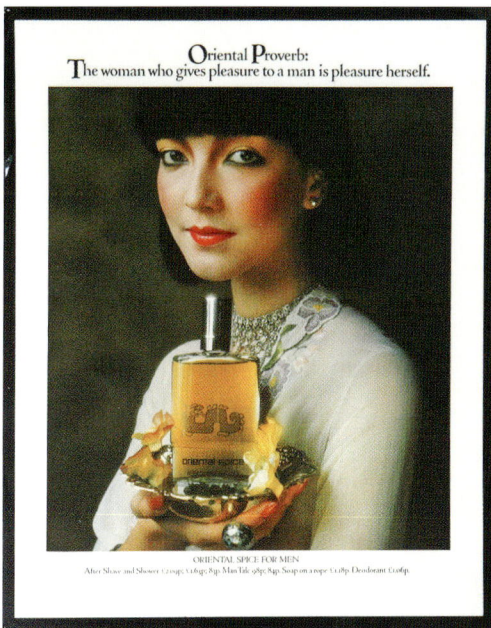

Credits: Copywriter, Mike Doyle; Art Director, Roger Cazemage; Photographer, Barry Lategan. Suit, lost in time, poor man. Hopefully he's not crying any more.

Facebook comments on the Oriental Spice ads:

Alan Orpin, Man who take 24 hours to climb up dunghill take 3 seconds to fall down other side.

My reply, Such wisdom from such an ancient soul. Your serfs must worship at your furry slippers Count.

Alan Orpin, Running a bit short on serfs as it happens. Had to burn a few at the stake last weekend. Usual reasons.... insubordination and dirty fingernails.

Roger Cazemage, Couple of crackers there Mike, I remember them well, cheers. My first ever shoot I went to was with Barry Lategan and Twiggy, I was 17, so was she. Oh, dear.

My reply, I was on the Lategan shoot also and as he had no assistant, I had to hold the white board as a reflector for infill or whatever it's called.

My photographic memory.

When I made my great mistake of leaving CDP for twice my previous salary and joining Dorland (or 'Deadland' as I later came to call it) I was teamed up with the Art Director, Mike Bradshaw[†].

His ancestry was actually Polish with a family name of Salotinkski but at the end of WW2 his Dad changed the family name as he couldn't get work with his surname. Ironically, Mike's kids changed their names back to the original later. He was given to wearing Cossack-Style shirts; most unusual. The only other person I knew with the same taste in shirts, was, Norman Berry, the Creative Director of Davidson, Berry, Pearce & Tuck.

Mike was AD on the Agfa ad. I quickly realised how lucky I had been at CDP with the great talents that I worked with.

As an aside, Mike was given the keys to the City of London for some reason and there was a photo in the papers of him walking sheep over London Bridge.

Credits: Copywriter, Mike Doyle; Art Director, Mike Bradshaw; Photographer, I don't know but he used Effie Howard-Johnston's stable of photographers almost exclusively.

Pitchin' & Bitchin'.

So much time and effort is put into pitching for new business in advertising, often with no great outcome. Except for one or two good stories.

Image: Daily Mail.

Tennent's Lager.

My first pitch worthy of note was at 'deadly' Dorland where I had left the warmth and security of a company where creativity was its main purpose in life, to one where 'service' was the ruler. Up until then I had never met a client, let alone present a concept or campaign.

The pitch was to retain the Tennent's Lager campaign in Scotland, a huge account with a spend equivalent to Kellogg's Corn Flakes. And the Scots, it seems, like a drop.

Only at the time the beer wasn't seen locally as any different to what was known as a pint of 'heavy' then, or 'Bitter' as it might be known as south of the border. That's how I remember it anyway.

I decided to emphasise the fact that it was a lager, a beer in the ascendant back then in the 70s.

I wrote a campaign based on the Scottish diaspora with one script set on the Starship Enterprise. It had 'Scotty' going to the ship's store only to find it empty of Tennents and beaming himself down to a Scottish pub to satisfy his thirst.

Other scripts were set in the wilds of Canada and another in the tropics on a tramp steamer.

Beautiful storyboards were created but then Nigel Seeley asked me to write another less expensive campaign.

This I did, to my later regret. It wasn't even original, it was a copy of a campaign Ridley Scott had shot in America for a US beer. The agency decided to invest in making one of the scripts, 'Ice Hockey'. Ridley agreed to film it and did a spectacular job, even having himself strapped to a sledge with a hand-held camera, being pushed around the ice, and in amongst the game.

After the pitch I went off to unwind and see a movie, *The Day of the Jackal*.

The next day I discovered that we had retained the business, and the Evening Standard reported it as being the most expensive commercial made at the time.

What was galling was the client kept on saying how they loved the diaspora campaign. I wasn't stubborn enough and the agency wasn't interested in doing the best work, only retaining the account. It was a very rude awakening to life outside of CDP and PKL

There were pluses however, such as having Roger Cazemage to work with and Judy White as a Planner, who I later ran into (in the nicest possible way) at Clemenger in Sydney.

The agency also had a wonderful Head of TV, Paul Mezulianick. He had been a musical infant prodigy in Vienna before the war. His family moved to England to escape the Nazis. As an 'alien' he and his family were shipped off from the UK to Australia for confinement, but the boat was torpedoed in the Indian Ocean.

Paul survived by clinging to some woodwork and, amazingly, stayed on in England after the war. He had fantastic taste in Music, and it was his hand in some of the agency's work that first attracted me.

The Dubonnet campaign, with *Songs of the Auvergne* sound track, being one outstanding example. Mike Bradshaw had been Art Director on that, to be fair, along with the Creative Director, Roy Taylor as copywriter.

After two years I decided to resign as I had been offered the post of Deputy Creative Director at SJIP/BMP. At my 'Exit' interview with Roy Taylor, he said he expected his staff to be acolytes working to his grand vision. Not the school I wished to work in, for sure.

My Dorland generation.

Roy Taylor (Creative Director), Mike Bradshaw, Bernie Phillips, Roger Cazemage, an Art Director whose name escapes me but was known as the 'Psychedelic Egg' because of his shape and the colourful clothes that he wore, think Hippy.   Apologies to anyone I have left out.

Facebook comments on Dorland.

Paul Carpenter I worked in the despatch dept of Chetwynd Haddons when Mike Bradshaw was CD there. He had a lovely P.A. who I was infatuated with.

Mike Doyle We were blessed with working with gorgeous girls. I married two of them.

Roger Cazemage Hi Mike, good to hear from you again, thanks for the mention. I'm sad to say I heard only last week that Mike Bradshaw passed away, couldn't make the funeral. A lovely man.

Rob Henderson Effie Howard-Johnston's stable of photographers she represented around then was probably John Claridge, John Bishop.

David Holmes Sorry to hijack this thread. I was briefly at Dorland and was privileged to know Mike Bradshaw. He told me he was Polish. And he told me also that everyone thought he was a lovely guy, but in reality he was right bastard. He was so wrong on the last count.

Adding to the gloom.

My time at Deadlands coincided with a series of strikes by coal miners and the introduction of the three-day-week.

Power would also be shut down in the late afternoons so we would often have to work in candlelight. Not the best of times, arguably the worst of times, to borrow from Dickens.

A solicitor's office, but you get the picture.
Image: express.co.uk

My leaving Dorland card.

Chapter
Eight

1975 to 1977. Much ado about almost nothing.

Samuels, Jones, Isaacson, Page/BMP (SJIP)

✝

The coupon and applause. Part One.

SJIP was partly owned by BMP, which made it attractive to me.

Lord Leverhulme is quoted as saying, "Half of my advertising is wasted, and the trouble is, I don't know which half."

Enter centre stage, Direct Response advertising.

Before online advertising, the business relied on having a sufficiently compelling argument in favour of the product for someone to fill in and post the coupon.

SCOTCADE.

One of our biggest accounts was Scotcade. The client, Bob Scott, had worked for Tower Cookware and realised there was a business opportunity in direct selling and appointed us as his agency.

Every weekend, in the colour supplements, one of our ads would appear. Then, a few days later there would be a War Council with Bob to track whether the ad had worked or not.

If it failed, we would test another concept and once we had a successful message, he would run that until the next offer.

No sale, no applause.

Dave Trott is reported as saying that working in the Creative Department at BMP was like being in the Marines of advertising. If one concept failed in research, then you had to come up with something new. Just like Scotcade, but a different mechanism.

The Tower ad I show was not one of my best headlines, but it was awarded the Best Direct Response Ad of its year by Campaign Magazine Press Awards.

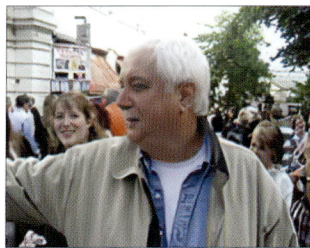

Roger Cazemage,
directing something.
Image: Facebook.

I hired another copywriter after a while, John Watson, who did a great job and eventually set up his own agency with our Production Manager, Bernie Varndell. I had long flown the coop by then.

Credits: *Copywriter, Mike Doyle; Art Director, Roger Cazemage; Photographer, Unknown.*

The name game.

One of our clients, Tetrosyl (not the catchiest of names), created a number of innovative products in the car care market. They had developed this remarkable car polish that could be applied even when wet, they just needed a name.

I came up with Triplewax and the rest is history as the cliché goes.

We made a commercial with Peter Webb about a diplomatic meeting where the chauffeurs are washing their cars and only the Triplewax driver is finished and ready for his minister when the meeting ends suddenly.

Triplewax is the number 1 selling car shampoo and polish with over 40 years heritage.
Taken from their 2019 website.

My SJIP/BMP generation.

Mike Isaacson (Creative Director), Roger Cazemage, Bernie Varndell, John Watson and the memory bank has run dry.
Apologies to anyone I have left out.

Chapter
Nine

1977, a very busy year but, again, sadly cut short.

French,
Gold, Abbott
(FGA)

†

Breakfast with Sir Terence Conran.

I apologise at the outset for more name dropping, I will see a doctor about that.

While at FGA I was assigned to the Habitat account, working with the wonderful Cathy Heng.

To present the creative concepts I would go with the Suit to Conran's London flat for early morning meetings.

He was very civilised, as you'd expect, and loved the work.

The Wythenshawe store was a breakthrough in the UK. This was before IKEA had arrived in the UK but the same concept.

Indeed, Habitat and IKEA ended up 'in bed' with each other in later years.

The cutaway illustration of the store was created by a neighbour of mine at the time in High Barnet, Peter Morter. He was best known for creating amazing cutaway illustrations of historical buildings such as palaces and cathedrals.

The commercial was directed by Des Sergeant. It featured people walking out of the store with things they had bought.

The shoot ended up with the crew walking out with featured items as they couldn't be sold having been put on 'display'. I came home with an armchair that did great service for many years but didn't make it to Australia.

Sir Terence Conran†.
Image: Dezeen.

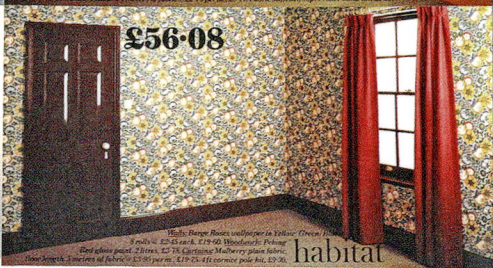

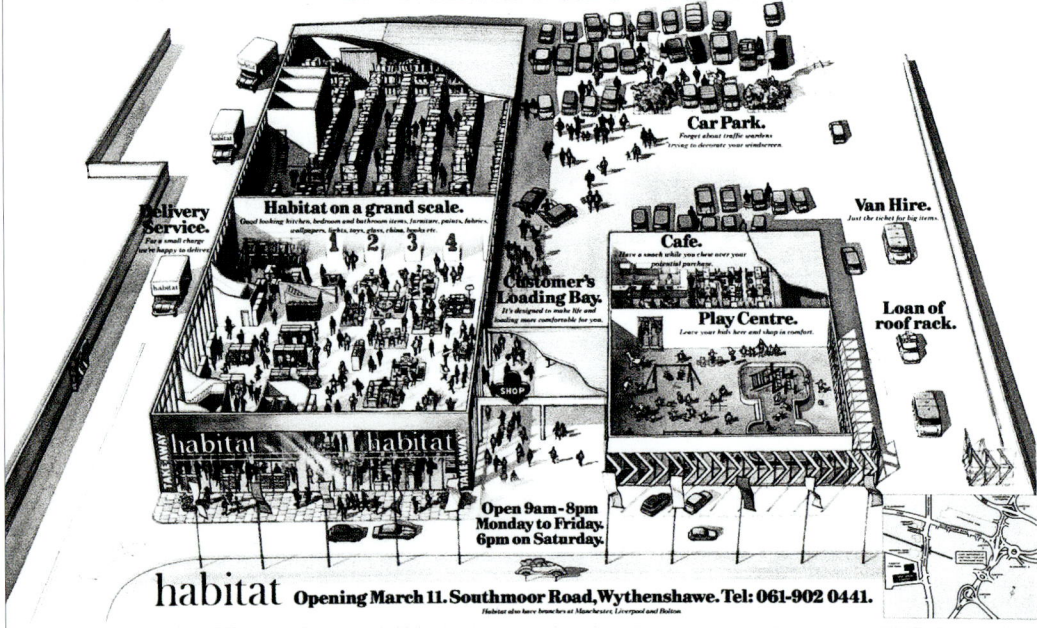

Germany calling.

I was also briefed to write a campaign for Crown beers. Cathy Heng and I were sent off to Hamburg to enjoy a "factory" visit.

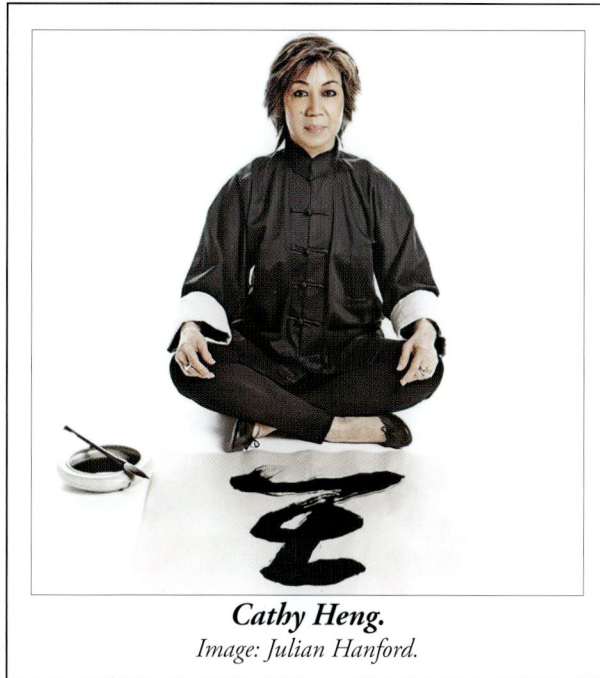

Cathy Heng.
Image: Julian Hanford.

We were treated to a lovely lunch by the brewery. The two men who treated us told us that Russian tanks were only an hour up the road in what was then East Germany; this was before the fall of Communism and was quiet sobering.

We didn't drink that much either as we were on our best behaviour, even with (men only) tours of the erotic Eros Centre laid on by the British salesforce.

I did try (and failed) to write an ad about the Reinheitsgebot; how a brewer could lose his head in Germany in the Middle Ages if he made a bad brew. Another copywriter, John Clive, did a better job of it I'm sad (and jealous) to say.

Stamp issued in 1983 celebrating the history of the Reinheitsgebot, and also commemorating its 450th anniversary. Image: en.wikipedia.org

The almost lost art of leaving cards.

Sad to say I've lost most of my leaving cards, of which I've had more than my fare share, as you will now have noticed. These cards were often a labour of love, taking much creativity and effort by those involved. Besides my Dorland card, I showed before, one of my favourites is from when I moved on to BBDO from FGA. Every year the Guardian newspaper ran a spoof feature on April Fool's Day about a fictitious island nation called Sans Serif.

Serif vs **Sans serif**

Alfredo Marcantonio, who shared my pleasure in this annual treat, created this for which I thank him and recommend his wonderful book, *Remember those great Volkswagen Ads?* Designed by John O'Driscoll and co-written with David Abbott.

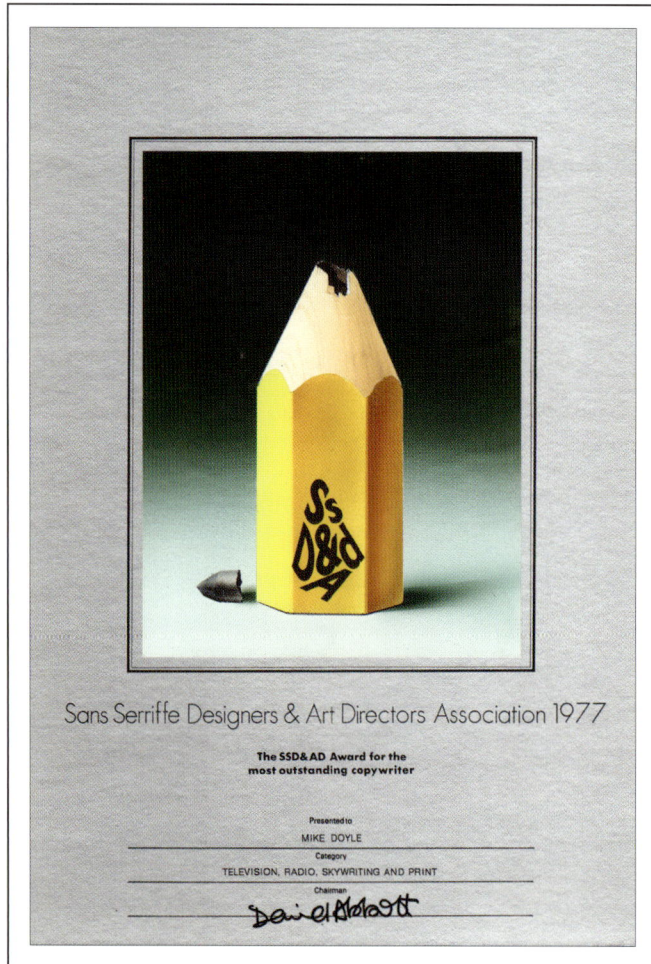

Sans Serriffe Designers & Art Directors Association 1977

The SSD&AD Award for the
most outstanding copywriter

Presented to
MIKE DOYLE
Category
TELEVISION, RADIO, SKYWRITING AND PRINT
Chairman

My FGA generation.

David Abbott (Creative Director), Alan Orpin, Alfredo Marcantonio, Cathy Heng,
John Clive, David Harrison, Judy Smith, Joe Hosa.
Apologies to anyone I have left out.

Note: It did amuse me that Richard French ended up working and living in Paris,
Mike Gold left to work in Finance and, saving the best to last, David Abbott
converted to Catholicism.

Vale David Abbott. I was so lucky to be taught by him and hired twice.

A tribute below by Campaign Brief editor Michael Lynch. MAY 18 2014, 1:34 PM.

The world's advertising industry will be saddened to hear of the death of David Abbott, arguably the greatest British copywriter of all time, who passed away yesterday aged 75.

Droga5 Australia creative chairman David Nobay and head of art Daryl Corps created the image below homage to Abbott's famous poster for The Economist as the most fitting tribute they could think of.

"I never heard of David Abbott."

Advertising trainee. Aged 42.

Corps worked at Abbott Mead Vickers, while Nobay ran Anthem in London, part of AMV Group, for a spell and had the honour of working under the great man for a week on a pitch.

David's early years.

He started as a copywriter at Mather & Crowther and then at DDB London. In 1966, he was sent to their New York office, then returned to London as a director.

In 1971, he founded French Gold Abbott. In 1978, he founded Abbott Mead Vickers (AMV), and went on to create famous advertising campaigns for clients including Volvo, Sainsbury's, Ikea, Chivas Regal, The Economist, Yellow Pages, and the RSPCA.

In 1991, BBDO acquired a stake in AMV and appended their name.

Abbott was awarded the D&AD President's Award in 1986 and The One Club for Art and Copy inducted Abbott into its Creative Hall of Fame in 2001.

His first novel, *The Upright Piano Player*, was published in 2010 by MacLehose Press.

One of the best compliments paid to Abbott came from Tony Brignull, another great British copywriter, when Abbott won the 1986 D&AD President's Award:

"He and John Webster, who won the award in 1982, are the undisputed masters of British creative advertising of our lifetimes.

"There are a few of us writers around who think of ourselves as the sons of Bill Bernbach. I have a feeling David is the only one who'd pass a blood test."

Abbott visited Australia in 1987 as a special guest of the AWARD Awards and appeared on the cover of Campaign Brief in October that year.

Note: the full story of the wonderful campaign for *The Economist* can be enjoyed by reading *Well-written and Red* by Alfredo Marcantonio.

Chapter Ten

1977 to 1978
(another all too short stay).

From PKL to BBDO (1)

A promise fulfilled.

Peter Mayle promised to rehire the four of us who were made redundant and he was true to his word, even though he had moved on to live and work in France and become a best-selling author with *A Year in Provence* being one of his best-sellers.

Peter appointed Tim Delaney to be his replacement and he hired me. So, in that way, Peter's promise came true.

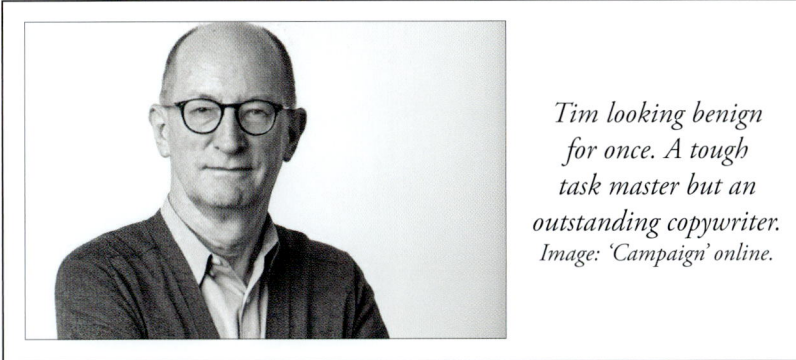

Tim looking benign for once. A tough task master but an outstanding copywriter.
Image: 'Campaign' online.

I was supposed to be working with my old LCP classmate, Martyn Walsh, but he was nowhere to be seen the day I started.

Tim apologised and explained that they had to 'let him go' and I was also free to look elsewhere if I wished.

However, he had just hired Alan Lofthouse ('Lofty') and I was more than happy to work with him, and did so for a couple of productive years.

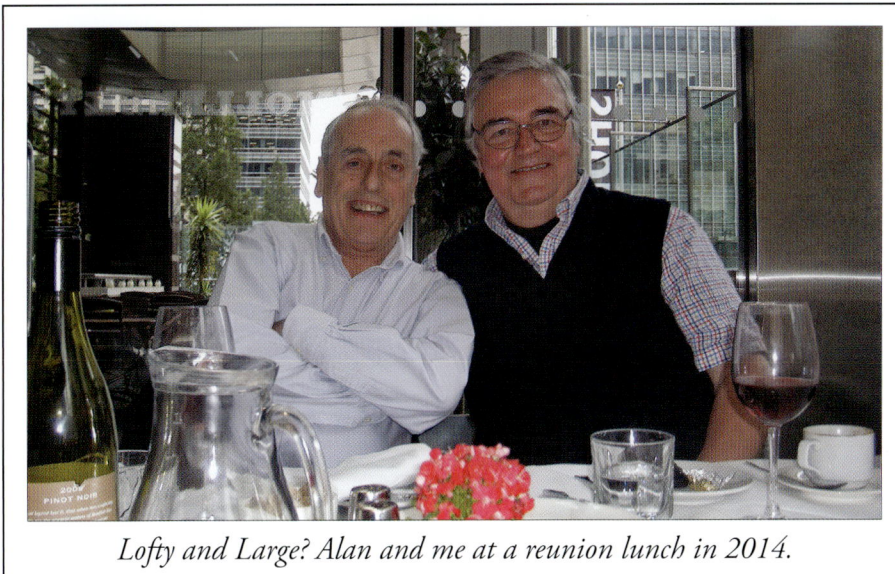

Lofty and Large? Alan and me at a reunion lunch in 2014.

It's practically impossible for Toyota to build a "Friday Car".

For the simple reason that just about everything on our production line is automated.

Computers, for example, are responsible for the Carina's 1600 engine being machined to a degree of precision few other car makers can match.

The same applies to the suspension, the transmission and the servo-assisted brakes.

Even the rust-proofing, undercoating and final paintwork are carried out by machine.

THE HUMAN TOUCH.

Humanity rules the day, however, on matters of quality control.

A journalist visiting a Toyota factory was staggered to see an ordinary assembly worker stop a whole production line.

Not because he fancied an impromptu tea break, but because he was dissatisfied with a piece of trim.

An extraordinary event in any other factory, but it's by no means unique on a Toyota assembly line.

Another aspect that sets Toyota apart from other makes is the impressive list of equipment offered with each car.

The Carina comes to you complete with tinted glass, a push-button LW/MW radio, quartz clock, cigar lighter, fitted carpets, two-speed wipers with intermittent wipe and reclining front seats with separate head restraints.

What's more, the driver's seat has been designed to not only adjust to and fro but also tilt up and down.

A feature the little lady will appreciate if she uses the car after you.

THE 20% DIFFERENCE.

Most of the Carina's parts are made by us.

Those that are not still have to match our own incredibly stringent production controls.

For example, we take the toughest safety standard set in the world and then ensure that whatever we make is 20% tougher.

No doubt this attitude had something to do with our recent success in a Swedish survey of 3 year-old cars.

Out of all the cars tested, including home-produced vehicles, a Toyota came out on top with the fewest faults.

A reassuring thought if you're hoping to buy a reliable car, but have no way of knowing which day of the week it was built.

TOYOTA
Everything keeps going right.

THE TOYOTA CARINA.

Their reliability doesn't depend on which day of the week they're built.

Accepted for the D&AD Award Annual, 1979.

THE TOYOTA CELICA.

Even flat out, you'll still hear the mother-in-law in the back seat.

The Celica Liftback's superbly engineered, 2 litre engine is no match for back seat drivers.

Flat out at 110 mph, it purrs along quietly at a mere 6000 revs.

While the stylish, aerodynamic shape maintains the peace by offering the wind the least resistance.

Inside you'll find it's a plush, fully-fledged four seater with bags of room.

The cloth-covered seats are amazingly versatile.

Those in the front not only recline, but also adjust fore and aft and up and down.

What's more, both have separate head restraints.

The driver's seat on the Celica XT and GT can also be adjusted for lumbar support.

And the rear seat backs fold individually to give you more room for awkward loads.

(No mother-in-law jokes here, please.)

There's wall to wall carpeting, including a carpeted luggage area complete with luggage straps to keep things secure.

To keep you secure there are inertia-reel seat belts.

There's a five-speed gearbox, a quartz clock, a LW/MW radio and tinted glass.

For a clear view ahead there are two-speed wipers with intermittent wipe, and washers which are actually built into the wiper arms.

And last but certainly not least, on the Celica XT there's the ultimate luxury: air-conditioning as a standard fitting.

All this is of little comfort though, if the car should prove unreliable.

A recent Swedish survey of 3-year old cars will put your mind at rest.

Out of all cars tested, including home-produced vehicles, a Toyota was found to have the fewest faults.

Rest assured, the Celica is built to the same exacting standards.

There's one raring to go for a test drive at your nearest Toyota dealer now.

Perhaps the mother-in-law would like to come too.

In a nagging capacity, of course.

TOYOTA
Everything keeps going right.

Credits: *Copywriter, Mike Doyle; Art Director, Alan Lofthouse; Photographer, Geoff Senior; Typographer, Ed Church. (He and I were teamed up later at Colman RSCG.)*

Keep your chauffeur in the style he's accustomed to. At a third of the price.

You are faced with a dilemma.

At £20,000 or thereabouts, your present means of transport is extravagant to say the least. But its creature comforts are dear to you.

What do you do?

Bid James farewell.

Or keep him, and a tidy sum in the bank, by prudently investing in the luxurious Toyota Crown.

Indeed, at £6,056 it should leave ample funds to cover his salary for a number of years.

YOUR STUDY ON WHEELS.

Sink into the plush comfort of our back seats, light a cigar and control your own air conditioning from the central console as you gently unwind.

Then if the F.T. seems a little too taxing, turn on the 3-band self-seeking stereo radio complete with your own volume control.

For the more studious there are individual reading lights.

Some say it's more comfortable than their own home but we feel that is pushing credibility too far.

JAMES' PERKS.

At the wheel, James will be pleased to find all his familiar travelling companions:

Automatic transmission, power-assisted steering, reclining seats with adjustable and removable head rests, individual map reading lights, stereo radio and cassette player, air conditioning, cigar lighter and electric windows.

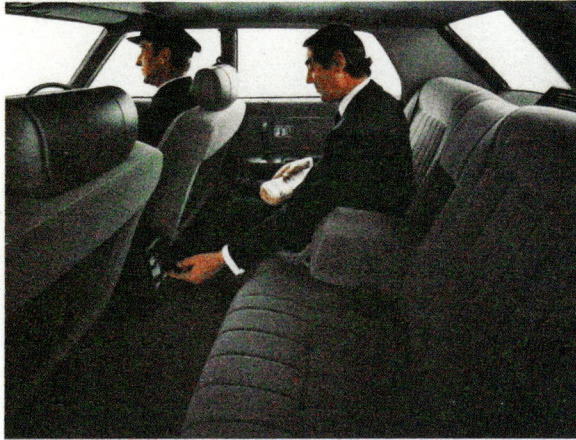

SAFE AS CASTLES.

The Toyota Crown is unique in having a door locking device that comes on automatically when the car reaches 15 mph.

We've also fitted tinted glass to cut down on glare from the sun and oncoming headlights at night.

Whilst on the subject of lights we have ones that warn of headlamp, tail or stop light failure and low brake fluid, plus hazard warning and rear door warning lights.

And to keep you both comfortably and safely in your place, there are front and rear seat belts fitted as standard.

Also, for your peace of mind, there's an unlimited warranty of 12 months.

As you can see the Toyota Crown is perfectly equipped for the awesome responsibility of carrying its Very Important Person from A to B.

And it can get you there at a very respectable 20 mpg* and with a performance that gives a top speed of 100 mph.

But as James would say, "It's always nice Sir, to have that little bit extra in hand."

If you'd like to test drive the Toyota Crown or the Estate version, ask James to take you along to your local Toyota dealer. (James will find them in the Yellow Pages.)

THE NEW TOYOTA CROWN

CROWN

TOYOTA
Everything keeps going right.

The original concept for the Toyota Crown had been created by another team, but it had been rejected by the client. However, the photography had been done and dusted. I had a morning to come up with a new concept and write the body copy. All went OK and the ad was published. Same credits as previous page but photographer is sadly unknown.

Pleasing Tim wasn't easy.

Lofty and I were briefed to create an ad for some new technology from Sony. They had a great system of having a tech guy to brief you and demonstrate how it all works, but in layman's language.

To say we slaved over this for the next few weeks would be an understatement. Tim's mind was elsewhere, as he was acting as a consultant to the British Labour Party, which meant he was hardly in the office and we had to grab him for his few spare minutes to present our thoughts. They kept on landing on barren soil.

However, after a couple of months he approved this; a concept we had presented a long time before. We didn't tell him that though.

We used to joke that the biggest job each year was designing the poster for the Labour Party jumble sale that Tim's Mum was involved with.

The truth according to most people.

The truth according to Sony.

Sony introduce truth in Hi-Fi.

The new TC K8B cassette deck.

Gone are the confusing inaccuracies of VU meters that bedevil other decks.

In their place we present our liquid crystal meter.

Changes in volume are faithfully registered by a bar of light: the louder the passage, the longer the bar.

If the signal is short and sharp, like a sudden clash of cymbals, it's clearly shown by the bar changing from blue to red.

In contrast, a VU meter's needle remains unmoved. It just sits there saying everything's fine, while the peak indicator frantically flashes away telling you otherwise.

Even if you've the trained eyes and ears of a sound engineer, it can all be very confusing.

Another factor that sets our meter apart is the fact that you can instantly identify which channel is peaking.

Furthermore, a peak hold facility memorises the loudest signal in the passage, so you can adjust the record level accordingly.

As an alternative, there's an automatic peak hold which keeps you up to date with the input's peak strength at 17 second intervals.

The beauty of it all, as you'll have gathered, is that you can get a truly accurate recording. To a fraction of a decibel, in fact.

In every respect, the TC K8B squeezes the maximum performance out of the tape itself.

Witness our wow and flutter figure of 0.045% wrms.

Credit for this is due to the incredibly accurate capstan motor.

Its accuracy is governed by our newly developed, precision engineered, servo-control electronics.

The machine also has an in-built protective logic. Even if you inadvertently asked the deck to switch from fast forward to fast rewind simultaneously, it could safely handle it.

Indeed, everything on the TC K8B is designed to protect the interests of both the tape and the quality of the recording.

At first glance, our price of £469 may seem a little steep.

But not when you consider the unfailing honesty of our liquid crystal.

SONY

Credits: Copywriter, Mike Doyle; Art Director, Alan Lofthouse; Photographer, Sadly unknown.

There was another campaign I was proud of but have no examples to show, as the client closed down their business.

It was for Homepride Bakeries and their rolls that stayed fresh for more than three days. Don't ask how. One headline was: *They stay fresh for two episodes of Coronation Street.* And another was a visual of a sign on a shop door saying, *Closed for Bank Holiday Weekend* with the headline saying: *Our rolls will still be fresh on Tuesday.*

Photography and artwork were all completed and ready to go to press when the announcement came. Lofty kicked a hole in our office wall in frustration.

We had a lot of our work turned down, maybe it wasn't that good, but I was proud of it. This included the Bubble Gum launch, commercials for Skol and various others that bit the dust; I felt we were not in favour.

I spoke to Phil Mason who was working with Rita Dempsey and it seemed they could do no wrong. I asked whether we (or I) were doing something wrong and he had no answer. I suspect he must have mentioned it to Tim because I was 'let go' not long after.

The evening I was leaving I realised that the car I had been paying for, before BBDO, and while there, wasn't in the severance package. So that delayed my exit but it was resolved within the hour with me paying the agency five pounds for the car. I was still sad to leave and, importantly, was proud of the work we did. Lofty stayed on to work with another writer.

Facebook comments on BBDO (1):

Gail Shaw Oh boy Mike! Tim was a just a lad when he turned up as a junior when I was working at Y&R London. Skinny, long reddish hair, duffle coat.....time doesn't fly, it skids along the floor and bites your…

Jonathan Yardley Great story. I miss my days at Crawford's ,Y&R, JWT, Saatchi's and Colmans. Yes my God it's now distant history. We were lucky to be part of it all. The business does not look any fun now.

Richard Kelley We were blessed with a great age of advertising, such fun, and wonderful work. And friendships that have spanned decades.

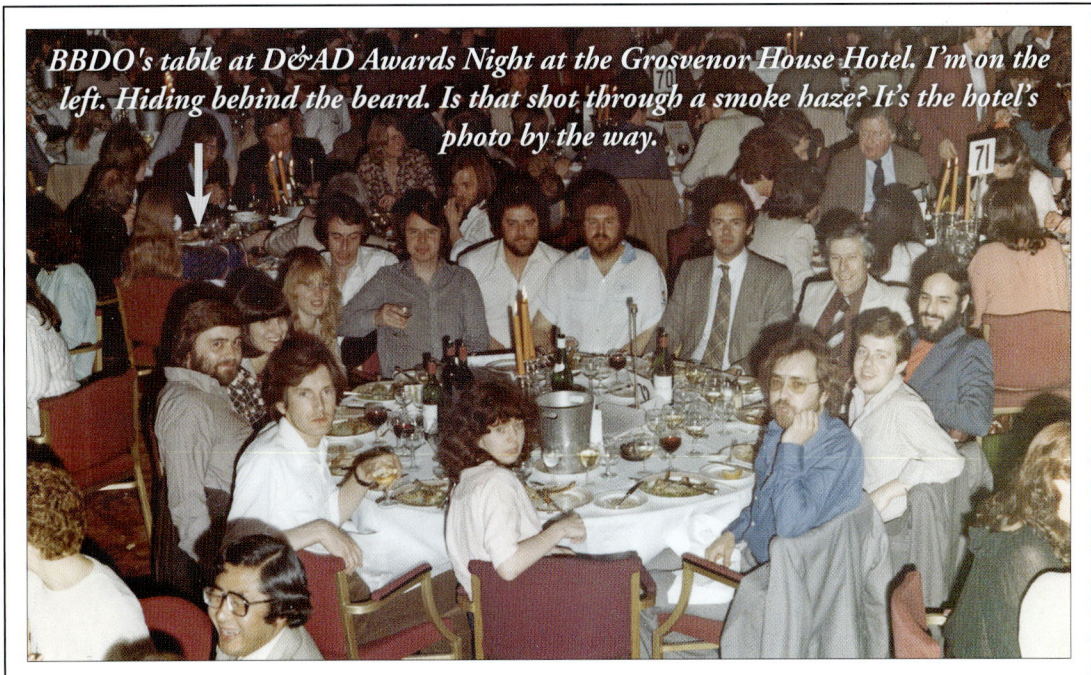

BBDO's table at D&AD Awards Night at the Grosvenor House Hotel. I'm on the left. Hiding behind the beard. Is that shot through a smoke haze? It's the hotel's photo by the way.

Amazing commemorative artwork by Jemmy Gray, another discovery by Peter Mayle, like Peter Gibb. I'm third row down on the left, next to Rita Dempsey. Tim Delaney's middle name is Brendan.

The Good Friday Club.

With my disenchantment with the Catholic Church, I won't be going to the Stations of the Cross on future Good Fridays.

A group of us at BBDO discovered that, along with British Rail, the Tate Gallery had the best wine cellars in the UK. So, we decided to do our bit to empty the Gallery vault.

It's first name, that I remember, was the *"Effing Good Friday Club"* (but a tad more Anglo-Saxon than that) as we met on the last Friday of every month at the Gallery restaurant. We were always served by a gorgeous Irish waitress, Trish, and there was a Jeroboam of champagne, followed by wines to Suit the various courses.

"Trish.", our Irish waitress.

The strict rule was not to return to the agency in the afternoon for obvious reasons.

Note: Richard Kelley came up with a much better name for the club, *Tate 'a' Tate*.

Members were me, the Kelley Brothers, Pete Andress, John O'Driscoll and Jemmy Gray. Derek Hass was always angling to be invited but never made it.

Life was like a Mars bar.

No, not like a box of chocolates, but it was like the product's slogan, *For work, rest and play*.

Lots of the first and last and, luckily, we were able to squeeze in a bit of the middle when we got a chance.

Work: There was always a deadline to meet for a campaign or even a single ad, let alone pitching for new business. If you weren't doing that, your business was in trouble.

Rest: My first day in advertising at Pritchard, Wood and Partners was going with my group heads, John Webster and Brian Mindell, to a wine auction. Although others spat out their wine, I held on to mine and was decidedly 'soft' around the edges that afternoon.

Play: usually meant long lunches at wonderful restaurants, mostly in London's Soho. Front of the queue to be honoured has to be Elena Salvoni[†] known as the "Queen of Soho", although she was too modest to say that.

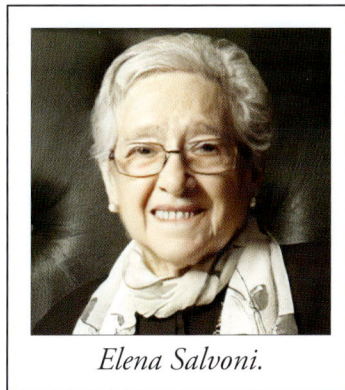

Elena Salvoni.

Her career spanned nine decades. She started out aged 14 at Café Bleu in London's Soho before following restaurant manager Joseph Paccino to Bianchi's where she worked for 30 years. Aged 65, Elena tried to retire, but her talents were so in demand that she continued to work for more than 20 years, first at L'Escargot and then at L'Etoile.

I proposed to Cherry at L'Escargot on Valentine's Day back in 1985, having got an awful 1984 out of the way with divorce, burglary and my agency closing, everything could only get better.

We held our reception in Elena's room and had many happy memories there.

They had 'snail' trails woven into the carpet and you got a chocolate snail covering a nut with your coffee.

Elena always made sure I had a small box of them to take home for the kids. The lampshades even had empty snail shells hanging from them

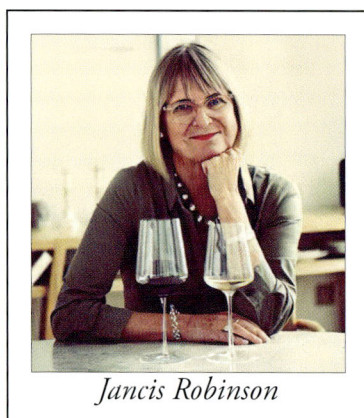

Jancis Robinson

L'Escargot was owned by Jancis Robinson who was the youngest 'Master of Wine' in the UK at the time. Jancis went on to become an author and also presented some excellent television programs on the subject.

Every month they would have wine from a grower from some part of the world with a matching cuisine served, and the grower would talk about the 'marriage' of the food and wine of the region. And, if memory serves me correctly, it was all for only 20 pounds.

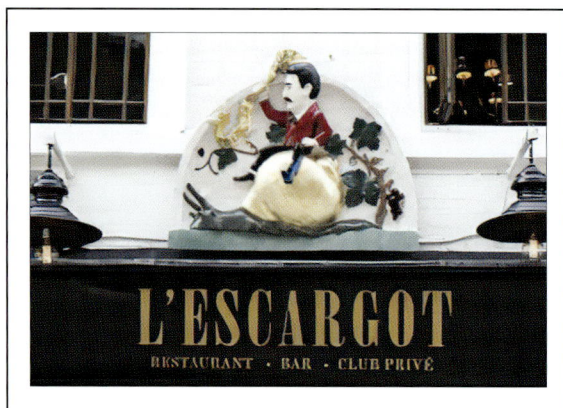

Other watering holes were the Kebab and Humus, Bertorelli's, Manzi's for great fish, Ketner's/Pizza Express with the Italian opera singing waiter, Schmidt's for the rudest waiters in London and the Tate Gallery for our monthly Tate 'a' Tate sessions.

Believe it or not we did also work and won many awards for our efforts. But wives and partners, sadly, had to carry the heavy loads because we would often be working late nights and weekends. Having said that, I wouldn't swap it for quids, as someone must have muttered somewhere. And many colleagues have been friends for life. Much as I like the occasional Mars bar, we achieved greater enjoyment during those years by creating outstanding and award-winning work. And many restaurants thrived with our dedicated support.

I'm forever blowing bubbles.

Bubble Yum is a brand of bubble gum marketed by The Hershey Company.

While I was working at BBDO my 'Grupenfurer' (Creative Director) Tim Delaney, was foolish enough to send me off to New York to be briefed for the launch of Bubble Yum into the UK.

Introduced in 1975 by Life Savers, the bubble gum was the first soft bubble gum created by a homemaker in Fisk, Missouri, who named it "rubber bubble gum." She gave some to her son to pass out at school. She soon sold the recipe to the Lifesavers candy division in St Louis.

We learnt that sales of Bubble Yum were so successful that salesmen from a rival company concocted a story about it being made from spider webs and the story spread around schools with a plummet in sales. They had to run a major campaign correcting the facts and sales returned to normal.

Note: *As we booked into the New York Hilton there was a scuffle at the front revolving door. A thief had walked in, and out, with a tourist's luggage that had been parked in the foyer. Welcome to the 'Big Apple'.*

With me on the trip, I had an agency Planner and the Account Director, both of whose names escape me. One was like a gasworks on legs and seemed to move forward down Broadway by jet power. Best not to walk behind, if you'll pardon the expression. We had our initial breakfast briefing at the Squibb Building with heaps of sugary doughnuts and filter coffee.

I spent a day in upper New York State with one of their salesmen visiting 'Mom and Pop stores' as he called them.

On another day we ended up at the town where they made the stuff. We drove in as dusk

187

was settling in and all I could see were pink bubbles sprouting out of everyone's mouths.

After the factory tour the client took us out for dinner at a local restaurant. He ordered a T-bone steak. They apologised that they had run out. I, jokingly, suggested a couple of filet steaks which he thought a great idea and ordered that. This from a man, who while breakfasting on piles of doughnuts, was as skinny as a string bean. There's no justice.

After that dive into Sugarland, we were welcomed by BBDO New York. Team BBDO from Germany were also with us. We were given the pep talk about how great the agency was (and still is) by a Suit whose sole job was to entertain overseas visitors. The next day there was a coach to take us to see Pele's last soccer game with a hostess serving drinks and nibbles on board.

Then it was back to the agency where I met Bruce Crawford. He had been smart enough to merge Papert, Koenig, Lois in London with BBDO and Tim became arguably the youngest, as far as I know, CD in the UK at the time.

Richard Kelley is the only other to have achieved such a thing being, being made CD of Needham's in Los Angeles in his early 20s.

We met the two company men they were sending to Europe to run the launch. The New York Jewish guy with a great sense of humour they sent to Germany. And, you guessed it, the sombre guy missing a funny bone they sent to the UK.

Why????

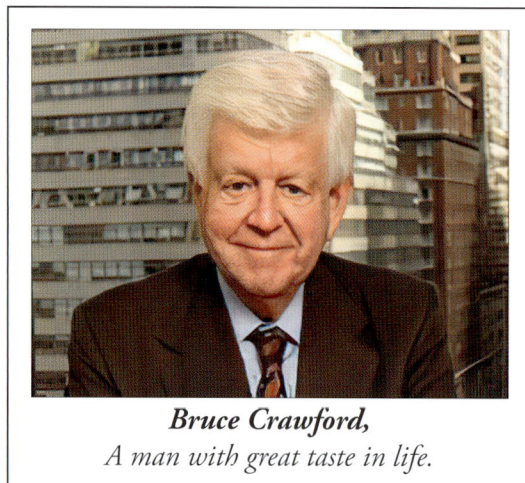

Bruce Crawford,
A man with great taste in life.

On our last night we were entertained at BBDO's special bar for senior staff and hosted by Bruce. Upon our return we all were sent copies of the New York newspaper reports of Pele's game. A nice touch.

Phil Mason and Rita Dempsey ended up creating the launch campaign. But I loved New York, so that was my reward.

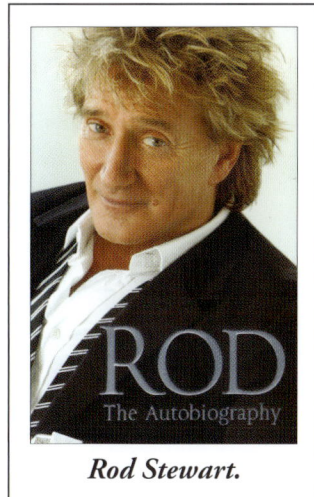

Rod Stewart.

Rod and Est!, Est!!, Est!!!

On one of my many holidays during the 80s in Los Angeles, visiting the BBDO Old Boys such as Richard Kelley, he treated me to a night out at an ice hockey game.

To me, in the warm embrace of a Californian evening, a trip to an ice hockey game was pretty exotic stuff. Let alone the crowd shouting "Gretski Sucks!".

Returning to Richard's home afterwards he pulled into an Italian restaurant and we joined a queue of blokes waiting to be admitted. We could hear English accents but thought no more about it until we were seated inside.

The Maître D had assumed from our accents that we were all together and sat Richard and I at a nearby table.

I then noticed that the head of the other table was Rod "The Mod" Stewart.

I knew him from blues clubs in London such as the Manor House Pub and The Refectory in Golders Green, where he sang with the Long John Baldry Band.

Recently, I bought his autobiography and discovered that, during his younger years, he lived close to me in London's Archway.

Anyway, to say thanks for some good musical nights I sent over a bottle of Est!, Est!!, Est!!! Italian wine.

No, it had nothing to do with EST, the program many ad folk got involved with in the 80s. This wine had an interesting story (see next page).

Anyway, Rod came over and said, "Thanks for the wine lads, over here on holiday are you?" After a brief chat he returned to the others who, we later discovered, were his band who had all been at a recording session earlier that day.

If you get the chance, listen to his rendition of *Grace*; one very moving song.

The wine's story.

Its unusual name, with its officially enshrined exclamation marks, is linked to a whimsical tale.

Legend has it that, in the year 1111, a German bishop called Johann Fugger was following the expedition of German King Henry V to Rome, where Henry was to be crowned as Holy Roman Emperor. Fugger, however, seemed more keen on sightseeing than politics.

As he travelled, he would send his manservant a day ahead of him in search of accommodation with quality wines. In order that the bishop knew which inns provided the best liquid refreshment, Martinus would write with chalk the word Est!, meaning "It is!", on the various inn doors.

Martinus was so taken with the wine from the village of Montefiascone that he wrote Est! Est!! Est!!! on the inn door.

On arriving, the bishop also fell in love with the wine, and from that day forth the wine from this area bore the name Est! Est!! Est!!! di Montefiascone. Moreover Bishop Fugger returned to live in the area until his death.

For centuries afterwards, the tradition to celebrate the anniversary of his death was to pour a bottle of this wine over his tombstone.

My BBDO (1) generation.

Richard Kelley and Pete Andress, Ron Brown, Phil Mason[†] and Rita Dempsey[†] , Frank Budgen, Mike Griffin, Caroline Bartle, Peter Gibb, John Sherfield[†] , Rick Cook[†] a.k.a. *Jackanory* as he always had a story to tell, often hilariously funny, to name but a few. Apologies if I've missed anyone.

A good time was always had by all.
L-R: Martin Reavley, Peter Gibb, Paul Delaney, Mike Griffin.

One of the many joys of working at BBDO was, ironically, the reunions, which are now seldom held and I had to miss a few being Downunder. The chant would go up, "Who's been fired by Tim Delaney once?" and we'd stand; 'Who's been fired by Tim Delaney twice?" and so it would go on.
Image: Paul Walter.

The St. Patrick's night rescue.

Wards Irish Drinking House at Piccadilly Circus, entrance to the left.
Image: Larry Franklin.

Lofty was a 'lifesaver' one St. Patrick's night. A number of creatives from BBDO had joined me at Wards Irish Drinking House in Piccadilly where a good time was had by all. At closing time the others said they were going to the Hard Rock Café to soak up the Guinness but I declined, as did Lofty.

It was Friday, with a pitch to work on the next day, and I just wanted to catch the last tube train home.

The important point to make here is I was legless, of which I'm not proud to admit.

Lofty guided me to try and get a taxi but, seeing the state I was in, none would stop. Lofty found a grubby hotel, off Baker Street, where I woke the next morning.

The pitch was for an Allied Breweries account (the irony of it with the Mum and Dad of all hangovers).

The others were in better shape than me and we didn't win the account. But I will be eternally grateful to Lofty for saving my Irish bacon that night. 'Saint Lofty?' I think so.

Chapter
Eleven

1978 to 1980 (two fantastic years).

The

Kirkwood

Company

†

Adland's 'grand impresario'.

Ronnie Kirkwood, hailed as one of adland's greatest showmen and leader of one of the most successful and fashionable agencies during its golden era, has died aged 87.

He passed away in his sleep on Saturday night at his home in Wincanton, Somerset, after a period of prolonged ill-health.

Dubbed "the grand impresario of the agency business" during the 60s and 70s, the one-time wannabe actor was flamboyant and stylish with an advertising career that was characterised by a swaggering self-confidence.

His launch of The Kirkwood Company in 1970 epitomised his approach. He insisted the agency would begin with nothing – no accounts, no staff and no office. "Nothing except my reputation".

Ronnie Kirkwood. †
Image: Campaign.

Yet there was much more to Kirkwood than mere hype and his legendary expense account.

He was also a leading advocate of a more subtle approach to TV advertising, describing early British commercials as intrusive and bad mannered and full of "loud-mouthed salesmen who confused shouting with communicating and bullying with persuading".

At the same time, he will be remembered as a pioneer of greater sexual tolerance in adland, having been openly gay at a time when many in the industry were still uncomfortable with gay lifestyles.

"I think it made him a solitary, austere and aloof figure who never went out of his way to be liked," a former associate says. "But he was a very shrewd judge of creative work which he knew how to sell to clients as well as being a great employer of creative talent."

Kirkwood's career began in 1950 when he started work as a visualiser, which is what art directors were called at the time, at SH Benson. He was one of the first generation of art school graduates to infiltrate a business dominated by Oxbridge types at a senior level.

His arrival at SH Benson came as commercial TV was about to launch in the UK and Kirkwood was tasked with setting up the agency's TV department. "That was when my advertising career took off," he later recalled.

He went on to head the TV department at Colman Prentis & Varley, then one of the country's hottest agencies. A commentator of the time described him as someone who "personifies the immediate, the visual, the instinctive approach of the art man in advertising".

His campaign for Breeze soap was regarded as a game-changer in the way women were featured in ads. Kirkwood chose not to portray them as the "wilting romantic young things" of the pre-war years but to communicate the sensual pleasure women got from soap.

This involved a radical creative strategy featuring a naked woman in a bath. The campaign was shot in Paris using a glass-sided bath full of detergent and Kirkwood keeping the model warm with glasses of gin.

Having quit as the McCann-Erickson executive creative director to launch The Kirkwood Company, its founder proved there was substance behind his showmanship. The agency consciously positioned itself as a grown-up operation able to deal with large advertisers as equal business partners.

Although the agency flourished it never recaptured its old zest after its sale to the Lopex Group in 1976.

It was said Kirkwood never enjoyed a comfortable relationship with the new management that succeeded Gordon Metcalfe and Tom O'Leary, his fellow founders.

And his problems were compounded by an acrimonious breakaway by John Horner, Graham Collis and Peter Kirvan, which resulted in a legal action over the Rowenta account.

Kirkwood left the industry in 1985 but remained busy. In 2002 his book, *The Travels of an Advertising Man*, was published. He also worked as a consultant for Marshall Cavendish while producing TV scripts.

"The business has been taken over by accountants and book-keepers," he lamented. "I had great fun."

'Campaign', John Tylee. *January 17, 2017.*

Tony Bodinetz[†], the creative Director, hired me. We had been in the same group at CDP with Lindsay Dale and Alan Waldie.

On the night I was hired, the Art Director (who shall remain nameless) that I was hired to work with, misbehaved in the pub around the corner of the agency and got thrown out. I had gone to the toilet and came out to find him hiding, shame-faced, in a doorway. He suffered the same fate at the agency the next day when they heard of his misbehaviour.

Lady Luck smiled on me again when they hired Paul Garrett to work with me.

Paul managed to talk the agency into providing him with a Lotus as part of his package. This caused much puzzlement with some of the company directors. I think Tony must have zipped his lips on the matter.

The offices were in Buckingham Gate with glimpses of the Buckingham Palace and the Changing of the Guard.

Postscript from Paul Garrett:

The car I persuaded Tony to allow me was a Lotus Eclat. I only mention it because it was a four seater and not a two plus two. So I ended up with a total tart trap of a car with room for Eileen and all three of my kids!

Note: Up until now Copywriters and Art Directors often had their own offices and only came together to work on briefs; maybe it was the tightening economy but we were now sharing a room. I loved it because I would get to see the work of photographers and illustrators brought in by agents such as: Julian Seddon, Harri Peccinotti's bother (can't remember his name) Dave Gardiner, Dave Tyler, Effie Howard-Johnson. Mary MacKillop, David Esser and Carol Acey (now Lofthouse), et al.

Julian would park his AC Cobra outside the CDP offices in Howland Street while visiting. We would discretely drool through the overlooking windows. Image: classicandsportscars. com

Pitchin' & Bitchin' cont'd.
Squeezing the grape, part one.

Mae West said "Beulah, peel me a grape" in her movie *I'm no angel.*

I spent much of my advertising life squeezing the grape in advertising wines, but also doing the noble thing in researching what the world has to offer.

We were invited to pitch for the French *Appellation Contrôlée* Wines account.

It was then at Bartle, Bogle, Hegarty, but the odds seemed to be in our favour.

Me, my Art Director Paul Garrett, the Creative Director, Tony Bodinetz, the Account Director and even the client had all worked at Collett Dickenson Pearce. So kindred spirits.

As the start of my 'research' I went to a wine trade fair and sampled some Beaujolais Villages wines. Then, to disturbed looks from the staff on the stand, I sampled Beaujolais wines. It should have been the other way around as the 'Villages' wines are a cut above. This provided me with the inspiration for the campaign. Namely, to be a French Wine primer. The lead ad headline being, *They look the same. Why don't they taste the same?*

As the competing agencies had to have the work researched, I wrote the body copy for each ad. We won the pitch and John Hegarty was very gracious in defeat and sent me a note congratulating us.

The account was very political, so the research worked in our favour. The ads had to be approved by the French Government agency for wines, the importers and each region featured. If any of them tried to change anything, our well-trained ex-CDP client told them they couldn't change a thing as it had all been tested, word for word.

The downside of all that was, I had been all ready to pack and join Paul touring France for the photography but the French said "Non!". They said my job had been done. I pleaded that I would be able to fine-tune, all to no avail.

The old typographer in me was inspired by Paul commissioning the typeface, Corvinus, to be recut by a lady in East Anglia, whose name escapes me.

Hc also had to have giant wine glasses made for depth of field reasons (simply put, this is the distance between the nearest and furthest of objects). Close scrutiny of the grape harvesters in the Beaujolais ad shows them grinning away at the extraordinary sight.

We also included photography of a local dish appropriate for the wine to further whet the appetite.

The client was also smart in being the first, to my knowledge, to import used wine barrels from France to be sold as planters at garden centres.

The campaign benefitted from a great media deal after another long printing strike. The ads appeared regularly in double page colour spreads in the Sunday Times Colour Magazine, and I was told that staff in off-licences (bottle shops in Oz) kept copies of the ads as reference sheets.

As icing on the cake, the entire campaign of six ads was accepted that year (1981) by D&AD in the Annual showcase of work.

Full marks to Paul who discovered that the agency was only entering three of them and made sure the entire campaign was entered. To recycle the strapline I came up with: *French Wines. To know them is to love them.*

Why is one Loire wine pink and another white?

are close to both the River Loire and the Atlantic Ocean.

And it's at its happiest being drunk young and chilled. Either with a meal or as an aperitif.

You'll find both wines easy on the pocket.

And both share the accolade Appellation Contrôlée.

This simply means that the quality and authenticity of each wine is guaranteed by the French Government.

Look for that and then, whichever wine you choose, you know it'll turn out just right.

No matter whether it's red, white or pink.

French Wines.
To know them is to love them.

The glass of Anjou Rosé to your right is clearly a blushing pink.

Not because it's a blend of red and white wine, as some mistakenly are led to believe.

Instead, it gets its pink colour from the skins of the red grapes from which it's made.

They spend only a few hours in the juice before being removed.

As a result you get a wine that's pink. And, furthermore, one that tastes light, medium-dry and crisply delicious when chilled.

'Delicious' is a description that equally applies to the Muscadet in

the glass to your left.

This fine French wine is white simply because it is made from nothing but white grapes.

It has a dry, deliciously soft taste that seems to belie the fact that the vineyards

What are French wines doing with names like these?

The answer is perfectly simple.

The names belong to the grapes that make these fine wines.

Only in this case they're French, from the region of Alsace, where the vineyards cling to mountain slopes overlooking the Rhine.

The local growers all share one ambition. Namely, to produce a wine that tastes as dry, crisp and clean as the mountain air.

Gewurztraminer is one perfect example of this.

It may be hard to say, but it is pleasurably easy to drink.

It also has a fruity, spicy scent, and a clean dry taste that happily lingers on.

Next in line stands Riesling. It's often described as the most balanced of Alsace wines, having a subtle, clean, dry taste with a delicate bouquet.

Bouquet does seem a particularly appropriate word, given that all these wines have a scent like that of Alpine flowers.

Last, but not least, is Sylvaner.

Lighter in taste than the other two, it's delicious on its own or with a picnic.

All these wines benefit from the Alsace growers' almost fanatical attention to detail.

Each of these three wines is made from one variety of grape, and one variety only.

The growers also keep a tight rein on their wine by bottling it in Alsace and nowhere else.

As a result Alsace wines are not that easy on your pocket. But they are rich in character.

Indeed, there's a guarantee with each wine concerning its quality and authenticity.

In short, Appellation Contrôlée. Two words that say a lot about our wine, whatever its name.

French Wines.
To know them is to love them.

Credits: Copywriter, Mike Doyle; Art Director, Paul Garrett; Type Cutter, Sorry, but unknown, Typographer, (besides Paul) Valerie Buckler; Location photography, Ken Griffiths; Food photography, Frank Farrelly.

Postscript from Paul Garrett on Facebook:

I blush at your praise, Mike. I'd like to think that the lovely Mike Chandler would have approved. Bill Thompson and I used to take turns using this typeface. As graduates of the Great Cal Swann, all of us cared (and still do) about these things. I like to think it showed. Great days for all of us!

Ed Church, what can I say? We had both previously worked at the unpleasant FCB. When I arrived at Boase Massimi Pollitt, Ed took me aside and said, "I know you! Hands off the typography!" While my hands were never fully off, I had great respect for Ed's taste, style (is that the word?) and terrific ability. I rank him as one of the greats!

The wine glasses in the ads, huge and handmade by Mr. Adnitt, the stammering glass blower, gave us the necessary depth of field and took almost two bottle of very nice Beaujolais each. No digital trickery for us.

Rob Henderson on Facebook: Lovely work. Interesting depth of field problem. Having two-bottle glasses made was a tasty solution.

Terry Comer[†] on Facebook: Don't forget the more recent heroes (Bobbi Gassey) who drove me crazy asking for a four letter word instead of the five letter word I had written (I always complied). And the unsung hero at Face, whose name I forget, because he was always in the background, but was another great typographer.

Germany calling, again.

Another account Paul and I worked on was Rowenta, in particular their new steam irons, which were innovative at the time with a detachable water tank and descaling pin. I had a visit to the factory and a taste of the local cuisine with boiled bacon and cider top of the menu list.

As a gift after visiting, Rowenta gave me this cider jug. I just need the bacon now to go with it.

We wrote two commercials which Mike "Rocky" Reynolds directed and Keith Benton produced. One was a spoof of the *Antiques Roadshow* TV series with our version of the legendary expert, Arthur Negus, singing the praises of the 'antique' in his hands in a future version of the programme. The second commercial was set in a future Museum of Domestic Appliances and a school visit with the teacher explaining how futuristic the product had been in its time.

◄ **Mike Reynolds.**
His Mum made a great St Patrick's cake using three heart-shaped baking tins.
Image: Mike Reynolds.

Keith Benton ▶
Image: Facebook

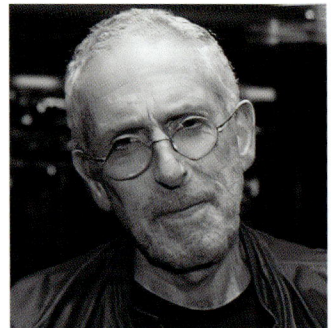

Sadly, I have no copies of the films but it was an enjoyable shoot and end result. However, the trade ad below does give some of the story.

TWO BRIGHT SPOTS AMIDST THE GLOOM AND DOOM.

Behold, our Christmas double act for T.V.
It's the final act, this year, in Rowenta's massive £1.1m investment in promoting our products.
Already, we're having to pinch ourselves to believe our sales figures.
Take, as an example, the biggest value sector in irons: steam and spray.
We've achieved 35% sales share. Or, to put it another way, more than one in every three steam/spray irons sold is made by Rowenta.
That's despite our premium price and the beleaguered state of the economy.
But we're not resting on our laurels, let alone our holly.
From November 17, right through to January, our revolutionary Aquasteam Tap Water Iron (DA21) is starring nationwide on T.V.

in tap water, by designing a unique pin valve to help clear lime scale away.
Second in our double act is the Filtermatic Coffee Maker (FK11). It'll be appearing on London, Southern and Midlands T.V. from November 10.
There's never been a better time for such an event.
Sales of coffee machines this year have already increased by leaps and bounds, and 65% of all the machines sold were of the filter variety.
Furthermore, Christmas is only 30 shopping days away.
And, even more to the point of this advertisement, it's even fewer stocking days away. So order now.
If our past experience is anything to go by, your cash register will be playing jingle bells.

Rowenta

The trade ad about the commercials in earlier, difficult economic times.

Credits: *Copywriter, Mike Doyle; Art Director, Paul Garrett; Photographer, possibly, Nigel Haynes.*

Postscript from Paul Garrett:

When we visited Rowenta I was carted off to be interrogated by their very German design director.
I was told I had to pass a test to prove that we were the right men for the job.
I was shown three prototypes of coffeemakers and had to decide which one they would produce. Fortunately I got it right.

Loving insurance?

Some, or even many, might say have I seen a Shrink? No, I haven't. Well, not yet.

It all started after my divorce from Mrs Doyle Mk#1.

I sold my home in High Barnet and moved closer into London, buying a small Gothic-style house at Torriano Cottages, Kentish Town.

One day, while I was at work, I was burgled, and they cleaned out most items I considered valuable. There was an access lane that ran along the end of all the gardens on my side of the street, and police said they drove a van up there and burgled every house, like a military operation. Certainly, a professional job.

I thought, foolishly, that my insurance would cover me, but in the chaos of the renovations to my new home, with a daily invasion of a team of Polish decorators, I found the renewal notice buried on a table and I had missed the renewal date by a day.

It took a couple of years to pay for the rental equipment they took, and, to my knowledge, they were never caught. It did teach me the value of making sure my insurance is up-to-date.

While I was working at Kirkwoods we were briefed to write a couple of ads for Legal & General Insurance.

The household ad speaks for itself, but the business ad may need explanation for those who haven't grown up with British comedy on TV. I chose three programs to illustrate my point: *Robin's Nest* which was about a restaurant with a one-armed Irish waiter, a walking disaster. *Fawlty Towers* may be more familiar with all its dysfunctions, and the third was The Fall and *Rise of Reginald Perrin* of Sunshine Deserts which was a dysfunctional food manufacturing company.

There seems to be a theme running there, not unlike Brexit, a recent comedy appearing on your screens as I write.

There was also a TV campaign called 'The Worries' with animated characters dealing with things that might go wrong at home with the building, but the authorities refused to approve it as they said it would frighten the public.

My other insurance campaign for Abbey Life, which Paul Garrett and I won from Boase Massimi Pollitt, came a tad later. I told the story about that previously in the Direct Response case study. Part two will come in Book Two, with tales of working on Australian insurance accounts.

Postscript from Paul Garrett:

'Likes'. This was the second ad and our lovely Kirkwoods Art Buyer (sadly can't remember her name) recommended illustrators for it. I don't recall who but I do remember being pleased with them. The previous 'plane crashing' ad was by Paul Sample which was magic!

Well, that seems to cover just about everything.

Illustrated here is a cross-section of the risks covered by the Legal and General Home Risks Policy.

(You would be cross if all this happened to you.)

The policy's great advantage is that it consists of eight separate sections.

So you can easily pick and choose the ones that suit your client's needs best.

The policy covers: Contents, All Risks, Personal Accident, Caravan, Small Craft, Personal Money, Deep Freezer Contents, and last, but not least, the fabric of the building itself.

All of which underlines what we have said in our headline.

Legal & General

Home Risks Insurance.

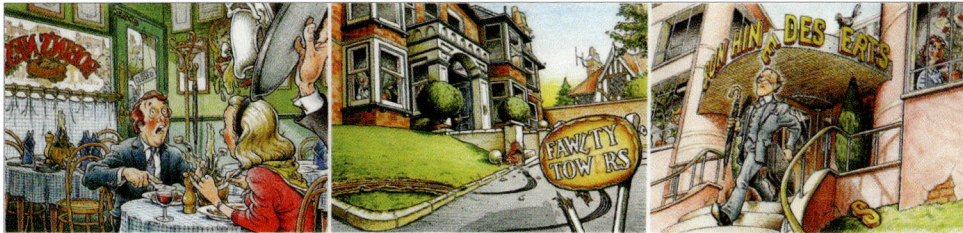

Even with the likes of them, there's little we can't insure.

Before you are three of the most accident-prone businesses known to man.

The majority of those accidents could be covered by our Business Package Policies.

There are three in all.

The first is for retailers; whether it's a cafe, shop or pub.

The second is for inns, guest houses and hotels. (Yes, even the likes of you, Mr. Fawlty.)

And the third is for offices.

All carry the basic cover you'd expect from such policies.

Also, for each kind of business, there are extra, especially relevant extensions.

But then, to paraphrase a certain TV executive, we didn't get where we are today by not being relevant.

Legal & General

We cover the things you care for.

Retail, Hotel and Office Insurance.

Credits: *Copywriter, Mike Doyle; Art Director, Paul Garrett; Illustrators (Cover) Paul Semple; (Likes of them) Sadly unknown.*

Another photographic memory.

Having mentioned the Agfa camera ad story previously, Paul and I were briefed to write an ad for the Sankyo client at Kirkwoods.

They also marketed Pentax and Paul was smart enough to get his hands on the mini Pentax system, which was an impressive bit of kit.

Good news for people with only one pair of hands.

The majority of sound-movie cameras seem to call for people with unnatural dexterity.

Conscious that you're not built this way, we at Sankyo had the bright idea of a sound-movie camera that works single-handed.

Despite its solid metal casing, it's surprisingly light.

By and large, this is due to our pioneering use of tiny integrated circuits.

To operate the camera is, literally, child's play. Which is another piece of good news if you'd like to see yourself on film for a change.

Simply set all the controls to green and off you go.

Which brings us to the truly impressive feature of this camera.

Whatever you choose to shoot, the camera focuses on it automatically. Even when you operate the 3 x power zoom lens. (You do have to use your other hand for this, or at least one finger.)

If you're wondering what to do with your free hand the rest of the time, there is a hand mike that comes as standard.

The boom mike in the picture is, in fact, an optional extra.

If it were fitted as standard, our camera would cost a bit more.

As it is, comparable cameras on the market cost way in excess of our asking price of £230.

Not that they're truly comparable. For the simple reason that very few manufacturers make all their own parts.

We do. And offer a hefty three-year guarantee on all the cameras in our range as proof of our confidence.

You have to hand it to us, that is good news.

Sankyo Cine
The way we make our cameras made our name.

Credits: Copywriter, Mike Doyle; Art Director, Paul Garrett; Photographer, Tim Brown.

A history lesson.

We were briefed to launch 'Double Diamond Burton Export Ale.

No one had ever explained the significance of Burton in brewing history and, with my love of history, I was set to go.

The first phase of this campaign was with Cathy Heng as Art Director, working as a freelancer with us at the time. Paul then took over for the second phase.

It wasn't this history, but the fickle finger of fate that flicked me on my way again.

Credits: *Copywriter,* Mike Doyle; *Art Directors,* Cathy Heng and Paul Garrett; *Photographer,* Barney Edwards.

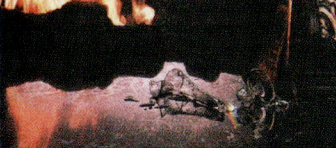

Postscript from Paul Garrett:

We did the second year of DDBEA campaign together.

You did year one with Cathy Heng who did a magnificent job in my opinion. I'd love to have done them. Our shoot with Barney Edwards was quite something coupled with the search that resulted in us finding an original wreck picture from the Gibson's of the Scilly Isles archive.

Note 1: Cathy was briefed to fly to the West Indies with Barney Edwards to create that year's campaign for Bacardi Rum. A tough assignment, but somebody had to do it.

Note 2: Paul Garrett and I worked on another beer, Arctic Lite; the research groups loved the creative but loathed the beer, so it was taken off the market. I had Ridley Scott excited to direct it, but it became another lost cause.

Barney heard in a phone message from the local lighthouse that night announcing that his partner had their baby and that all was well.

Credits: Copywriter, Mike Doyle, a microscopic and keen eye may be able to see me modelling as a 'wrecker' in the bottom of the photo.

Art Director, Paul Garrett; Photographer, Barney Edwards.

Pitchin' & Bitchin', cont'd.

Budweiser.

Paul Garrett and I pitched for the launch of Budweiser into the UK. The creative idea was to see America from the eye of an Eagle.

Tony Scott[†] agreed to shoot it and found an eagle wrangler who could make it happen, I also had the idea to get the group The Eagles to record the sound track.

Ronnie Bond recorded and sang the demo and we presented to August Busch III, the head of the brewery, who got very excited about the idea and the music, even punching his fist in his excitement. I think it was positive.

We actually won the account but Allied Breweries couldn't manage the wood-chip brewing process, so the business and the account were handed elsewhere.

So near, yet so far.

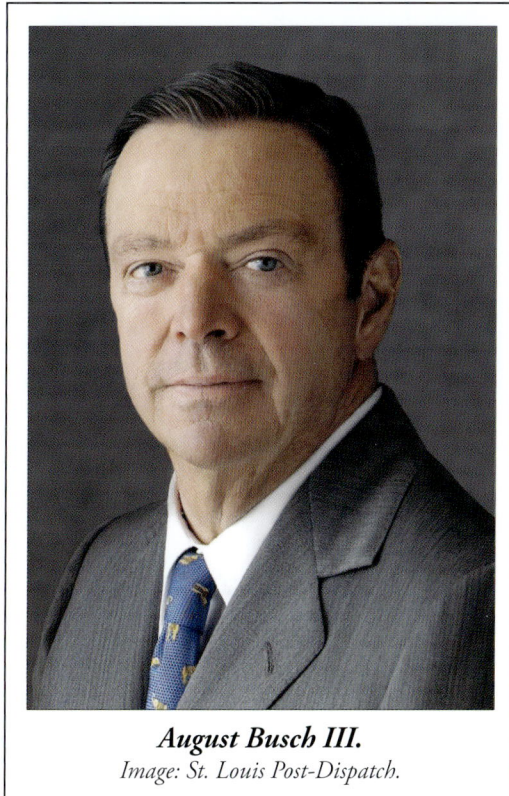

August Busch III.
Image: St. Louis Post-Dispatch.

August Anheuser Busch III is a great-grandson of Anheuser-Busch founder Adolphus Busch and was the company's Chairman until November 30, 2006. August Busch III is informally known as "Auggie" and as "The Third" or "Three Sticks" by subordinates and employees at Anheuser-Busch. He is the father of August Busch IV. **Wikipedia**

The day of the Magical Mystery Tour. *A coach turned up at the agency and took us down to Brighton for a day at the beach, fish & chips (of course) and rides in the fun fair.*

The Kirkwoods table at the annual D&AD Awards Night at the Grosvenor House Hotel.

My Kirkwoods generation.

I would like to give credit to the other team at Kirkwoods in my time: **Derek Apps** and **Mike Stephenson**. They were the 'punk' band to our 'classical duet'. But we loved their work for Vladivar Vodka, and Foster Grants to name only two. **Imelda O'Donovan** who created a great 'St Michael's Night' audio tape of Irish music for me and went on to marry Derek. Paul and I did hire **John Merriman** who went on to have an agency of his own. I seem to recall he had an amazing collection of enamel advertising signs. Apologies to anyone I have left out.

Postscript from Paul Garrett: I remember Derek tying his own shoelaces together out of boredom in a presentation, and then falling flat on his face when he attempted to leave having forgotten them. So endearing. It was impossible not to like them in spite of the obvious talent they both had.

Postscript from Mike Stephenson: From Kirkwoods we moved to BMP then to Lowe's where we won all our awards for our Heineken work and Whitbread Best ads. Also Lloyds Bank and Hula Hoops. The Heineken ads included 'Bins', 'Comet' and 'Mona Lisa'. I then went on to direct, winning more awards for COI Army ads, Police and TTA for instance. In 2001 I started my own production company MOON. (I also have my own memoirs book available on Amazon called *ADLAND AND ME*.

The fuel crisis.

The 1979 'oil crisis' (our second) occurred in the world due to decreased oil output in the wake of the Iranian Revolution. The price of crude oil more than doubled to US$39.50 per barrel over the next 12 months, and long queues once again appeared at petrol stations, as they had in 1973.

The agency Directors were kind enough to refer me to the local garage who supplied me with the petrol that I needed to keep mobile. The Government did give us fuel stamps but I can't remember having to use them. They weren't of any use anyway, if no petrol was available.

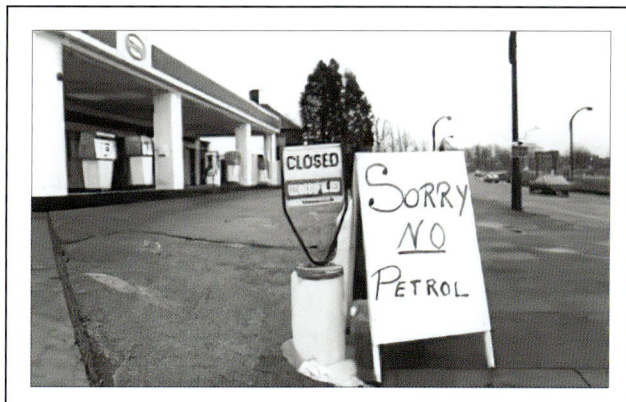

Chapter
Twelve

1981 to 1984.

Wright
& Partners

✝

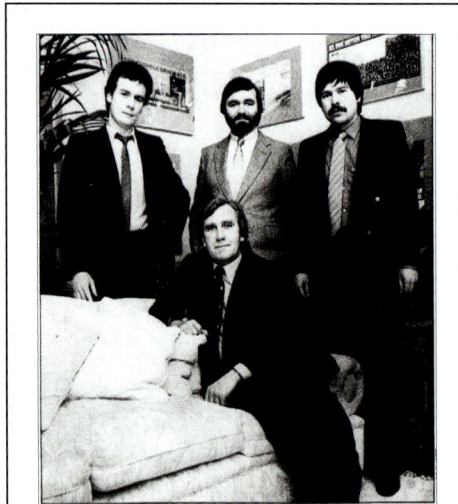

L-R: Garnet Edwards, Yours truly,
Keith Smith with Johnny Wright, in
pride of place, seated.
Image: *Press cutting from* Campaign.

My road to Monte Carlo.

First things first, I had been freelancing after leaving Kirkwoods and was invited to help the team at a new agency with a pitch for Irish Distillers and Jameson Whiskey. They had all been working together at Grey Advertising and had decided to go out on their own, forming the new agency, Wright & Partners. Johnny Wright had succeeded in persuading Irish Distillers to include the new agency on its pitch list.

Our first offices had previously been the home and office of the award-winning Shirt Sleeve Studio.

When I joined them at Wright & Partners, in 1981, the agency had already been appointed by Crown Paints to their Trade Paints division as well as the wallpaper products such as Anaglypta and Lincrusta.

The advertising was directed to painters and decorators, factory owners and architects to name but a few. My Dad had been a painter, so I felt an affinity with the product and I had already been active in painting the various homes I had restored.

We used to go up by train to Darwen to visit the clients at Crown. They were a pleasure to deal with and we had the bonus of a British Rail breakfast into the bargain. Although, one day there was none served as the announcement on the train said, "The cook has forgotten his frying pan". Monte Carlo wasn't anything to do with Bob Hope or Bing Crosby and their Road movies, but a sales conference Crown held there, hosted by the lovely Sue Lawley.

It must have felt cold to the locals as they were all rugged up, but we were in shorts and short-sleeved shirts.

The Monte Carlo branch office of W&P?

Ladies, look away. I must, briefly, bring your attention to the 'pig' ad below. My Art Director, and Joint Creative Director (partner in crime?), Garnet Edwards, had his photo taken with the pig and that Christmas sent a card to close friends with the shot and message, "Merry Christmas from the wife and I." Ouch!

216

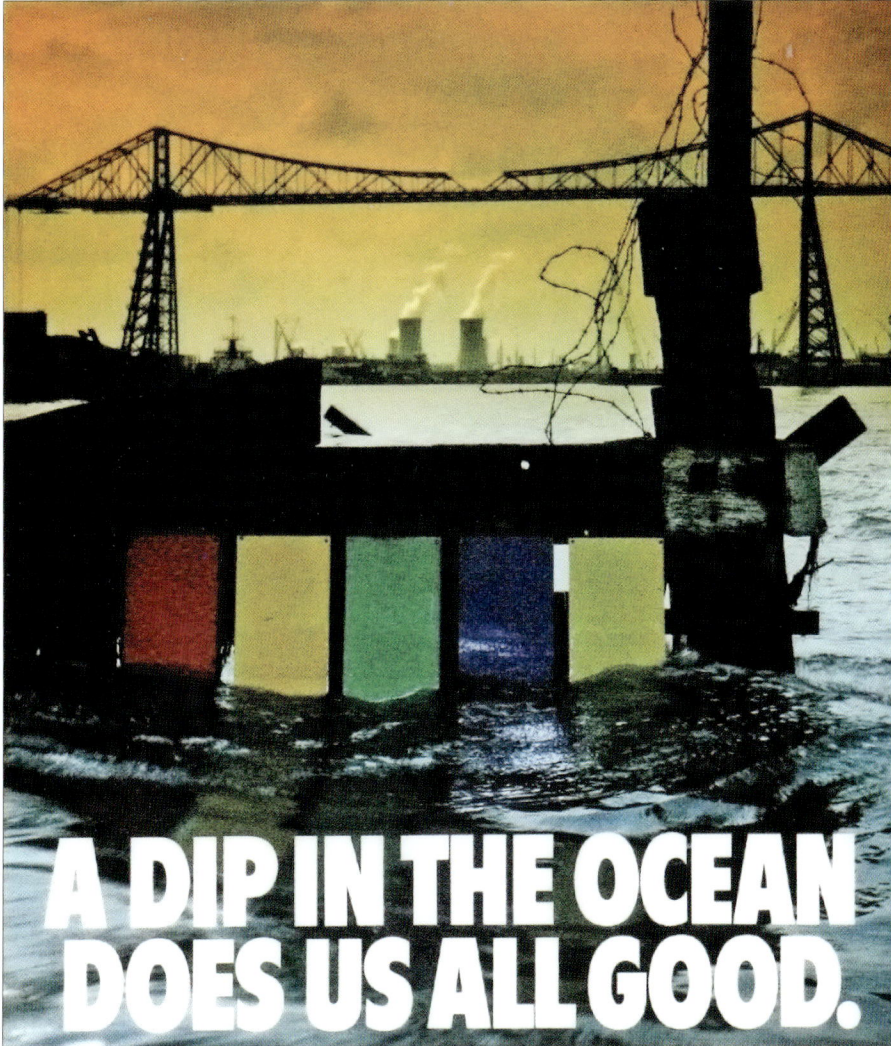

A DIP IN THE OCEAN DOES US ALL GOOD.

The acid test of any paint is how well it performs in an aggressive environment.

The worst, in the view of our boffins, is this sorry place on the banks of the Tees.

Metal panels, coated with various Crown Paints, are fixed to a jetty there and left to the mercy of the elements.

In this instance they are excessively cruel.

The salt in the air is corrosive enough but to make matters worse, at high tide the panels are completely immersed in sea water.

To add injury to injury, the air also contains sulphur dioxide.

Of all the industrial pollutants this is certainly one of the worst. When it contacts metal it turns to sulphuric acid.

If both, panels and paint can survive that, they'll survive practically anything.

One of Crown's latest developments is totally concerned with survival.

Oil rigs suffer endless assaults from the North Sea.

Their vulnerable splash zones usually have a product called Two-Pack, Coal-Tar Epoxy to protect them.

This relies on the painter mixing both the base product and the curing agent in exactly the right proportions. Often in dreadful weather.

Inevitably the paintwork suffers. A fact which naturally gave us cause for concern.

So, in company with Bayer we developed a One-Pack Polyurethane System.

It's as near to fool-proof as you can get. What's more, when subjected to a series of rigorous tests, it passed them all with flying colours.

Speaking of colours, yet another Crown development with extensive research behind it is Crown Colour Plan.

This range of paints is available in 960 colours, all computer-controlled to guarantee consistency.

Order 50 litres now, and then reorder in a year's time, and the colour will be exactly the same.

All things considered, our attention to detail has to be good for everyone concerned.

crown paints

CROWN DECORATIVE PRODUCTS LTD., DEPT. RKG, P.O. BOX 37, DARWEN, LANCASHIRE BB3 0BG.

This ad was criticised in Parliament by the Member for Middlesbrough who complained that it gave a bad impression of his town. It was a true story nevertheless.

Crown credits: *Copywriter, Mike Doyle; Art Director, Garnet Edwards; Photographer/ Illustrator, usually Stak but the rest are sadly unknown.*

W&P in the 'Pink'.

Being in advertising it makes sense to advertise your wares. Charlie Saatchi was famous for his chutzpah in promoting Saatchi & Saatchi London with full page ads in *The Times*. We were told he was amazed to see a four-page, ad promoting a new agency called Wright & Partners.

Our client, Securicor, agreed to run a four-page, glossy colour, corporate ad in *The Financial Times* highlighting the extraordinary range of services they offered under my banner headline: *Securicor, our other national trust.* Securicor was like the brand 'Hoover' that became synonymous with vacuum cleaners. It was the carrier for precious cargoes such as human transplants as well as money. It even built armoured vehicles. Little of which the public were aware.

In case of production problems the paper required a black and white standby. Securicor didn't feel this would be right for them, so we took the opportunity to create the alternative material for us.

Well , bless my cotton undergarments, the presses did actually fail, and our ad ran (free to us) to readers all over the country and Europe. (page 221)

Thousands of copies of The Financial Times, with its distinctive pink pages, carried a four-page ad for this tiny, new agency.

Whether we got any business because of it, it's hard to say. With 20/20 hindsight

Edwards (l) and Doyle . . . team

Securicor makes ad debut with one-off FT drive

Securicor launched its first corporate advertising this week with a four-page colour ad in the *Financial Times* created by Wright and Partners, which won the business two months ago (*Campaign*, 4 February).

The aim of the campaign is to extend Securicor's reputation as a parcel and cash-carrying company to a multi-faceted organisation covering alarm systems, vehicle-building, hotel management and mobile communications.

The four-page special ad, which ran only once, on Wednesday, is aimed at businessmen in order to generate greater awareness of the full range of Securicor services and to encourage businessmen to use Securicor more widely. The ad was designed by the agency's creative partners Garnet Edwards and Mike Doyle.

The next advertising for Securicor by Wrights will break at the end of this month and will run through until July with colour pages in the Sunday supplements. This £120,000 campaign will promote Securicor's mobile communications. The two ads were created by Tim Batten and Andrew Smart.

campaign, knocking both Labour and Conservative and Saatchi and Saatchi is sitting tight on its ideas for the Tories—but has a campaign ready to go when needed.

Four pages of advertising appeared in the Financial Times last Wednesday extolling the virtues of Wright and Partners—all due to a happy accident.

The space was scheduled for a big full colour ad for Securicor, but the colour printing broke down and the normal black and white substitute was not available. The agency hurriedly filled the space with their own house ad, getting the media bargain of the week, and Securicor gets its colour ad free next week.

Edwards . . . 'it didn't cost much'

Not in the pink

There can be few of you still left under the illusion that Wright and Partners actually forked out 30-odd grand for its four-page house ad in the *Financial Times* last week. But Wrights creative partner Garnet Edwards reckons there are far-reaching implications to the *FT*'s "buy one, get one free if the machine breaks down" proposition.

Just in case you are totally oblivious to this little saga, what happened was that Wrights had booked a four-page colour space for client Securicor. The *FT* said fine, but you'll have to provide us with a black and white version (or should that be black and pink?) in case the colour machinery gives up on us. Adamant that this particular ad would not work in mono, Edwards came up with the compromise of producing a house ad as a standby. "It didn't cost much and we could always use it as a mailer if it didn't run," he reasoned.

The machine duly broke down, the house ad ran (free) and Securicor will get its colour ad this Friday. But did you know, says Edwards, that to warm up the colour machine the *FT* always uses the black and white ad for something like 10,000 copies, which then get distributed to far-flung places like Europe and Wales?

FT readers in Europe and Wales be warned. You could be in for a surfeit of agency house ads.

In the black, in the pink

BROKERS and bankers were scratching their heads over the cornflakes on Wednesday last week, because the centre four pages of their beloved Financial Times were devoted to a house advert for Wright and Partners, a two-year-old ad agency little known outside the media business.

The going rate for such largesse is more than £38,000 and even then it is normally affordable only by big corporate spenders.

This time, however, it cost nothing. According to Johnny Wright, the agency's boss, the space was originally booked for one of his clients, Securicor, as a glossy four-colour extravaganza. In case of printing mishaps, the FT requires that a black-and-white backup be available.

Securicor did not feel that its message could translate to monochrome – hence the Wright house ad. Lo and behold, the colour version failed.

Incidentally, the level of reponse to the ad is a cautionary tale for any firm which is really thinking of spending so much in one go. Two days after it appeared, Wright said that he had business inquiries from "an hotel group, a publishing house, an oil company and a financial group". Early days, of course, but that works out at £9,500 a call.

Press cutting from 'Campaign'.

219

FUNNY HOW ONE NAME ALWAYS SPRINGS TO MIND.

Wants a lift – says he's just bought a Krugerrand

Securicor's status as a household name was certainly not achieved by employing the untrustworthy.

Every one of our employees is security screened. This stretches back twenty years. Or, for younger recruits, to school-leaving age.

Such screening means that everything in our power is done to ensure the integrity of our employees and the divisions in which they serve.

The end result of all this effort is an enviable staff reputation. One that we are proud to say is definitely second to none.

Our attention to detail runs to fashion shows where our guardettes keep an eye on things.

So that your staff needn't run any risk, we collect and deliver cash from the banks and will also make up wage packets and distribute them.

In addition, we'll take care of high-value items such as furs, jewellery, or art treasures; keeping them in our vaults as well as ensuring their safe delivery.

OUR AIR COURIER SERVICE.

Remember, if you have any documents or packages that require safe delivery, anywhere in the world, our Air Courier service is just the ticket.

For valuables, Securicor Global Couriers only employ highly trained and discreet staff with at least five year's Securicor experience behind each one of them.

As part of this service we operate a 24-hour Air Courier Information Hotline (01-844 0404).

BEADY EYES.

On the home front, Securicor will patrol and protect your premises at night and at weekends.

And if you have your own night security staff they can call Securicor's local Control Centre at pre-arranged times throughout the length of the night.

This ensures that they keep alert and, in the absence of their scheduled call, we know that they may need the help of the long arm of the law.

After all, the last laugh ought to be at the expense of the criminal, not you.

'Please leave, Mr Evans, your redundancy money is blocking up the street'

✕ SECURICOR
ONE OF OUR NATIONAL TRUSTS

Credits: *Copywriter, Mike Doyle; Art Director, Garnet Edwards; Cartoonists, Various*

THE NEW CURIOSITY SHOP.

Founded at the end of 1980, we've rocketed from zero to 118 in the 'Campaign' league of the top 300 UK agencies.

By anyone's standards that is a dramatic growth record, one that we're understandably proud of.

This pride also extends to our client list and the work we've produced for them.

OUR CLIENT LIST.

Canada Dry International, Crown Paints, Dixons, EMI Music Video, Labour Party, Miln Marsters, Orlane, Prime Computer, Securicor, Tolly Cobbold.

A FEW POTTED CASE HISTORIES.

CANADA DRY (Middle East/S. Europe). Overall they have brand leadership in most of the region and in their key market, Egypt, they have enjoyed a significant increase in sales. The complexity of our task is logistically awesome: 12 markets, with their Cola having three different names, besides having to work in four different languages.

CROWN PAINTS. (Protective Coatings/Factory Maintenance). We directed our ads at a broad cross-section of decision makers; Managing Directors through to consulting engineers and painting contractors. To reach them we used newspapers such as 'The Daily Telegraph' backed by specialist press.

The advertising brought in an enormously high degree of quality responses: 51% of the total on Protective Coatings came from the national press, 40% in the instance of Factory Maintenance.

The PRIME COMPUTER campaign appears as double page spreads in the colour supplements, with a TV test in Granada. In a mere six weeks pre- and post-awareness figures have shown a very healthy shift from 13% to 36% at a fraction of their competitors' spend.

ORLANE (Cosmetics and Halston Fragances) briefed us to advertise a special offer that was exclusive to Selfridges. The medium chosen was TV-AM. Foolhardy? Far from it. Orlane and Selfridges have seldom, if ever, seen such a positive response, or one of such quality. Proof that, in the right circumstances, TV-AM can work.

Selfridges actually sold out!

TOLLY COBBOLD, the Ipswich brewer and the second oldest in the land, wished to give support to the London Free Trade. Our mix of posters, tube cards, and colour pages in TV Times, Time Out and LAM saw a 20% improvement in accounts opened over the previous year. That's certainly not small beer.

For a fuller picture of these case histories and a look at the work of the Nosey Agency 'phone or write to either Johnny Wright or Keith Smith.

WRIGHT & PARTNERS, 62 BERNERS STREET, LONDON W1P 3AR. TELEPHONE: 01-631 4808. TELEX: 24512.

WHAT SETS ONE ADVERTISING AGENCY APART FROM THE REST?

WRIGHT AND PARTNERS. AHEAD BY A NOSE.

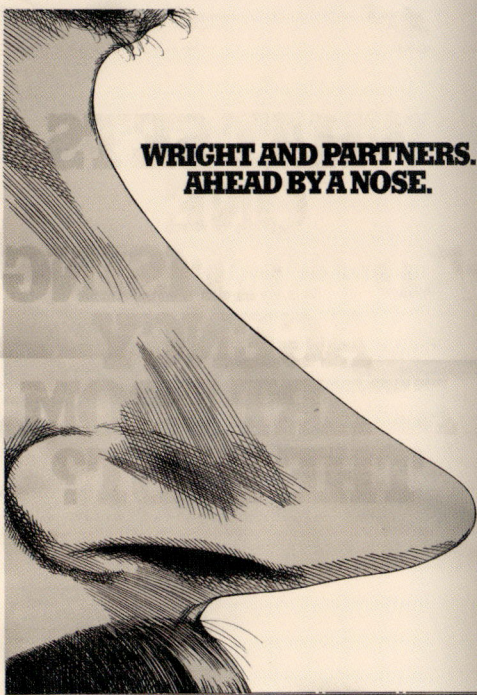

If you're looking for an agency that offers you that little bit extra, our large hooter beats the rest any day.

Being nosey about our clients' business is the very essence of our working method.

In addition to the usual desk research, copious probing questions are asked of our clients.

Factory visits are deemed especially important. Our Planning Department organises research groups to search for facts about consumer attitudes before a single ad is briefed into the Creative Department.

Only by fully understanding all the ramifications of our clients' marketing objectives can we really start the advertising process.

METHOD ADVERTISING.

At Wright and Partners we believe our ads must measure up to three criteria.

One: the ads should be relevant to the needs of the consumer. Identifying those needs is part of our initial homework.

Two: the ads should be competitive. This can be achieved either by creatively highlighting the product benefits or in their absence as with a "me-too" product, by developing a competitive positioning.

(e.g. For the introduction of Petcraft Riscrok into supermarkets our creative solution was "Healthy-Diet Dog Biscuits Keeps Noses Nice 'n' Wet." Look in Sainsburys and you will see just how competitive the packaging and positioning is.)

Our third criterion is that the ads should look distinctive. Creating a unique look for a brand can be hard work but the end result is always rewarding.

Given the fact that more than 90% of advertising is said to be ignored, these three measures of our work have even greater relevance.

We don't stop there, however. Accountability on our accounts and campaigns is of paramount importance.

Hit and run advertising is not for us, pre- and post-testing being an integral part of our way of working.

If you're spending money in the media you and we have to be sure it's working and is money well spent.

HEAVYWEIGHTS VS LIGHTWEIGHTS.

Another edge we have over many of our competitors is the fact that at least two directors will always work on your business.

Work being the operative word. All the directors are actively involved on our accounts, on a daily basis. They are not just agency front men who you meet once in a blue moon.

This is no idle statement as our present clients will testify.

To give you some idea of our agency experience forgive us if we do a little name and initial dropping.

Miles Doyle (Creative Director, Copy) counts DDB, CDP, BJIP as Deputy Creative Director/Copy Chief, BBDO and Kirkwoods amongst his agencies.

To name but a few of his past accounts: Benson & Hedges, Scotcade, National Panasonic, Smiths Crisps, Ben Truman, Habitat, Toyota, Sony, Rowenta and French Wines.

Garnet Edwards (Creative Director, Art) worked at CPV, Benton & Bowles, DDB, Euro as Head of Art and Grey as Creative Director.

His blue-chip account experience includes Pepsi, Teflon, KBM, Cover Plus Paints, Avis, Audi, Aiwa, Swissair, Mercedes, General Foods, Yellow Pages and Timex.

Keith Smith (Client Services Director) was also at DDB, then McCann Erickson followed by Grey where he was a board director.

Over the years his accounts have included OCI, Skol, Van den Berghs, Prestige, Lyons Tetley, P&G, Nestlé and the Mirror Group Newspapers. Yet more blue chips.

Last, but certainly not least, of the partners is Johnny Wright, our Managing Director. His background is more client biased.

He started as a Production Controller at Metal Box. From there he went to Cheesebrough-Ponds as Brand/Marketing Manager. His next stop was Grey where he spent ten years, rising through the agency ranks to become the Deputy Managing Director.

His particular account responsibilities were P&G, General Foods, John West, Airwick and Revlon. Clearly our blue chips runneth over.

Heavyweight experience such as this does not just apply to the partners.

Take Rob Britton, our Planning Director as just one example.

At McCanns he was a Media Planner/Buyer. Next he was a Media Group Head at Grey London.

READING FROM LEFT TO RIGHT: JOHNNY WRIGHT, KEITH SMITH, MIKE DOYLE, GARNET EDWARDS.

From there he went to Tokyo where he was Grey's Media Director.

His next port of call was Grey New York where he moved over to account handling and became Account Executive on General Foods.

He then returned to the UK where Grey made him Account Director on Nestlé and British Telecom.

A wealth of experience that equips him perfectly for planning; an essential part of our advertising mix.

OUR WORK ETHIC.

The combination of the afore-mentioned, multi-faceted talents adds up to a hefty team working on our clients' business.

A team dedicated to producing advertising that is not only effective, but also highly distinctive.

Furthermore, a team motivated by the greatest incentive of all—being our own master.

This creates an enthusiasm that is seldom seen in multi-national agencies. And, more to the point, those agencies seldom put such enthusiasm and experience to work on your business.

That, if you like, is your greatest incentive to come and visit Wright and Partners, the Nosey Agency.

maybe we should have included a coupon.

Nevertheless, any publicity is good publicity as the old saying goes.

Before we rattled Mr Saatchi, we had run the 'Cat' ad (see below) in our trade magazine *Campaign*, to announce we had grown and were moving to new, improved offices.

Securicor's ad ran a few days later. Keen eyes will see in the press cuttings that Johnny Wright, our MD, reported 'Business enquiries from an hotel group, a publishing house, an oil company and a financial group'.

Credits: *Copywriter, Mike Doyle; Art Director, Garnet Edwards; Illustrator/Cartoonist, Arthur Robbins.*

The business of politics.

The agency was appointed by the British Labour Party in 1983.

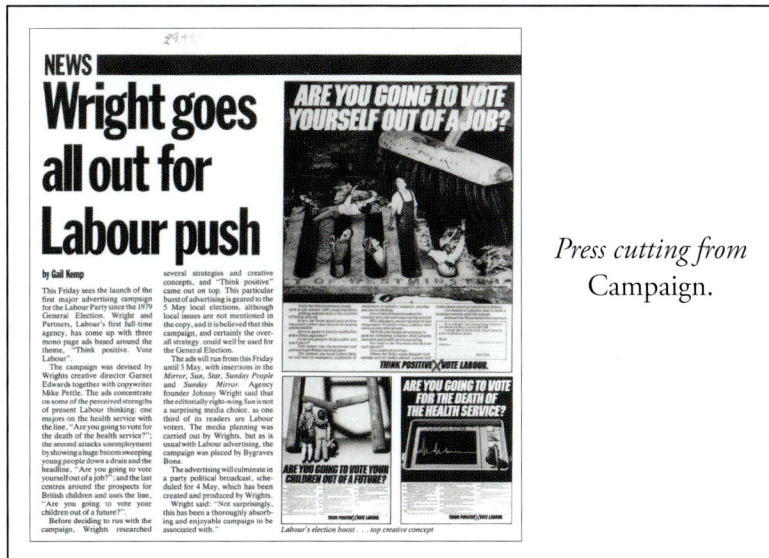

Press cutting from Campaign.

I had joined the Social Democrats so had to step aside while Garnet Edwards, my Art Director Partner, and Johnny Wright, ran that account leaving the rest of the business, briefly, to Keith Smith and myself.

We were approached by what were then Socialist/Communist block companies like Sekonda Watches and Skoda cars, but nothing came of it.

We were even approached by the Maltese Tourist Board and Air Malta. Dom Mintoff, the Maltese Prime Minister, discovered that Saatchi's, the Conservative Party agency, was handing the island's account. He instructed the department of tourism to find the Labour Party agency.

Garnet went off with a freelance writer, Barry Smith, and came back with a brilliant campaign about how foreign, but familiar, a holiday in Malta is.

However the consortium of hoteliers and tour guides lobbied, and succeeded, in keeping the account where it was.

I do remember getting a buzz when we had the great American journalist, Walter Cronkite[†], talking live to America from our reception about us and the election. Broadcasting to a worldwide audience he opened by calling Johnny, "Jimmy"!

Garnet had done a brilliant job with the agency decor and had even painted, by hand, the cornucopia over the entrance door. We were next to the Sanderson Fabrics Showroom and people would often come in asking to buy the Designers Guild furniture in our reception. You can see in the illustration in the house ad that we had a 'shopwindow', corner location.

Image: CBS.

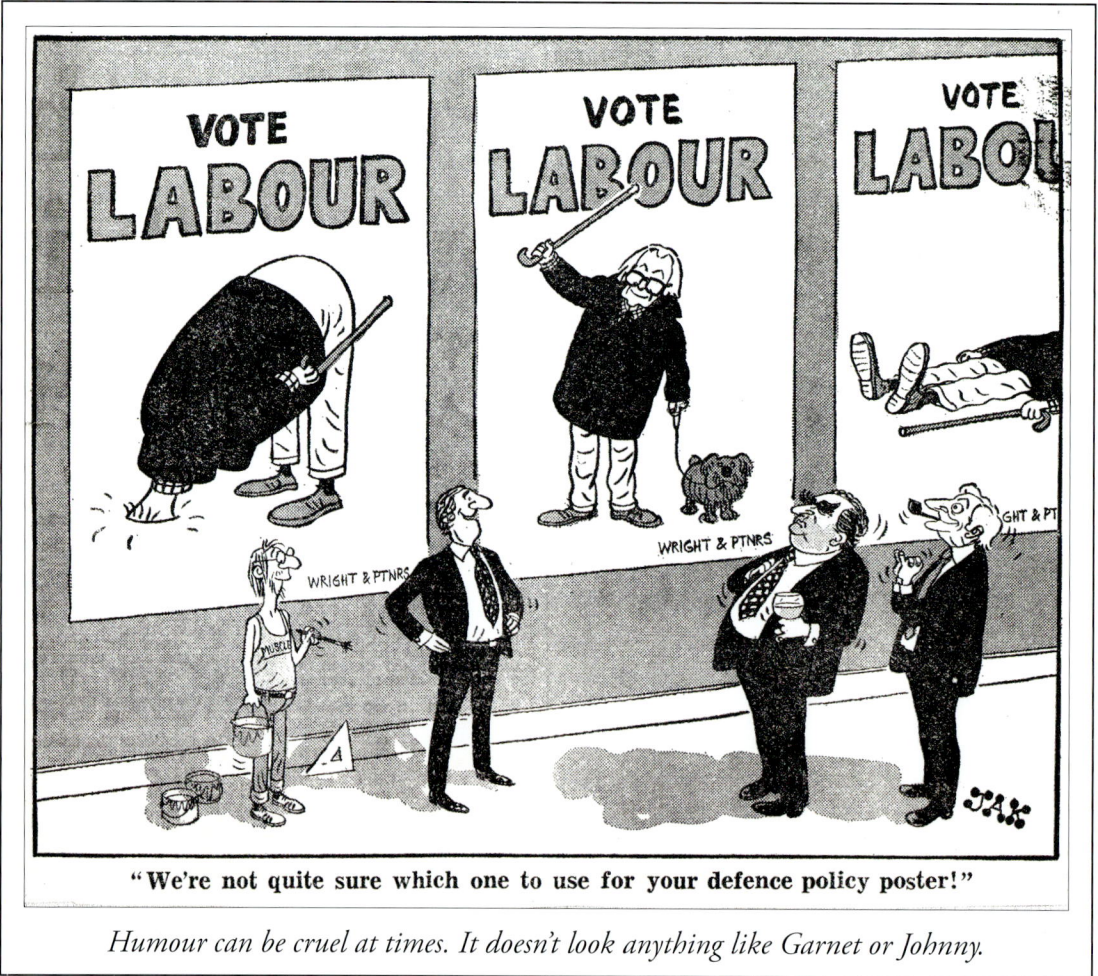

"We're not quite sure which one to use for your defence policy poster!"

Humour can be cruel at times. It doesn't look anything like Garnet or Johnny.

Germ warfare and the 'miracle'.

With Australia's 'Coalman' Morrison, defying the polls and pundits with a victory in our 2019 election, a win that he described as a miracle, it reminded me of a product I helped launch while at Wright & Partners in London way back when.

The product, Wipex†, was described as being a miracle as it wiped out all known germs. It had been featured on the BBC *Tomorrow's World* program, which featured products and inventions that could change the way we lived.

My job was to come up with a campaign aimed at the catering industry with all its risks of salmonella and food poisoning.

It also reminds me of a story I heard about the Arab/Israeli 6-day war where more Israelis were reported as dying because, it was said, they came from a cleaner environment and didn't have the anti-bodies to protect them like the Egyptians.

It's probably apocryphal, but maybe Quentin Crisp was right in living in grubby homes and then moving on to new premises whenever the dirt got too bad.

Johnny told me in 2019 that the product failed and left the 'fledgling' agency with its first, biggish bad debt. Not something to be proud of but I still like the ads.

Creatively, I think this is a good example of what Garnet used to call, "Shouty loud typography". It has to be said with a Welsh accent to fully appreciate it.

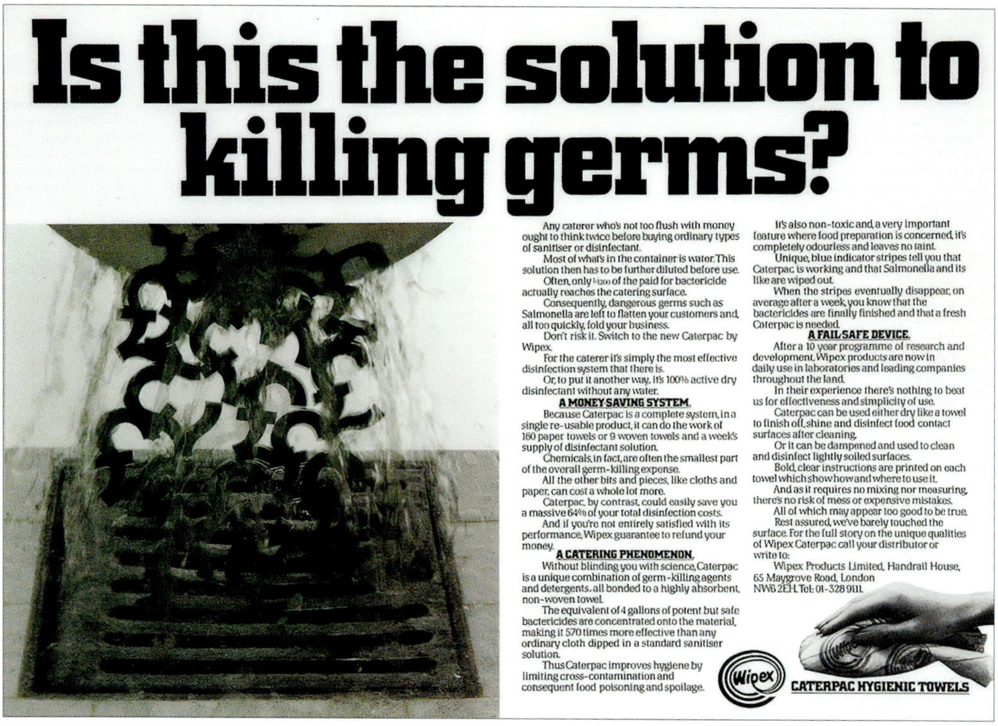

Is this the solution to killing germs?

Any caterer who's not too flush with money ought to think twice before buying ordinary types of sanitiser or disinfectant.

Most of what's in the container is water. This solution then has to be further diluted before use.

Often, only ⅓₀₀ of the paid for bactericide actually reaches the catering surface.

Consequently, dangerous germs such as Salmonella are left to flatten your customers and, all too quickly, fold your business.

Don't risk it. Switch to the new Caterpac by Wipex.

For the caterer it's simply the most effective disinfection system that there is.

Or, to put it another way, it's 100% active dry disinfectant without any water.

A MONEY SAVING SYSTEM.

Because Caterpac is a complete system, in a single re-usable product, it can do the work of 160 paper towels or 9 woven towels and a week's supply of disinfectant solution.

Chemicals, in fact, are often the smallest part of the overall germ-killing expense.

All the other bits and pieces, like cloths and paper, can cost a whole lot more.

Caterpac, by contrast, could easily save you a massive 64% of your total disinfection costs.

And if you're not entirely satisfied with its performance, Wipex guarantee to refund your money.

A CATERING PHENOMENON.

Without blinding you with science, Caterpac is a unique combination of germ-killing agents and detergents, all bonded to a highly absorbent, non-woven towel.

The equivalent of 4 gallons of potent but safe bactericides are concentrated onto the material, making it 570 times more effective than any ordinary cloth dipped in a standard sanitiser solution.

Thus Caterpac improves hygiene by limiting cross-contamination and consequent food poisoning and spoilage.

It's also non-toxic and, a very important feature where food preparation is concerned, it's completely odourless and leaves no taint.

Unique, blue indicator stripes tell you that Caterpac is working and that Salmonella and its like are wiped out.

When the stripes eventually disappear, on average after a week, you know that the bactericides are finally finished and that a fresh Caterpac is needed.

A FAIL-SAFE DEVICE.

After a 10 year programme of research and development, Wipex products are now in daily use in laboratories and leading companies throughout the land.

In their experience there's nothing to beat us for effectiveness and simplicity of use.

Caterpac can be used either dry like a towel to finish off, shine and disinfect food contact surfaces after cleaning.

Or it can be dampened and used to clean and disinfect lightly soiled surfaces.

Bold, clear instructions are printed on each towel which show how and where to use it.

And as it requires no mixing nor measuring, there's no risk of mess or expensive mistakes.

All of which may appear too good to be true. Rest assured, we've barely touched the surface. For the full story on the unique qualities of Wipex Caterpac call your distributor or write to:

Wipex Products Limited, Handrail House, 65 Maygrove Road, London NW6 2EH. Tel: 01-328 9111.

Wipex — CATERPAC HYGIENIC TOWELS

Their arguments really are paper thin.

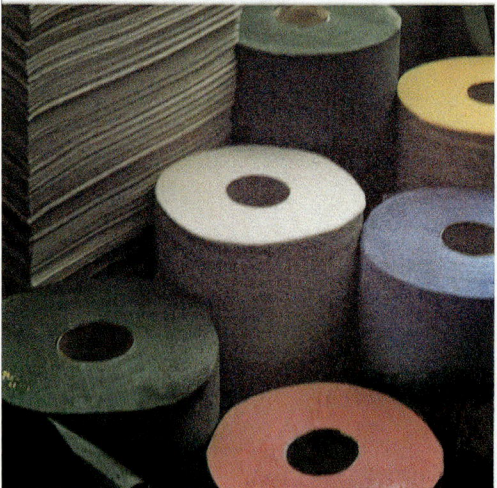

The arguments in favour of paper are that it's a cheap and effective means of drying.

[remaining body text illegible]

Wipex — CATERPAC HYGIENIC TOWELS

Credits: Copywriter, Mike Doyle; Art Director, Garnet Edwards; Photographer, not sure, it was usually Stak.

The client in a war zone.

One truly unusual client was Canada Dry in the Middle East, which was based in Lebanon with Beirut as their headquarters. The whole country was going through a vicious civil war at the time.

Conversations with the client would have to be halted while explosions were happening outside their offices.

We made commercials for them and the one stipulation was that a blonde girl had to appear somewhere in the story.

These were always footage of sports with the drink as a reward.

There was next to no budget but our TV Producer, Terry Fry, always found an affordable way to make the films.

Terry later left the agency as we didn't have enough TV work to keep him busy and he set up his own production company, acting as a consultant to agencies. I can't recall its name only the brand image of a pearl in a case.

Jean genies.

We won the Western Jeans Company† account; a company started by two young guys who had begun with a stall at Kensington Market selling jeans they had designed themselves.

They progressed to owning a chain of shops across the country.

Garnet and I would travel up to their offices in the Midlands on a fairly regular basis to be briefed, and then often go on to Manchester to work on some promotional concepts.

Always short lead times and tight budgets, so we had to work some magic with only print as an option at the time.

We would often squeeze in an evening at Manchester Art College where we would meet up with one of the key lecturers, John Driver.

To the best of my knowledge these are the people he taught there who went on to successful careers in advertising:

Garnet Edwards, Alan Lofthouse, Paul Garrett, Paul Fonteyne, David Christenson, Rick Cook, Alan Midgely, Bill Thompson, Phil Waddicor, Ken Grimshaw, John Donnelly and Bernie Thornton. Any additions to the 'Hall of Fame'?

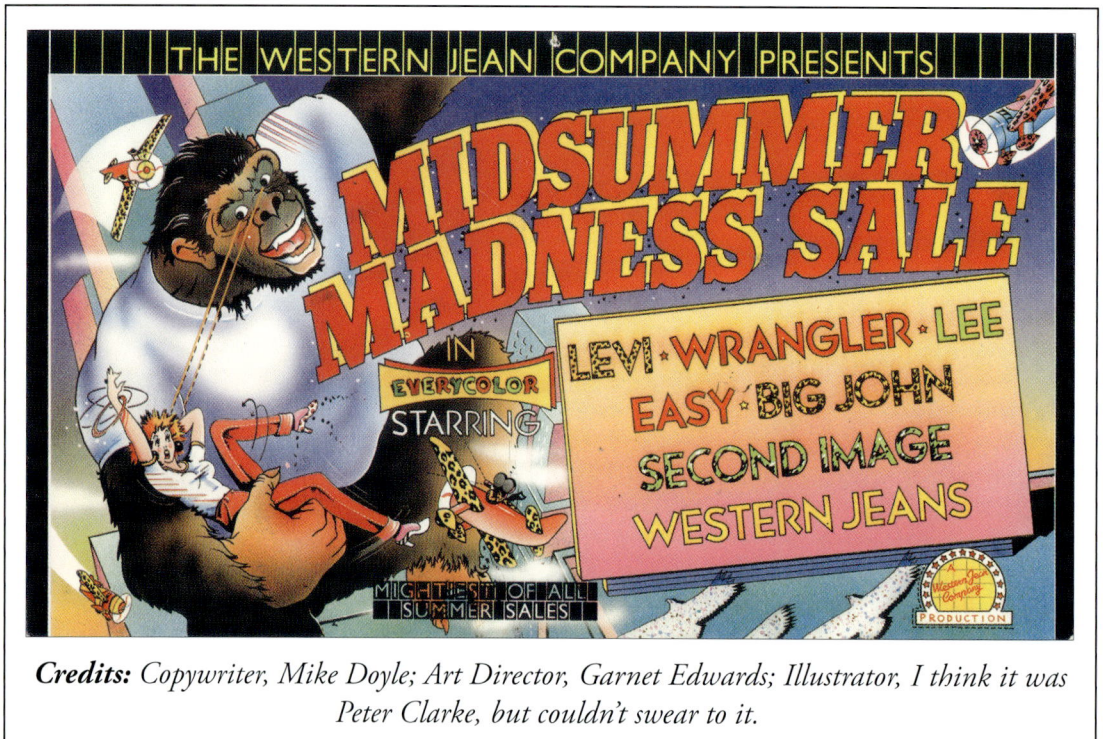

Credits: *Copywriter, Mike Doyle; Art Director, Garnet Edwards; Illustrator, I think it was Peter Clarke, but couldn't swear to it.*

Other W&P stories.

We had a few smaller accounts such as Foster Beard, a Finchley company that acted as a wholesaler for Blanco appliances and Duropal laminates, JetClean who had a steam cleaning franchise, the Alfred Marks employment agencies as well as the double glazing company, Astraseal, for whom we ran a series of small ads.

We also had a kitchen/bathroom retailer in Oxford who, along with Foster Beard, gave me 'mates rates' for renovating my houses in Kentish Town and Shropshire.

Going Japanese.

The Dixons chain of electronic goods stores gave us a brief to rebrand their range of products, some with silly names like Miranda. Given most of the Dixons' products were sourced from Japan and the Far East, it made sense to give it a Japanese name. I hit the dictionary and came up with a selection of names but recommended the name Saisho, which in Japanese meant 'first'. Garnet designed the logo and packaging but we never got to advertise it as a brand in its own right. They ended up changing the name to Matsui many years later and then killed it.

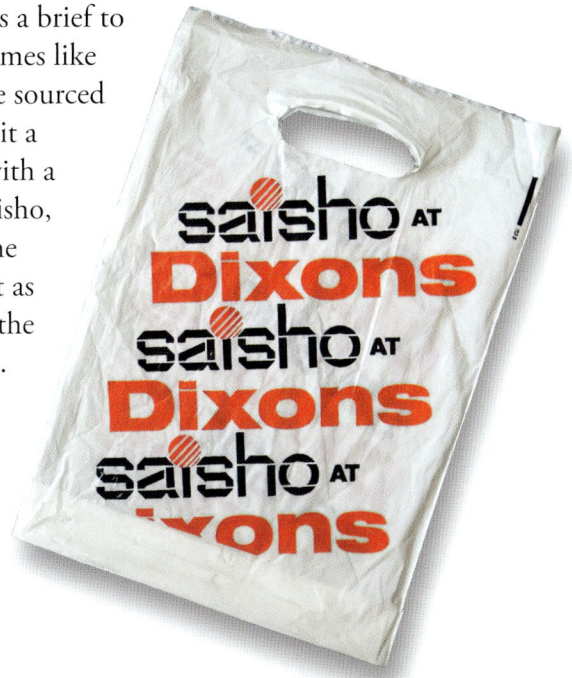

Pitchin' & Bitchin', cont'd.
Irish Distillers.

W&P had just split from Grey Advertising (condemned by its name at the outset, although good work was done) and they had managed to get on the pitch list for Jameson's Whiskey.

I was freelancing at the time and was invited to work with Garnet Edwards (whom I already knew) on the pitch.

The briefing was in Dublin but my train was delayed, so I missed the others and their flight, despite running through Heathrow. A rare sight indeed.

I caught the next flight and they parked me in the theatre with a glass of the falling down water while I watched a video the others had already seen.

Keith Smith and I stayed on in Dublin and did a pub crawl (research) before catching the last flight back. In one pub, a girl I was chatting to sobered me up by telling me that I wasn't Irish (despite both parents being born in the Emerald Isle) as I hadn't been born there.

The agency building was owned by a production company (whose name escapes me) who had offices in the mews at the back.

This proved to be useful. Carpets had been laid on the weekend before the pitch. But on the morning itself they discovered that the new boardroom table wouldn't go up the stairs. The owner's carpenter had to come to our rescue; saw off the leg and then reattach it once it was in the room.

Not the actual table mentioned, but you get the idea.

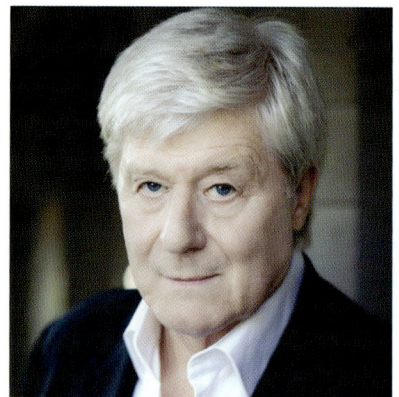

Martin Jarvis.
Photo: recordedbooks.com

For appearances, we asked the media company we had an arrangement with to occupy one room so that the phones would be going. We also had people to walk up and down the stairs.

Our MD, Johnny Wright, was good friends with the actor Martin Jarvis who was starring in the hugely popular TV series, *The Forsyte Saga* resulting in churches having to reschedule their services. Martin kindly came in to see Terry Fry, the agency producer, as if he was in for a casting session. Bless him.

The Irish stayed for hours and consumed a fair amount of their own product, which we provided. As they left they said "it was a great craic, just like being at home".

Foolishly, we thought we were in with a chance but they went with a boring campaign out of Davidson Pearce, showing just a bottle and glass without even a memorable headline. Grey won Blackbush, the other brand, which Paul Martin and Kenny Nicholas, actually did some fine work on.

Napolina.

Still at W&P we pitched for Napolina, an Italian brand of canned food. The memory of the pitch still hurts.

Alan Brady & Marsh seemed to be winning business by adding some 'theatre' to their presentations so we decided to take a leaf out of their book.

We set up the boardroom (the leg was still staying strong and attached) as an Italian restaurant with chianti bottles, check tablecloths (it was the look at the time) and we each had a role to play. I was typecast as the chef I seem to remember.

As soon as the prospective client entered the room it was abundantly clear that we should have done a lot more homework in getting to know this person.

He just froze and clearly couldn't wait to get out.

Luckily, I don't think we had done any creative work for the pitch. And, yes, we didn't get the business.

We were growing. So were seed sales.

As the business grew we had to hire another creative team and we struck it lucky with the copywriter Andrew Smart (living up to his last name, he was a high scorer in MENSA), and his Art Director, Tim Batton, who had great taste even if he did get excited about garden sheds. They also worked on UNICEF, for which I have no examples.

One of the first accounts we put then to work on was Miln Masters, a seed merchant from Norfolk. I show just a few examples of their great work, some of which was accepted for the Communication Arts Awards magazine

Credits: *Copywriter, Andrew Smart; Art Director, Tim Batten; Photographers, sadly unknown*

Pitchin' & Bitchin', cont'd.

A Prime time.

I can't remember who we pitched against for Prime Computer but we won and Andrew and Tim did a great job. As did Richard Williams†, whose company created a wonderful animated commercial about the ascent of Man. Sadly, again, I have no copy of the film.

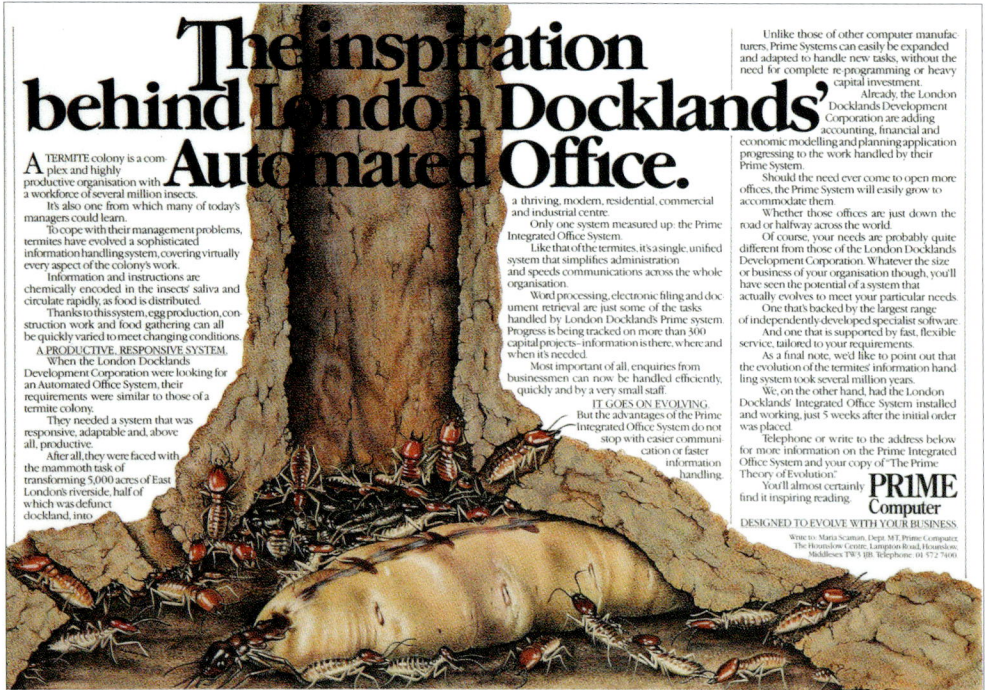

Credits for all Prime ads: Copywriter, Andrew Smart; Art Director, Tim Batton; Illustrators, sadly unknown. The campaign did win a Clio Award. In 1998 Prime sadly closed for business

Westward Ho!

Before the agency merged with Ayer Barker and I disappeared to new horizons, we had presented to Taunton Cider, who gave us a project.

Basically it was to rebrand Pomagne, a sparking alcoholic pear drink or cider. To Garnet's credit he came up with the name, Diamond White Cider and it was then handed to another agency becoming the UK's best-selling cider at one time.

By a strange twist of fate, I would be working on a competing brand later in Oz.

My days in East Anglia and a fine beer.

While at Wright & Partners, in the 1980s, we won the East Anglian Brewer, Tolly-Cobbold.

This entailed many day trips to the brewery where we were forced to sample the product, all in the name of research of course. This resulted in the *Four Suffolk Originals.*, which ran as posters on the London Underground at stations close to their pubs, some around Baker Street.

We spent a week making a commercial for them, directed by Johnny Thornton[†].

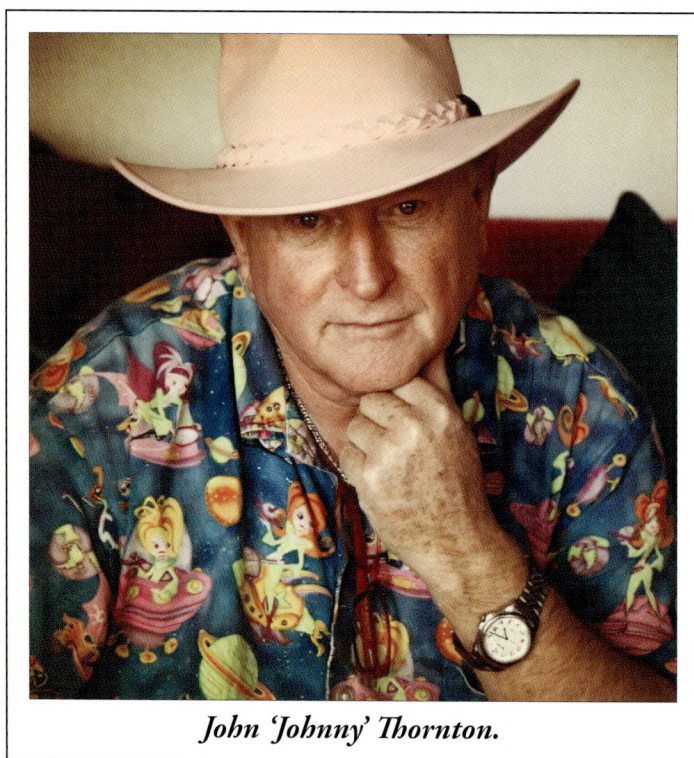

John 'Johnny' Thornton.

It featured locations painted by Constable, Suffolk Punch horses ploughing fields and Thames Barges with their distinctive red sails. We also found a local folk group that played music specific to the area. Then, to top that, we had the wonderful East Anglian, Johnny Morris, to record the voiceover.

To the best of my knowledge, it never ran. We had to shut up shop.

Note: It always tickled me that our 'house wine' at W&P was a brand called *Machiavelli*.

FOUR SUFFOLK ORIGINALS.
Thomas Gainsborough
John Constable
Benjamin Britten
TOLLY'S ORIGINAL BITTER
TOLLY·COBBOLD Brewers of fine Suffolk ales since 1723.

IT PACKS A LOVELY PUNCH.
TOLLY'S
WINTER ALE
WINTER ALE
OLD STRONG
TOLLY·COBBOLD
Brewers of fine Suffolk ales since 1723.

We also had the perennial challenge of communicating the fact that one of their beers had a stronger alcohol content, hence 'Oomph' was a solution.

Credits for all posters: *Copywriter, Mike Doyle; Art Director, Garnet Edwards; Illustrator/Photographer, sadly unknown*

YOU'RE INVITED TO

THE ANNUAL ST. PATRICK'S NIGHT HOOLEY

AT WRIGHT & PARTNERS, 62 BERNERS STREET, W1. TEL: 01-631 4602
MARCH 17, STARTING 6.30pm. ENTRANCE BY INVITATION ONLY. (TO BE SURE, TO BE SURE)
R.S.V.P. MIKE DOYLE.

Having a huge cellar in the agency with a bar serving beer from our client Tolly-Cobbold and cider from our cider client, Taunton meant we could celebrate each year (and each St. Patrick's night) with folk from the business, having a great night out.
The illustrator may have been Jack Reeser

Pitchin' & Bitchin', cont'd.

Lonsdale cars.

Again at W&P we pitched for an Australian arm of Mitsubishi. The factory, if I remember correctly, was in South Australia in a suburb called Lonsdale, hence the name. As it happened, Garnet Edwards was on holiday in Queensland and dug out some information to help. I did some research into Australian road conditions and the car's technology designed to cope with harsh environments. We pitched, but the account went to Yellowhammer who came up with posters showing the car upside down. Perleeeese!!!????

R.I.P. W&P.

Another agency, Ayer Barker, approached the agency with a takeover proposal, which the other partners agreed to.

There was no role for me and the agency was not my cup of tea, creatively, so I left. But W&P were a great bunch of people to work with and we had some excellent clients and produced work I was proud of.

My W&P generation.

Johnny Wright, Keith Smith, Terry Fry†, Rob Britton†, Garnet Edwards, Andrew Smart, Tim Batten, Jim Hubbard, Tim *Boomer* Baynes, Andy Palmer, Sid Tomkins, Roz Bicen, Anne-Marie Carlyle and Mark Wood†.
Apologies to anyone I have left out.

The diaspora: After Ayer Barker, Johnny went on to run Lintas and then his own consultancy, advising the likes of Bartle, Bogle, Hegarty. Keith went on to be Founder and International President for the non-American world of TBWA, setting up the Asia/Pacific office, based in Hong King and now Zurich. While Garnet became Creative Director of Cogent Elliott, the industrial accounts agency based in Slough. He is now back in his beloved homeland of Wales.

The Wright & Partners table at the D&AD Awards Night Dinner at the Royal Albert Hall.

The other side of the political and economic coin.

While Brezhnev was still in power, Mrs Doyle Mk #1 and I went for a holiday tour including Moscow and Leningrad.

Talk about another world. No ads other than political posters. No shops, as we would recognise them. The Gum department store in Red Square was unbelievably depressing but it was a remarkable experience.

Every morning as we left the hotel overlooking Red Square, a swarm of Russian kids would pounce on us trying to trade Russian badges for chewing gum or anything else we were willing to trade.

It was the middle of winter but building work was still going on amidst clouds of steam; presumably providing heat for the building materials and workers.

Everywhere you could see small stalls selling vodka.

A visiting group of American women, wives of husbands working at the Vauxhall car factory in England, were closely watched by 'advisors', no doubt KGB officers.

The train journey to Leningrad was very romantic; it brought back memories of *Doctor Zhivago.*

Fellow passengers sent us carafes of wine as a welcome.

A short stay, but it did help us appreciate what we had in the West.

Leonid Brezhnev.
Former General Secretary of the Central Committee of the Communist Party of the Soviet Union

Leonid Ilyich Brezhnev was a Soviet politician. The fifth leader of the Soviet Union, he served as General Secretary of the Central Committee of the governing Communist Party of the Soviet Union from 1964 until his death in 1982. His 18-year term as general secretary was second only to Joseph Stalin's in duration. **Wikipedia**

The Kremlin walls behind me, standing in Red Square and very grateful for my Swedish Army coat.

Lenin leaving the Gum department store with not a shopping bag in sight.

Chapter
Thirteen
Lucky for me.

1984 to 1986.

Colman RSCG

✝

Friend/Boss/Lodger/Best Man.

(Note: We are <u>not</u> holding hands.)

Richard Kelley had been a friend ever since I worked at PKL where he used to drop in to see his brother John. Richard had been lured by Colman RSCG from living in Los Angeles to be the agency's new Creative Director. He needed somewhere to stay so he rented a room from me in my new home in Torriano Cottages, Kentish Town.

He regularly had to fly back to his family in Los Angeles. He asked me to freelance for the agency while he was away. When he returned, he asked me how it went, and I told him. I loved it.

He offered me a job but it was a challenge as, he was a good friend, I was his landlord, and he was my boss. What would happen if it all went pear shaped? I told him I would rather walk than endanger the friendship.

So, I was hired. I met the love of my life, Cherry, and Richard was my Best Man at our wedding. It couldn't be any other way. Graeme Robertson was my Second Best-Man though. He had been my Best Man at my first marriage.

My first dip into the Medicine Chest.

I had my first taste of pharmaceutical advertising (which later was to become a major part of my career in Australia) at Colman RSCG when I was assigned to Ciba-Geigy (Now Novartis). The two products I was given were *Proflex* for back pain and the cutely named *Do-Do,* a cough medicine.

With Proflex I discovered the client had a huge number of brochures about how to manage back pain, so included in the ads was an invitation to apply for a free brochure. I was told that the ads cleared the stock from the warehouse. Whether they reprinted them is something I don't know.

The creation of the Dodo campaign coincided with the birth of my daughter Zoë, and the illustrations still delight to this day.

Credits: *(Proflex), Copywriter, Mike Doyle; Art Director, Ed Church, Illustrator, Unknown. (Dodo), Copywriter, Mike Doyle; Art Director, Ed Church; Illustrator, Peter Brookes.*

COLMAN RSCG & PARTNERS

HOUSENOTE

To: Mike Doyle
        Ed Church

From: Simon Billington

cc: Val Hodgart
        Alan Swindells
        Sholto Douglas-Home

11th July, 1985

Do-Do Alive & Kicking

During a recent Ciba visit to Boots H/O is was noted that April medicine deliveries into retail stores were down 70% on same month year ago. Trading conditions have been difficult. More recent information is not yet available.

Boots also indicated that May/June deliveries of Do-Do into retail stores are up 15% versus year ago. Both Ciba and Boots agree that this increase is solely attributable to the current Do-Do bird advertising campaign. Naturally both parties are very pleased with this success.

    Well done!

    Regards

    Simon

    Simon

So rewarding when you know the ads have worked.

249

"Secret Women's Business."

Women of Australia's First Nation's people have this saying for their customs that are not for our prying eyes.

All I knew about 'periods' was gleaned from a stretch of time at school in art, English or history lessons, leaving me a tad short on detail.

While at Colman RSCG in London I was assigned to the Tampax account for Ireland. Is it my name or heritage?

Anyway, it seems the nuns across the water were telling their girls not to use tampons as they could lose their virginity.

How any of us are still even admitting to be Catholic beats me but I will, for my sins, die as an RC.

We were away up in Shropshire for a long weekend at our holiday cottage in Bishops Castle (1.5 rooms up and 1.5 rooms down, hardly a palace) when I came up with a solution.

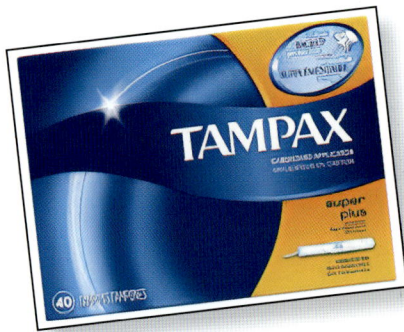

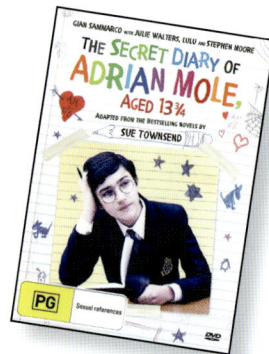

Adrian Mole and his diary about a 13+-year old boy was a best seller at the time and I had the idea of writing the radio campaign from the point of view of his girlfriend.

Luckily the town's second-hand bookshop had a copy, so I set to work.

The client, who was a nurse, approved the idea and scripts.

I had already written to the author, Sue Townsend, who gave her approval for the campaign but Tampax wouldn't pay her a fee.

So, I had to adapt the script, dropping the name of Mole's girlfriend. I can't remember for sure, but it was either Sheila Hancock or Miriam Margolyes who read and recorded the scripts, which went to air. Sadly, I have no copies.

I don't know how effective they were, but Ireland certainly has advanced by leaps and bounds, passing things like same sex marriage.

Man or woman power?

While at Colman RSCG in London I worked on the Manpower recruitment account.

The posters, with shorthand as part of the creative, were designed for cross-tracks on the London Underground, while the press ads went into business magazines.

We did make one commercial with the title of *The Perils of Pauline* highlighting the superior service offered to temps. Funnily enough, the producer on the job was the wonderful, and appropriately named, Pauline Rose (Crane at the time). Sadly, I don't have a copy of it to show.

WORD PROCESSOR OPERATORS

VDU

VDU WORK

Temporary office jobs where you can make your mark.

Credits: Copywriter, Mike Doyle; Art Director, Ed Church; Illustrator/ Photographer, Unknown.

HOLIDAY PLANNER

CHERRY
JOYCE
DAVID
DEBBIE
BEVERLEY
JOHN
PAULINE
BARBIE
SALLY

Now is the season of temporary discontent.

An IT fruit salad?

Apples, Apricots; was there ever a Banana Computer?

At the time, Apricot Computers had Collett, Dickenson, Pearce as their agency and were seriously unhappy.

They had started off dealing with senior members of staff and then felt neglected, as every time they dealt with the agency it was with someone of lesser rank. Call it the 'slippery pole syndrome'.

Richard Kelley, assigned me to the Apricot account and my first task was to visit our head office in Paris where the Apricot clients were already having discussions.

A very pleasant day was spent learning about the client and admiring RSCG's magnificent offices. They were housed in a warehouse designed by Eiffel (yes, he of Tower fame) with cast iron girders and pillars with his name cast in them all over the place.

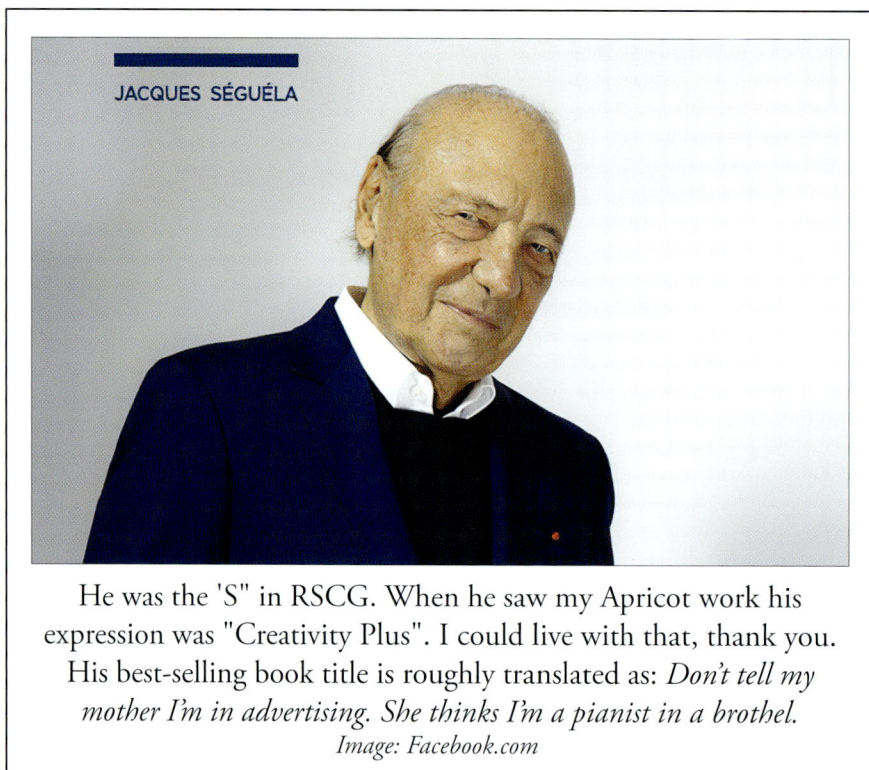

JACQUES SÉGUÉLA

He was the 'S" in RSCG. When he saw my Apricot work his expression was "Creativity Plus". I could live with that, thank you. His best-selling book title is roughly translated as: *Don't tell my mother I'm in advertising. She thinks I'm a pianist in a brothel.*
Image: Facebook.com

Returning to London, we were given the task of redesigning the Apricot logo. It was not a pitch in the traditional sense, they just needed reassurance that they would always be dealing with the same people.

My Art Director, Ed Church, as always, did a magnificent job. And I was sent off to the Birmingham International Exhibition Centre with the designs to present, where they had a stand at an IT exhibition.

Unfortunately, the rocking of the train sent me to sleep and I awoke with a start at the station leaving the portfolio on the train.

I only realised this as the train chuffed off on its way to Wales. It was never handed in as lost property. The client must have felt for me and my distress, and never made me suffer by reminding me of my gaffe.

Later, when I did present the designs, they loved them and we were appointed as their agency.

Taking a leaf out of David Abbott's book for his Sainsbury's campaign where the client's name was always in the headline, I chose to include an apricot in every visual to help in recall.

This proved not as easy as it sounds. We discovered that the fruit was not in season. So, the agency Art Buyer, Cherry (soon to be Mrs Doyle Mk 2) had a realistic model made that appeared in every ad from then on. The Suit was the lovely Brendan Payne[†], but I often had to fill that role as well in visits to the client's HQ in Birmingham.

Many years later, while at another agency, I watched a BBC series on companies in trouble that needed help, like Morgan cars and, yes, Apricot. The presenter had been head of ICI and advised Apricot to get out of hardware and return to where they had started in accounting software. They took his advice and, to the best of my knowledge, ceased to be an advertised brand.

Credits: *Copywriter, Mike Doyle; Art Director, Edward Church; Photographer, Unknown; Model Maker, also, sadly unknown and Cherry can't remember either.*

Here comes the Sun.

Working with Ed Church was great. However, it pleased my infantile mind by answering his phone, if he was out of our office, by saying, "Church of England's Answering Service, how can I help you?".

Our brief for the Piz Buin advertising was that we had to use the same image they reproduced world-wide, their *'Perfect for longer exposure'* copy, and we had a double-page spread to fill.

We gave the left-hand page as a brief to the brilliant illustrator, John Graham, and in my opinion, he did us proud. The poor (maybe not) photographer was unknown to us.

PERFECT DAY.

PERFECT EXPOSURE.

LONGEST DAY.

LONGER EXPOSURE.

Facebook comments on the Piz Buin ads:

Alan Orpin Class, dear boy. Pure class. Haven't seen this before. Very lovely.

Jonathan Yardley super.

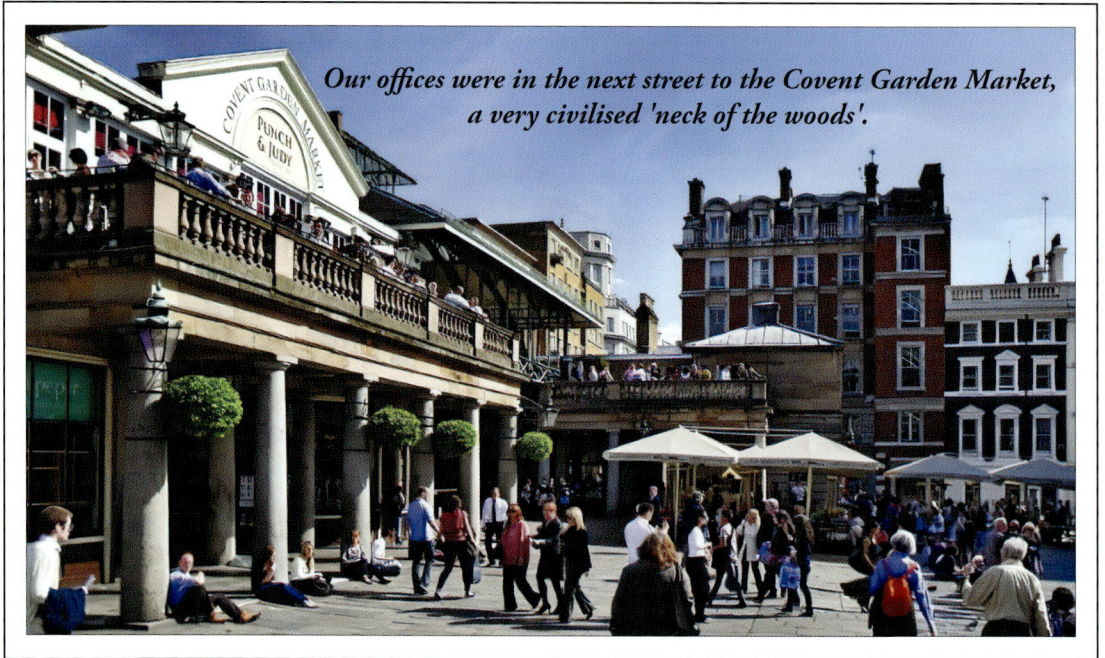

*Our offices were in the next street to the Covent Garden Market,
a very civilised 'neck of the woods'.*

"Ma Cherie amore."

The dark side of the agency moon?

The failure of the Indian rocket to land on the dark side of the moon in 2019 reminded me that there is often an account (or two) at an agency that creatives try to steer clear of.

Lurking in the shadows of Colman RSCG was the Credit Plan account, which I worked on with Ed Church. I vividly remember one Art Director at the agency sneering that he wouldn't work on the account, and he was a director at the agency. Furthermore, the account was a constant source of income from which we all benefitted. Another account some 'creatives' were 'sniffy' about was the British Telecom Linkline account, which was business to business.

Note: The torn page above for Linkline is my homage to the El Ad created by DDB New York

257

Ed Church.
Looking philosophical, or for inspiration, at our wedding reception.

My Colman RSCG generation.

Richard Kelley (Creative Director), Tony Riggs, Steve Hooper, Dennis Lewis (the 'Handyman?'), Scott Waterhouse, Danny Higgins, Roger Holdsworth 'The Vicar" and, of course, Cherry Drumm (Doyle), Debbie Williams, Pauline Crane (Rose) and Joyce Rennie.
Apologies to anyone I have left out.

The Colman's Creative Department.

California dreaming.

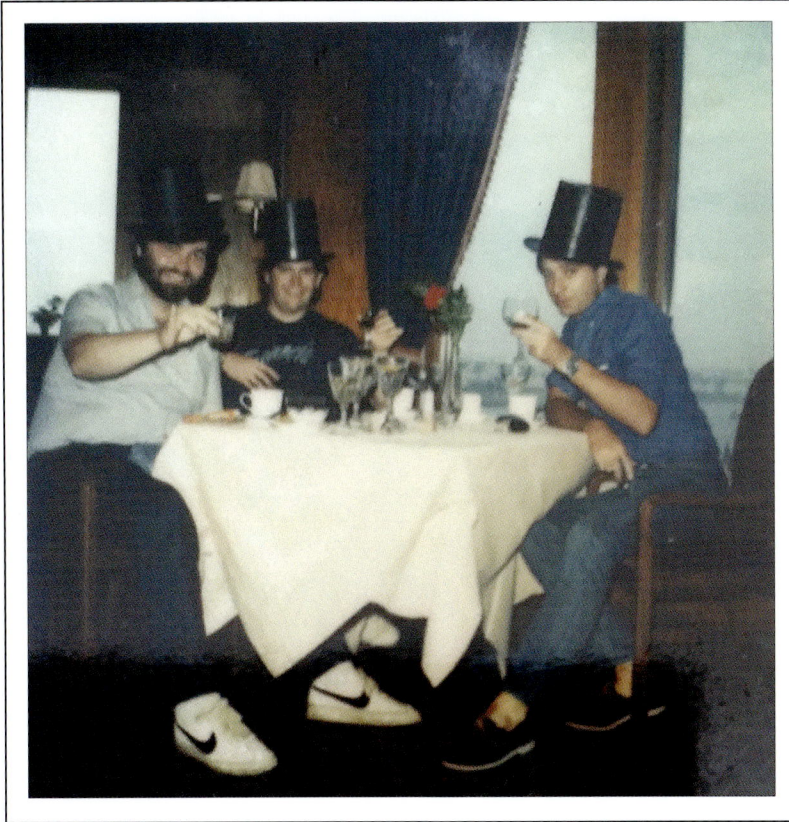

Post Colmans, with Richard back in the U.S. and us playing silly buggers in the 80s on the Queen Mary in Los Angeles Harbour with Richard Kelley and, far right, Pete Andress, Richard's Art Director for many years in the UK and the US.
We had bought the ice buckets off the restaurant to wear as top hats. Well we thought it funny at the time, champagne and wine probably helped.

Facebook comment:

Richard Kelley What a night that was, Mike. Pete Andress was there too. The meal was after a day out to see the Howard Hughes Spruce Goose plane and a lunch on the Queen Mary that ended with us bribing the waiter so we could take home the plastic ice bucket in the shape of a top hat. Such fun.

At the wedding reception in Elena's Room at L'Escargot restaurant.
Cherry is giving me one of those looks she's given me often in our many years of being married. I haven't the foggiest what I said on the day, sad to say

Note: Cherry's Dad, Val Drumm (and not in the picture), had taught photography first at the Regent Street Polytechnic, followed by the London College of Printing, (after I had left), and ending his career at the Royal College of Art.

For several years he had also been a photographer at *Country Life* magazine, visiting and recording historic buildings and country houses.

Chapter
Fourteen

1986 to 1988.

Garrett, Doyle, Fugler (GDF)

†

Happy days.

Paul Garrett already had a creative consultancy with Tim Braybrooks who decided he didn't want to build an agency. Tim was going to pull up stumps and head off to the US with his impressive guitar collection.

Tim suggested me as a substitute and Paul agreed. He had also talked with a Suit, Jeff Fugler, who'd been at CDP and French Gold Abbott and who was keen to join. That's how Garrett, Doyle, Fugler came to be born.

I reunited with Paul for a second time in the UK in 2016.

Note: We quickly realised that we needed someone to answer the phones and run the office. Caroline Ryan, a beautiful Irish girl (pictured below, well I admit I am biased) came in as a temp. Her first task was to source some office materials and somehow or other she found a cost-saving solution. We made her a permanent part of the 'family' and she was a joy to have around in those 'interesting' years.

Caroline.

Postscript from Caroline.

"I am very touched that you would think of mentioning me. It was a really special time for me, pivotal in sending me down the path I've travelled! I desperately wanted GDF to work; it is both rare and fabulous to find yourself completely driven and carried along on a wave of enthusiasm and passion. That role was so multi-faceted.

I was reminiscing recently with Anne (do you remember Belfast Anne who joined us for a summer as an intern during her last year in uni?). You three took us on our very first trip to The Ivy for lunch. We weren't much impressed with the darkness but bowled over by strawberries with black pepper and Armagnac on the rocks!

Anne has risen to great heights, became a very talented planner and now heads her own global innovations company, BIG Innovations.

You might remember that I went with Jeff to DDB as New Business Assistant and fought to get myself taken seriously! It worked but I soon realised that it was so not me! I think it was a presentation on Fish and Tetrapak that nailed it for me. I couldn't quite believe the amount of sycophancy involved. I spent a lot of time in the creative department and realised I could probably combine my interests and left to become a photographic agent. Best move! I represented Seamus for a number of years. I'm now heading up Republic Of Photography (ROP) with Seamus (he is very much a portrait photographer but lends his creative direction to the ROP).

It is funny when you stop to reflect. It seems like only yesterday and crazy that 30 years has passed."

Images: Caroline O'Byrne.

A toilet stop.

One client GDF inherited from Braybrooks Garrett was the magnificently named Thrislington Cubicles. (Tim had already written the headline; my job was to write the text.)

Thrislington were very design conscious and marketed themselves to similarly-minded architects. They had even won awards for their calendars.

Credits: Copywriters, Tim Braybrooks, Mike Doyle; Art Director, Paul Garrett; Photographer, Tim Brown.

The coupon and applause (cont'd).

Before online advertising, we relied on having a sufficiently compelling argument in favour of the product for someone to fill in and post the coupon.

ABBEY LIFE LIVING ASSURANCE.

BMP had the Abbey account for months with no success, so the client responded to a mailing from us, giving us a fortnight to develop a campaign to launch the product. We had as a freelance planning consultant Prosper Riley-Smith. I loved his first name as it lent a certain edge to our business.

Given the delicacy of writing about death and disease, I created a number of concept statements to gauge people's reactions to various messages.

The ads ran on schedule and did remarkably well, to the point where we were mentioned at the launch for doing such a remarkable job.

Credits: *Copywriter, Mike Doyle; Art Director, Paul Garrett; Photographer, Tim Brown.*

The story was so good we even ran an ad for ourselves in *Campaign* magazine.

One instance where selling really was a matter of life and death.

We can help you be less of a burden on your family.

Many people contract cancer and live.

You're probably insured for when you die. What happens if you live?

Is there life before death?

"If I must die please let it be slow."

When Abbey Life appointed us this summer to launch their new life policy we took a deep breath.

We needed to. Abbey briefed us on May 21st and wanted the campaign to run in June and July.

Despite the tight time constraints we felt it necessary to do some research.

The tone of the advertising had to be exactly right given that the policy, Living Assurance, dealt with rather delicate and taboo subjects.

Like ordinary life insurance, it pays out if you die. Where it differs is in also paying out if you contract one of the dreaded major diseases such as cancer, or if you suffer an accident and severe disablement.

With the research in mind we created these five ads which were up and running sixteen days after being briefed.

The resulting sales were 75% above the target Abbey had set, making the launch their most successful ever.

If selling your product is a matter of life and death to your business shouldn't you be talking to us? GARRETT DOYLE FUGLER

Telephone: 01-379 7049. (Ask for Jeff Fugler.) 40 Drury Lane, London WC2B 5RR.

Credits: *As previous page.*

True to the fickleness of advertising, the client's Marketing Director left, and they appointed a new one. He hired the recently opened Australian agency MOJO who, true to form in Oz, gave him a jingle and the product swiftly disappeared.

As did we sadly, shortly after, owing to an unfortunate series of events. Ho, and a huge hum. However, if that hadn't happened, I might never have come to live and work in Australia. Life does have its rewards, despite our Australian Government.

Who was Roy Scot?

One day at GDF my partner, Geoff Fugler, said a Roy Scot was coming in to talk us about advertising.

What he didn't say was that this was a branch of the Royal Bank of Scotland.

I can't remember how they came to visit us or whether we had to pitch, but we must have done something right as they appointed us as their agency.

Oh, and there was no Roy by the way as I quickly discovered. Always quick off the mark this one.

It was another account that I was sad to say goodbye to when we were forced to shut our doors.

Geoff had a lovely story of when he was an Account Executive at Lowe Howard-Spink when they pitched for Toys R Us. The creative work was presented, and the client then commented, " It's all very nice but where's Geoffrey?"

Everyone looked to Geoff and said, "He's here."

They meant their brand character "Geoffrey, the Giraffe".

The account went elsewhere. I don't know whether the Giraffe is still with them.

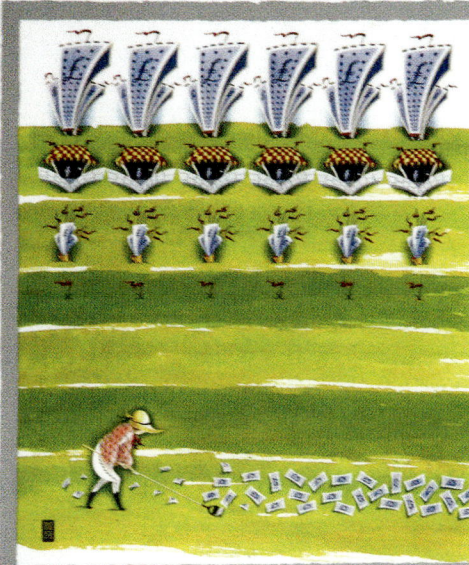

Credits: *Copywriter: Mike Doyle; Art Director: Paul Garrett; Illustrators: Sadly unknown, however I do remember they were a husband and wife team.*

The second squeeze of the grape.

I had a contact with a wine client from a former agency (Dorland) who was impressed enough with our French Wine work to appoint us for the launch of Baden Wines into the UK.

Most Brits were raised on German Riesling, and a sweet version at that. So, we had to explain the difference. Paul went off to Bavaria with a fantastic photographer Nadav Kander.

The client in Germany found the photographer's ancestral home, which as Jews, the family had to escape from and go to South Africa. The occupiers of the property were a tad nervous as you can expect, but all passed off pleasantly.

As with the French Wine campaign, I had written the copy for the pitch so the client wouldn't pay for me to tour the wine regions. And, further proof of my stupidity (if needed), I wrote the copy before photography and was left holding the fort of our fledgling agency.

Paul designed the labels and I wrote the copy for the descriptive back labels.

Initially, we had white, elegant designs but checking on retail outlets, others had thought likewise. I think he came up with a very stylish solution.

Proof of the campaign's success can be seen in the distributor list at the foot of the page, which got steadily longer. It didn't hurt that it was a very tasty drop.

Not everything that comes from the Black Forest is sweet.

Visitors to our region come to drink in the sights, the waters at spas like Baden Baden and the clean air, which many say is as sweet as our gateaux.

What often comes as a pleasant surprise is both our fine cuisine and the complementary dryness of Baden wines.

This characteristic, unusual in a German wine, is caused by both our climate and location. Baden's vineyards are the southernmost in Germany in what is known as the 'Sunshine State'.

The EEC classify us as being in the warmth of winegrowing Zone B together with the vineyards of the Loire, Alsace and Champagne. All the other German wines come from the cooler Zone A, where sugar is often added to compensate for their grapes' lack of sun. Our grapes ripen with their own natural sugars to make a drier, slightly stronger wine.

If you're wondering why you've never heard of us before, the explanation is simple.

Until recently, almost our entire production was consumed by appreciative customers in Germany. (In Baden we drink twice as much as the rest of Germany who, in turn, drink twice as much as the British.)

Regrettably, for our German customers, word has spread on the grapevine with requests to export a selection of our wines to you.

Baden Dry is but one example. This refreshing wine is ideal with a meal or as an aperitif.

Whilst you may have to pay a few pence more, the only sweet thing will be the joy of discovery.

WE REGRET TO SAY THE PLEASURE CAN NOW BE YOURS.

What we hope to do to your view of German wine.

Your perspective of German wine will alter by 180 degrees after just one glass of Baden wine.

The reason being, it offers you a deliciously dry alternative to the sweeter wines you may be used to.

Relatively unknown over here (up until now), Baden wines have enjoyed enormous success in our home market.

We now produce about 15 per cent of all German wines.

Part of the reason for our success has to be our long tradition of creating "Trocken" or "Totally Dry" wine.

Our southern location certainly helps. (We are in the same sunbelt as the Loire, Alsace, Burgundy and Champagne regions.)

Our dryness also stems from the fact that we pick our grapes early for that certain edge that makes our wine make a meal.

Oz Clarke, the noted wine writer and critic, was impressed enough to write, "The Baden whites can easily achieve the flavour of ripe fruit and the relatively low acidity necessary to make good dry wine. No other German wine area does it so well."

An excellent example of our skill being Baden Dry.

Served chilled, with a meal or as an aperitif, it has much of the elegance of our local spa, Baden-Baden.

It certainly gives the notion of "taking the waters" a new dimension.

BADEN

WE REGRET TO SAY THE PLEASURE CAN NOW BE YOURS.

BADEN WINES ARE AVAILABLE FROM: ASDA, E. H. BOOTH, HOUSE OF FRASER, ARMY & NAVY, DINGLE'S OF BRISTOL, HOWELL'S OF CARDIFF, RACKHAMS OF BIRMINGHAM, GODDINS, PETER DOMINIC, BOTTOMS UP, ROBERTS & COOPER, SAINSBURY'S, THRESHER'S, VICTORIA WINE, WAITROSE.

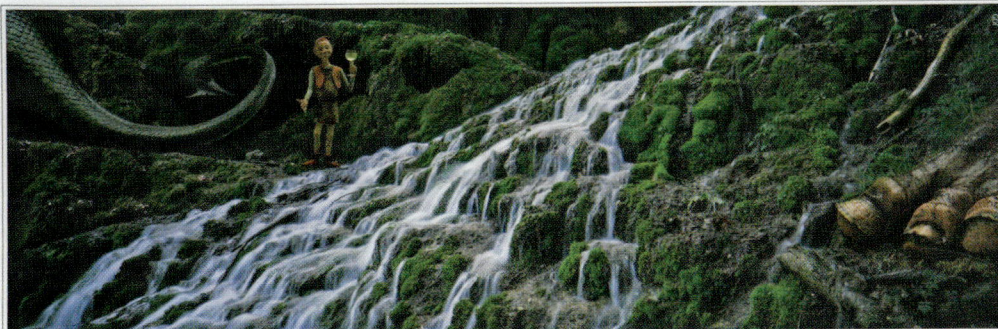

Fire-breathing dragons, giants and pixies. What were they drinking in the Black Forest?

The region that created Grimm's extraordinary tales also produces an extraordinary range of wines.

Extraordinary in that Baden wines are slightly stronger, drier and better in quality than Germany's other offerings.

These qualities have created an enormous demand at home.

On the subject of size, the cafes in Baden serve wine in some of the biggest wine glasses to be found in Germany.

Couple that with the fact that we drink twice as much wine as the rest of Germany who, in turn, drink twice as much as the British and it may go some way towards explaining our unfamiliarity on these shores.

(It certainly helps to explain some of those fairy tales.)

A situation which is now changing thanks to our increase in exports to you.

The welcome dryness of our wines is caused by a happy accident of geography.

Baden's vineyards are the southernmost in Germany, sharing the same sunshine as the Alsace, Loire, Burgundy and Champagne regions.

Baden grapes reach their own natural ripeness in the southern sun to make a drier, slightly stronger, better quality wine.

Just one example being Baden Qualitatswein.

As befits a region famous as Germany's Gourmet Corner, this wine complements a meal perfectly as well as being a crisp, refreshing aperitif.

Beware of over-indulging, however, as the resulting tales may seem rather far-fetched.

BADEN

WE REGRET TO SAY THE PLEASURE CAN NOW BE YOURS.

BADEN WINES ARE AVAILABLE FROM: ASDA, E. H. BOOTH, HOUSE OF FRASER, ARMY & NAVY, DINGLE'S OF BRISTOL, HOWELL'S OF CARDIFF, RACKHAMS OF BIRMINGHAM, GODDINS, PETER DOMINIC, BOTTOMS UP, ROBERTS & COOPER, SAINSBURY'S, THRESHER'S, VICTORIA WINE, WAITROSE.

Credits: *Copywriter, Mike Doyle; Art Director, Paul Garrett; Photographer, Nadav Kander.*

Do you remember Filofax?

While at GDF I had been invited to be a tutor for the student training scheme run by the British Design and Art Direction Association (D&AD).

While at lunch with my two partners, I talked about how the brief I had written for the students to create an ad campaign for Filofax was actually an opportunity for us to approach them to handle their business.

At the time, it seemed everybody was carrying one (well, OK, certainly ad and media folk).

Retail chain stores like W.H. Smith and Boots were selling rip-offs and there was a danger for the brand to disappear into obscurity when it ceased to be 'trendy'.

Army officers and police had a special pocket in which to carry them. Directors like Woody Allen created one for every movie that he made. But there was an opportunity to throw the net wider.

So, I approached them, and, by coincidence, they had already talked with the agency run by Tim Delaney, Leagas Delaney.

To cut to the chase, they awarded us the business. It wasn't big bucks but had potential. And we were all 'card-carrying members' already. Indeed, I still use the travel version when returning to the UK.

While I was a junior copywriter at Doyle Dane Bernbach in London, we used to get a staff magazine out of the head office in New York. One issue's cover image has stayed with me throughout my professional life. It was of two women staff members, standing in a corridor, carrying examples of two outstanding campaigns created by the agency, and in particular by the Art Director, Helmut Krone. One was of VW and another was of Avis.

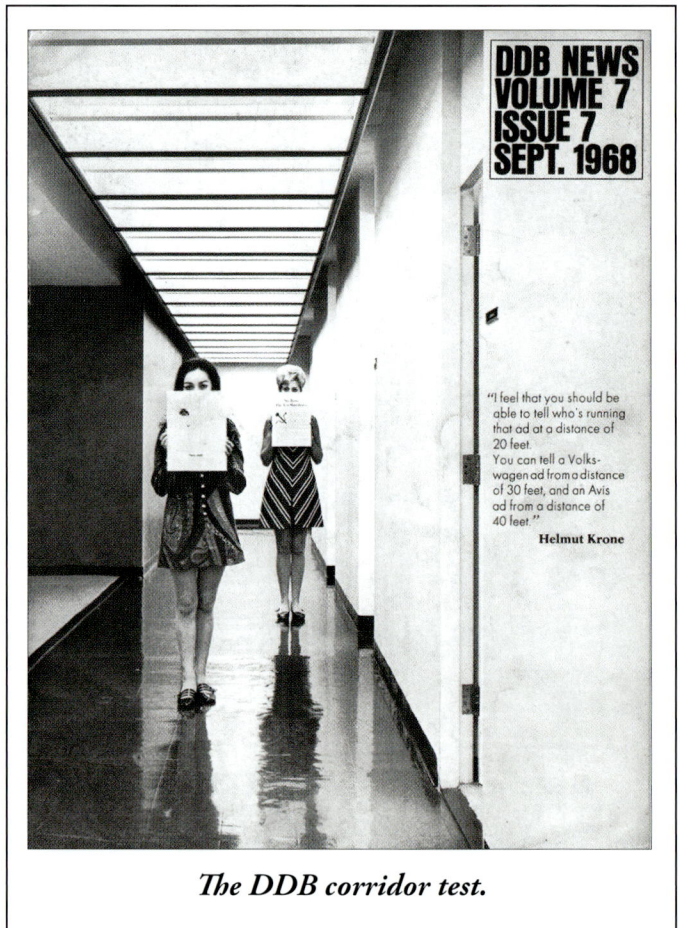

DDB NEWS VOLUME 7 ISSUE 7 SEPT. 1968

"I feel that you should be able to tell who's running that ad at a distance of 20 feet.
You can tell a Volkswagen ad from a distance of 30 feet, and an Avis ad from a distance of 40 feet."

Helmut Krone

The DDB corridor test.

The point being, you could identify the advertiser from a distance before you even got to the message. My Art Director and Partner, Paul Garrett, did a magnificent job in achieving this. The frame to every ad being made up of Filofax pages. I would start the copy with the distinctive 'F" of the logo. (Yes, an homage to what David Abbott had done with Sainsburys). My wife, Cherry, came up with a great idea. It was to create pages for women to record their pregnancy and birth record.

Credits: *Copywriter, Mike Doyle; Art Director, Paul Garret; Photographer, Nigel Haynes.*

The client and the fireman's pole.

We were appointed by a company that made a range of vegetarian foods, The Realeat Company. My wife being a 'vegie' didn't hurt.

There were some logistical challenges with this client, however, as he was a paraplegic, confined to a wheel chair, and our offices in Drury Lane were up a long flight of stairs. Fortunately he had helpers who carried him up for our meeting.

We must have done something right as he overlooked this hurdle. The point being that most meetings after our appointment were at his home.

He had been disabled in America when his twin brother pushed him out of a tree.

He had adapted his home to meet his needs with a fireman's pole between floors so in the morning he could shimmy down and carry on business from there.

I can't remember how he got back upstairs, presumably with his carer's help.

The product was outstanding and ahead of its time. The proof of the pudding being John Webster and his wife, Maureen, came for dinner at our place in Torriano Cottages. Cherry had made two lasagne dishes.; one with the Realeat mix and the other with meat. John went for a second helping of the Realeat version. I rest my case. With the sad ending of the agency, the trade ad here is all I have to show for the account. It had great promise but now doesn't show in a Google search.

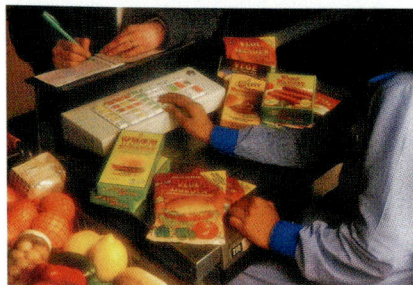

There's a revolution happening right under your nose.

Credits:
Copywriter, Mike Doyle; Art Director, Paul Garrett; Photographer, Unknown.

Postscript from Paul Garrett:

I do remember the first meeting with the American client.

We had no knowledge of his plan to arrive by wheelchair and I helped push him all the way to Aldwych and via the cellar lift into the Waldorf Hotel.

Then having the meeting in the Grand Salon during a tea dance. Accompanied by a small orchestra and a large number of elderly couples waltzing.

Pitchin' & Bitchin', cont'd.

Department of Trade Debt?

A couple from the Department (I may be wrong about the exact department name at the time) came in for a credentials presentation. But were very specific that they could only give us 45 minutes as they had another appointment to go to.

One of my partners, who shall remain nameless, went on for an hour, despite irritated expressions on the faces of the audience.

They stood up, apologised and left. We never heard from then again, as far as I remember. Lesson: always listen to your audience.

One very, very well organised Art Director.

Many Art Directors work best in a mess. But Paul has to count as one of the most tidy and organised Art Directors I have ever worked with.

He had his Magic markers organised like organ stops with a colour chart on his wall.

Image: christianmontone/flickr.com

At home he was into war games with toy soldiers and each regiment had a drawer to themselves.

And he had a VHS collection of Formula One and (I think) Le Mans races all coded. So impressive.

Our swan song.

We can sell the unsellable. What can we do for you?

Garrett, Doyle,

Chairman and Art Director.

A Londoner who went north of Watford (even Watford Gap) to graduate from Manchester College of Art. He then spent the next 18 years working at many of London's top creative agencies.

These include JWT, BMP, CDP (where he was a group head on Parker Pens, Stella Artois and various other accounts), Kirkwoods and SJIP/BBDO as Head of Art.

At Kirkwoods Paul first worked with Mike Doyle successfully pitching for, and working on, business in excess of £5 million.

Some of the campaigns Paul art directed include P&O Ferries, Iran Air, Kimberly Clark, St Ivel/Unigate, Wilkinson Sword, Spillers Homepride, Parker Pens, Whitbread, Courage, Allied Breweries, Evening Standard, IDV, Food & Wine from France, Anheuser Busch, Hamlet Cigars.

Paul's work has consistently won awards down through the years, especially those that are respected by the industry.

In November 1981 he formed Braybrooks & Garrett with SJIP/BBDO's Creative Director, Tim Braybrooks.

It was, arguably, Britain's most successful consultancy.

In August 1986 this became the agency: Garrett, Doyle, Fugler.

Creative Director and Copywriter.

Unusual for a copywriter, Mike studied Typography and then Graphic Design at the London College of Printing. Mike also fits the description 'heavyweight' in every way.

He started in advertising in 1967, playing an active part in the start of Britain's creative revolution in advertising back in the Sixties.

The agencies Mike has worked at are DDB, PKL, BBDO, CDP, Dorlands, SJIP (where he was Deputy Creative Director), FGA, Kirkwoods (working with Paul), Wright & Partners (Partner and Joint Creative Director), Colmans (Joint Creative Director).

Mike's work has regularly featured in D&AD (even as far back as 1968) including the campaign he and Paul created for French Wine.

Mike also won the D&AD silver award for a Benson & Hedges film as well as having it voted one of the 100 best ever commercials.

The 'Campaign' award for the best Direct Response ad went to Mike for Scotcade.

Together, he and Paul have won a vast raft of awards both at home and internationally.

Fugler, Unlimited.

Managing Director and Account Director.

After what he laughingly calls an education at London University, Jeff graduated to being an account handler 14 years ago.

Starting at Boase, Massimi, Pollitt he then spent several years at Collett, Dickenson, Pearce followed by Abbott, Mead, Vickers where he was Account Director on Sainsbury's for the first three years of its now legendary 'quality' campaign.

(A recent survey by Marplan for 'Marketing Week' put Sainsbury's on top, in the Top Ten of the very best of British marketing.)

After AMV Jeff moved to TBWA and then to Lowe Howard-Spink to set up and run their second agency.

During those intervening years Jeff (in addition to crossing paths, not swords, with Paul and Mike) managed accounts such as Birds Eye, Carnation, Courage, Daily Express, Dunn's, Fiat, The Metropolitan Police, Ovaltine, Rawlings, St Ivel, Smiths Foods and Whitbread.

All accounts known for the strength of their marketing, the incisiveness of their strategic direction and the quality of their creative work.

Two centuries ago Doctor Johnson said that "the soul of an advertisement is promise, large promise?"

We offer advertisers a very large promise indeed.

Despite our relative newness our media buying power is not limited. We have a working arrangement with the very best of the media independents.

Take TMD as an example. They feature amongst the top ten spending agencies in MEAL. In fact they are the UK's largest media independent. As a result we can buy space just as effectively as the mega-agencies.

Where we differ significantly from them is we offer you the benefit of working directly with the agency principals.

Our vast experience means a rich cross-fertilization on all our clients' business. Business to Business accounts benefiting from our consumer experience, and vice versa.

Paul Garrett, Mike Doyle and Jeff Fugler will always be working on, and involved in, your account.

Our plans for the future include the appointment of a Planning Director with a similar pedigree to ourselves.

In the meantime we have the pleasure of working with two research companies: Davies Riley-Smith and Analysis.

Prosper Riley-Smith (we like his Christian name) started his career at BMP during the formative days of account planning under Stanley Pollitt.

He then became a research fellow at Strathclyde University, lecturing in consumer behaviour. After that he went to SJIP before becoming Managing Director of Q-Search, since when he has established his present companies.

What Prosper brings to the party is a wealth of experience in marketing and strategic thinking as well as a finely-tuned knowledge of the consumer. In the latter role he acts as a representive of the public, helping the agency to target our campaigns in the most accurate way.

Finally, to quote Campaign magazine "It would appear that with...the industry's pre-occupation with making mega-bucks, there is danger of advertising emerging as the last item on the (agency) agenda.

Agencies who fall into this trap and allow their creative product to slip will suffer.

After all, mediocrity, according to the clients, is not good enough."

In our unlimited view, we couldn't agree more.

Sadly, we had to shut up shop as a couple of key accounts failed to materialise, but we did have the comfort of our agency brochure (it was the size of Campaign Magazine) being voted into The One Show Awards in New York in 1989.

The 'Unsellable'?

That was the Britoil share float that all the pundits said would not sell if it went as a public company.

The sale of the first 50% had not been a success.

With our campaign the share issue was over-subscribed many times, raising a billion pounds sterling.

At long last, The Treasury had struck oil. They later remarked that we had succeeded in selling what they, at times, had considered unsellable.

Copywriter Tim Braybrooks should take much of the credit, along with Paul Garrett, for the success of the Britoil campaign. A case study we inherited.

Chapter
Fifteen

1988 to 1989.

BBDO, second time around

I returned to BBDO London for the second time to be hired by Cedric *"Three Wigs"* Vidler[†], he preferred to be called "Ced". He had previously had his own agency which had been bought by BBDO who retained him as Creative Director.

Ced Vidler.

Ced's hobby was driving racing cars and he was involved in a crash where the engine caught fire and fried his hair. He would wear the long wig for a while and then the shorter version and people would complement him on his haircut.

Funny how some Art Director's last names match their talents.

I was hired by to work with the former typographer turned art director, Barry Woodcraft. Barry is now an award-winning carver of decoy ducks of which I've included some examples. The late, great naturalist, Peter Scott, thought Barry was one of the best, which is not to be sniffed at.

You can see examples of his work at ***www.woodcraft-art.com***

Barry Woodcraft.

Barry's handicraft. *Image: woodworkersinstitute.com*

Barry and I worked on a number of campaigns including Apple, with full pages in the Financial Times, and the relaunch of the British Home Stores chain.

Barry and I were of similar build, think Tweedledum and Tweedledee.

The offices were overlooking Regents Park and we often took a break with a walk in the Park, with Barry studying our feathered friends.

He would occasionally come down to our barn in Kent to work on campaigns, but we could not offer many ducks.

During my time at BBDO I also had the pleasure of working with Tini 'Chandler, daughter of Mike. Happy memories.

The Barn in Kent, it was divided into three homes of which we had the one on the left. You may just about see me cutting the grass.

The more acceptable face of IBM.

Apple altered the face of computing for the better in 1984 with the launch of Macintosh.

At last there was a computer that could talk in a language you could understand.

And not the mumbo-jumbo of mainframes.

Not content with that, we felt it should be able to talk to IBM, DEC, minicomputers, mainframes and a host of the communication networks. This is easily done through a wide choice of Macintosh communication programs.

You're confronted by an easily-understood vocabulary of words and intuitively familiar graphic symbols such as your friend to your left.

The Macintosh Toolbox also gives you interface options such as multiple type fonts, dialogue boxes and pull-down menus.

So your working tools are familiar ones that in practice can boost productivity by as much as 24%. To assist you in this we introduced AppleTalk in 1985, the very first low-cost, local area network. Unlike most networks, setting up couldn't be simpler. In a matter of minutes you can connect up to 32 Macintosh computers, giving your workgroup access to one of our LaserWriter II printers.

Whether across the office or across the world.

The system is incredibly easy to maintain and remarkably inexpensive. For instance, to network five Macintosh's costs £335.

To do the same with five IBM PC's would cost you £4,725.

You could say its the more unacceptable face of IBM.

 Apple. The power to succeed.

Conclusive proof that Apples are good for you.

The well-respected Gartner Group recently published a report on the role of the Apple Macintosh in business.

It demonstrated many of the reasons for our increasing share of the pie.

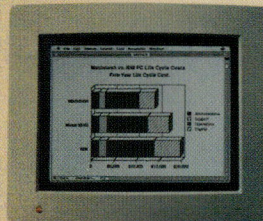

For example, an Apple Macintosh was shown to cost 28% less to run than an IBM PC over five years. That worked out as a saving of almost £3,027 per user.

The Gartner Group's report also demonstrated that even in a mixed IBM/Macintosh environment, computing costs could be dramatically reduced.

They estimated that a company with 600 personal computer users (half IBM and half Apple Macintosh) will have a fully burdened, five-year life cycle cost per user that is 15% less than that of an all-IBM environment.

This worked out at a saving of £830,000 over five years.

Standardising on Macintosh would cost 20% less, saving £1.8 million over five years.

KPMG Peat Marwick carried out a survey which highlighted some of our other strengths.

They found that people using Macintosh were actually up to 24% more productive than their IBM counterparts.

The main reason for this is Macintosh's system of easily understood words and symbols such as files, folders and menus which, with the help of a mouse, speeds and simplifies operating.

So no matter what software is being used, there's a consistent vocabulary and methodology to work with. All of which makes it easy to switch from one program to another.

A fact which was demonstrated in another recent in-depth study. This proved that training costs on Apple Macintosh are 60% lower than those of IBM or other MS-DOS computers.

Furthermore, they found that only half the time is needed in support. For full details dial 100 and ask for Freefone Apple.

We rest our case on health and wealth in business.

 Apple. The power to succeed.

Executives can now improve their creativity by 24%.

That extra percentage can make all the difference when exercising your grey matter.

It can easily get frustrated with conventional computers previous five years, with unimpressive consequences. Let loose on Macintosh all changed. Productivity and creativity increased by leaps and bounds. And because they actually began to enjoy

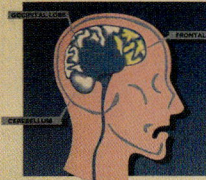

The conventional PC brain.   The Macintosh brain.

and lose heart. Often losing an opportunity in the process.

Whereas the Apple Macintosh encourages creative juices to flow and can lead to winning a contract with a more imaginative presentation. Or creating a sales report that graphically knocks the socks off anybody else's.

The 24% above wasn't plucked out of thin air, incidentally. Its based on an in-depth study by the accountants KPMG Peat Marwick.

Participating companies reported a gain equal to an extra week per month in increased productivity from employees using Macintosh. It was also noted that managers with access to IBM or other MS-DOS computers had reluctantly used them in the their work, they used more software. As a consequence they were able to extend themselves to their full potential.

The reason is simple. From day one they were looking at a screen that could be intuitively understood.

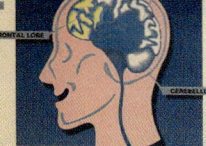

It resembled their desk top with files, pieces of paper and even a wastepaper basket at the side.

This familiarity bred improved sales documents and analyses, spreadsheets and technical drawings such as those above created on the Macintosh II.

For more information dial 100 and ask for Freefone Apple. It will be one executive decision you'll never regret.

 Apple. The power to succeed.

In 1989 IBM just might catch up with our performance in 1984.

When Apple introduced Macintosh to the world back in 1984, IBM greeted it with a blank stare.

We caught them on the hop, initially, in 1977 when we launched the world's very first personal computer.

In '84 Macintosh set yet another standard in speaking your language instead of double-dutch. Macintosh talked to you in words and intuitively familiar symbols.

All orchestrated by a mouse which we first introduced in 1983. This freed your mind from the drudgery of the keyboard.

Back in '84, another innovation was our pocket-size 3½" disk which IBM have only just adopted. (Existing customers will presumably be left up the 5¼" creek.) DeskTop Publishing was created by us the following year to help businessmen produce professionally-printed documents in-house.

In 1985 the first low-cost networking became possible with AppleTalk. It also gave Macintosh its first opportunity to talk to IBM.

MultiFinder in 1987 allowed you to do more than one job at a time. Yet again for the first time. The same year our HyperCard caused quite a stir by helping you build databases quickly and easily while easing you into the art of programming.

Next year IBM hope to adopt our standard of 1984. Where will we be? Suffice to say, old habits die hard.

 Apple. The power to succeed.

Apple and **BHS Credits**: *Copywriter, Mike Doyle; Art Director; Barry Woodcraft; Apple Photographer/ Illustrator, sadly unknown; Illustrator: sadly unknown. BHS Photographer, Paul Redmond (?).*

BBDO & 'The Truman Show'.

I wrote before about the many talented people I met and worked with during my time in advertising.

Another who deserves a mention has to be Andrew 'Andy' Niccol who I encountered while I was working at BBDO London for the second time.

He was one very strong-willed Kiwi but with good reason. (I include Andy's profile from Wikipedia below.)

He created a campaign for the agency's publicity (one of the toughest briefs always), which consisted of sending prospective clients a book of wallpaper samples saying 'that's what you get from other agencies. We offer a unique solution to your marketing challenges'.

In the agency foyer off regent's Park sat a giant wallpaper scraper with our client's brand names engraved on the huge gleaming blade. Deservedly, it got into the D&AD Annual that year. He also created an amazing campaign for Pepsi that they shot in America. However, it was so American everyone thought it was an imported campaign.

Andrew Niccol.
Image: Wikipedia

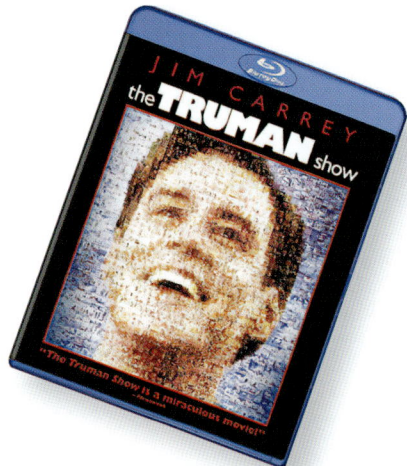

Andrew M. Niccol (born 10 June 1964) is a New Zealand screenwriter, producer, and director. He wrote and directed *Gattaca* (1997), *Simone* (2002), *Lord of War* (2005), *In Time* (2011), *The Host* (2013), and *Good Kill* (2014). He also wrote and co-produced *The Truman Show*, which earned an Academy Award nomination for Best Original Screenplay in 1999 and won a BAFTA award for Best Screenplay. His films tend to explore social, cultural and political issues, as well as artificial realities or simulations. His film *Good Kill* was selected to compete for the Golden Lion at the 71st Venice International Film Festival. Then came Reality TV? -*Wikipedia*

Facebook comment on BBDO:

Terry Comer Vidler hired me and then fired me for telling a Suit who was trying to be creative to stop wasting his time. Shame cos I was doing some good work up there, the Daily Mail radio campaign with Patricia Hodge and a campaign for the French Wool Board which had a Miles Davis style version of Ba Ba Black sheep as its backing track.

My BBDO (2) generation.

Cedric Vidler (Creative Director), Barry Woodcraft, Andrew Niccol, Tina Chandler.
Apologies to anyone I have left out.

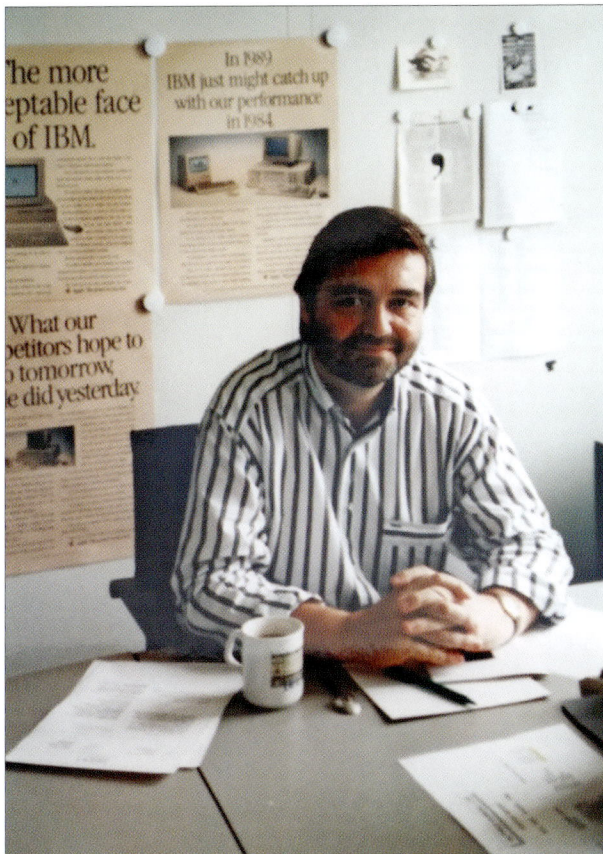

At the BBDO coal face. No typewriter or desktop computer. You would still give your copy to a copy typist. The irony is I was writing copy for Apple.

"Ohh.! So you're the one who,

took all our jobs."

My generation went from typewriters, to laptops, to a phone with enough AI to get those first men to the Moon.

We had our perks.

Life at BBDO had its challenges but it also had many rewards.

Our client, Pepsi Cola, promoted the UK tour of Michael Jackson[†], this was before all the unpleasantness was uncovered.

We had reserved seats for employees and 'other halves', at his concert at Wembley and a coach to take us there and back to the office afterwards. No trouble with drinks, non-alcoholic, being supplied of course. It was a truly great night and performance.

Another summer treat for staff, courtesy of Pepsi, was front row seats at the Queens Club for the tennis tournament warm-up before Wimbledon started.

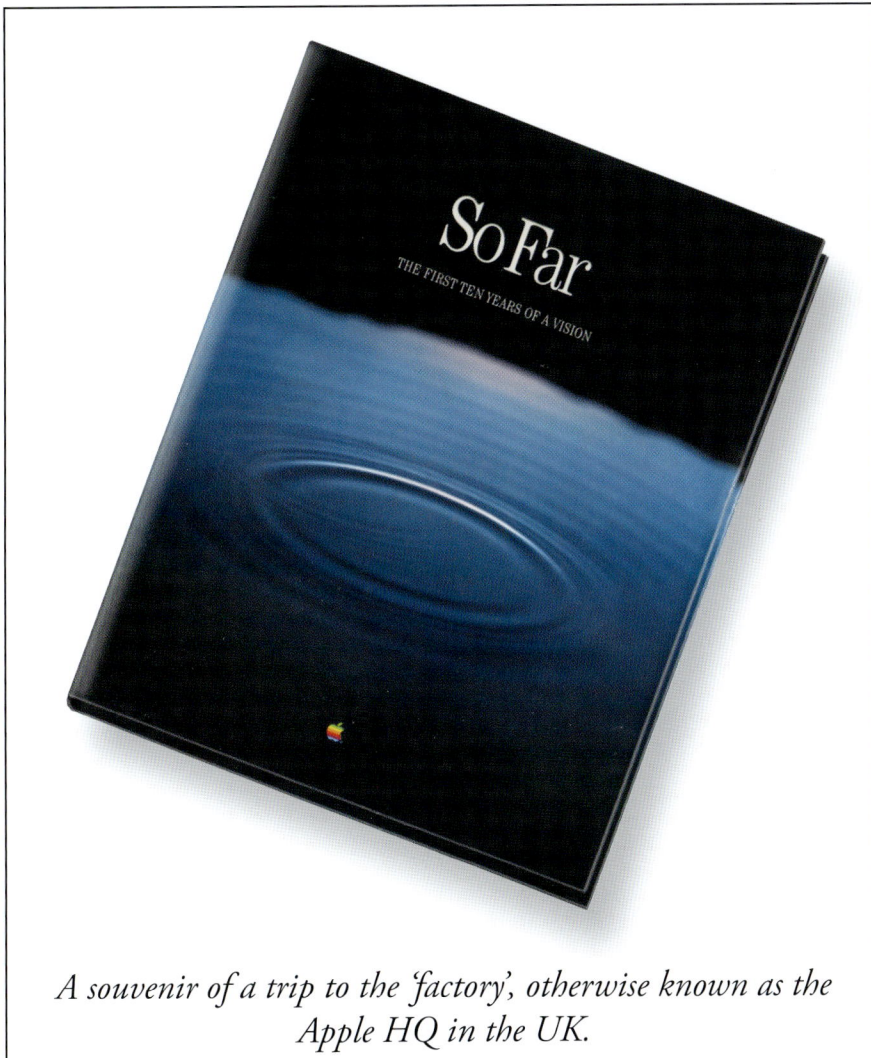

A souvenir of a trip to the 'factory', otherwise known as the Apple HQ in the UK.

Chapter
Sixteen

1989 to 1990.

Laing, Henry, HHCC

✝

While I was briefly at Laing, Henry, Hill, Holliday, Connors, Cosmopolis (phew! Pity the person answering the phone) in London in the 80s, I was hired to work with the very talented Gary Denham[†].

Sadly, he left the agency shortly after we had created a skin cancer campaign where all the information came from Australia. Was it something I said?

Gary Denham.
The Man in Black (and a dash of white).
Image: giving.com

Unfortunately, I have only this one example of the work we did together. Gary was the first and only (to my best knowledge) 'Goth' AD that I've worked with, having skull rings and a skull on his desk and always dressed in black.

The skin cancer campaign we created originally had a visual of a bare-breasted woman. That was felt to be too confronting, and I prefer the 'crucifix' version anyway.

The phenomenon of Brits rushing to Spain, and the like, and covering themselves in olive oil had led to a huge increase in skin cancer diagnoses in the UK, hence the campaign.

ARE YOU DYING TO GET A SUNTAN?

At the first sight of the sun the typical British holidaymaker tends to throw caution to the wind.

What they don't realise is that they're in danger of getting skin cancer if they sunbathe for too long. Skin cancer is now even more common than breast cancer in the UK.

Happily, most skin cancers are curable.

Malignant Melanoma can be another matter. If neglected, it may spread through your body causing secondary cancers and can be fatal. If treated early, however, it is also curable.

SAVE YOUR SKIN.

Most at risk from the sun's rays are those with fair skins. Although people with darker complexions, or whose skin tans easily, should still take care.

Babies and children should also be protected as their skin is particularly vulnerable.

Fortunately, there are various measures you can take, without putting a dampener on your holiday.

HOW TO PROTECT YOURSELF.

For instance, before you venture out into the sun, apply a sunscreen with a high Sun Protection Factor or SPF. The higher the number, generally, the greater the protection.

It's also important to reapply your sunscreen after swimming and at regular intervals while sunbathing.

Too much sun can be dangerous. For your skin's sake move about, see the sights but, above all, cover up when you feel yourself burning.

Equally, in the middle of the day, when the sun is at its most aggressive, you should make as much use of the shade as you can.

For further advice, visit your local pharmacist before setting off on holiday.

Your skin will thank you for it.

PROTECT YOURSELF AGAINST SKIN CANCER.

Credits: *Copywriter, Mike Doyle; Art Director, Gary Denham; Photographer, Seamus Ryan.*

Another glass of wine can't hurt.

My new Art Director, Andy McKay, and me were briefed to create a campaign for French Vin de Pays wines for the London Underground cross-track poster sites. These were inspired by my love of the great French posters of yesteryear such as by Cassandre. A pale imitation perhaps, but I was pleased.

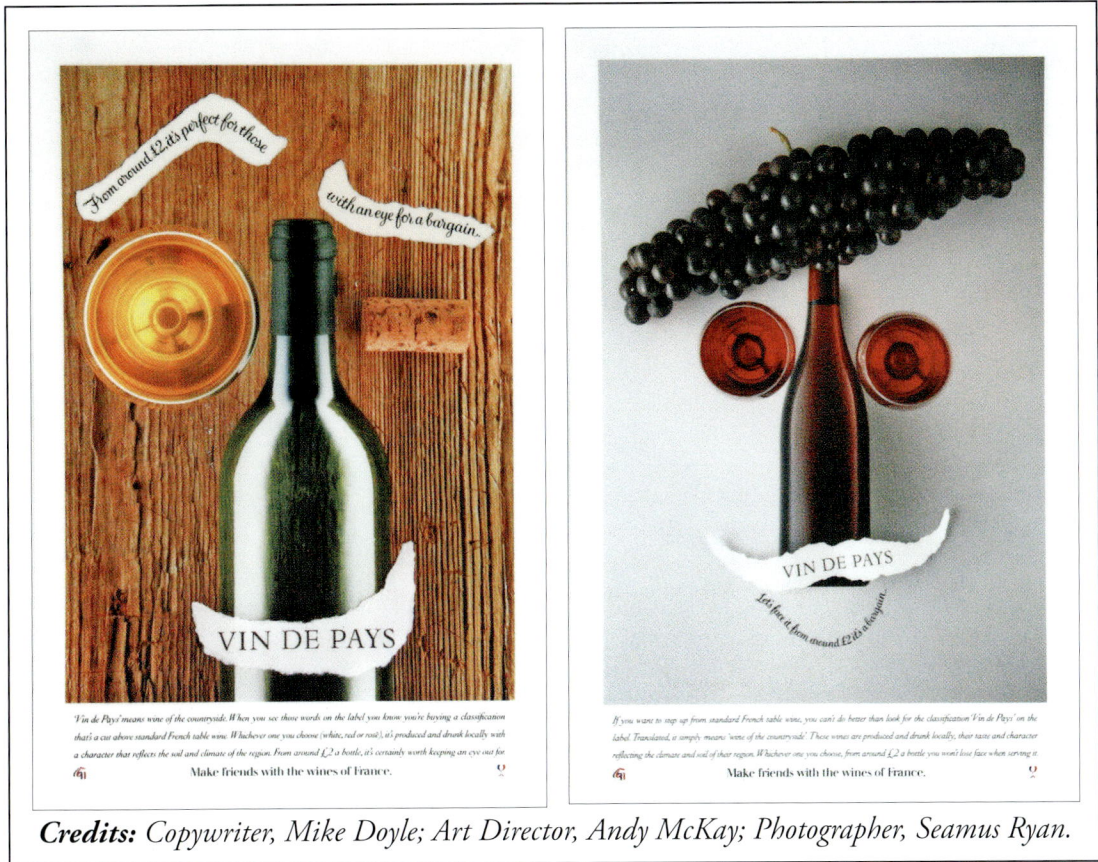

Credits: Copywriter, Mike Doyle; Art Director, Andy McKay; Photographer, Seamus Ryan.

Facebook comments on the Vin de Pays Wine ads:

Paul Carpenter When art direction and copywriting work together it makes for memorable work.

Mike Doyle It doesn't matter how good the copy is if no one wants to read it, it's pretty much a waste of time and effort.

Andy McKay Hi Mike, the snapper was Seamus Ryan. It seems like eons ago that we did these.

The perennial challenge of creating advertising for yourselves, in this case Laing Henry. I used the fact that Jennifer Laing had been a director of Saatchi & Saatchi while Max Henry had been a Senior Art Director at J. Walter Thompson, positioning them, and the agency, as 'thoroughbreds'.

We filmed a promotional video at a stable in Newmarket, following the care and training that happens with a thoroughbred to make it become a winner

A messy location.

Our offices overlooked Leicester Square; an elegant corner of London and centre for cinemas and theatres. Unfortunately, it soon became a dumping ground for the city's rubbish when a rash of strikes meant the piling up throughout the city of waste, including that from hospitals.

Not a pleasant, or healthy, time at all. What with that and people sleeping in carboard boxes everywhere, Australia was looking even more attractive.

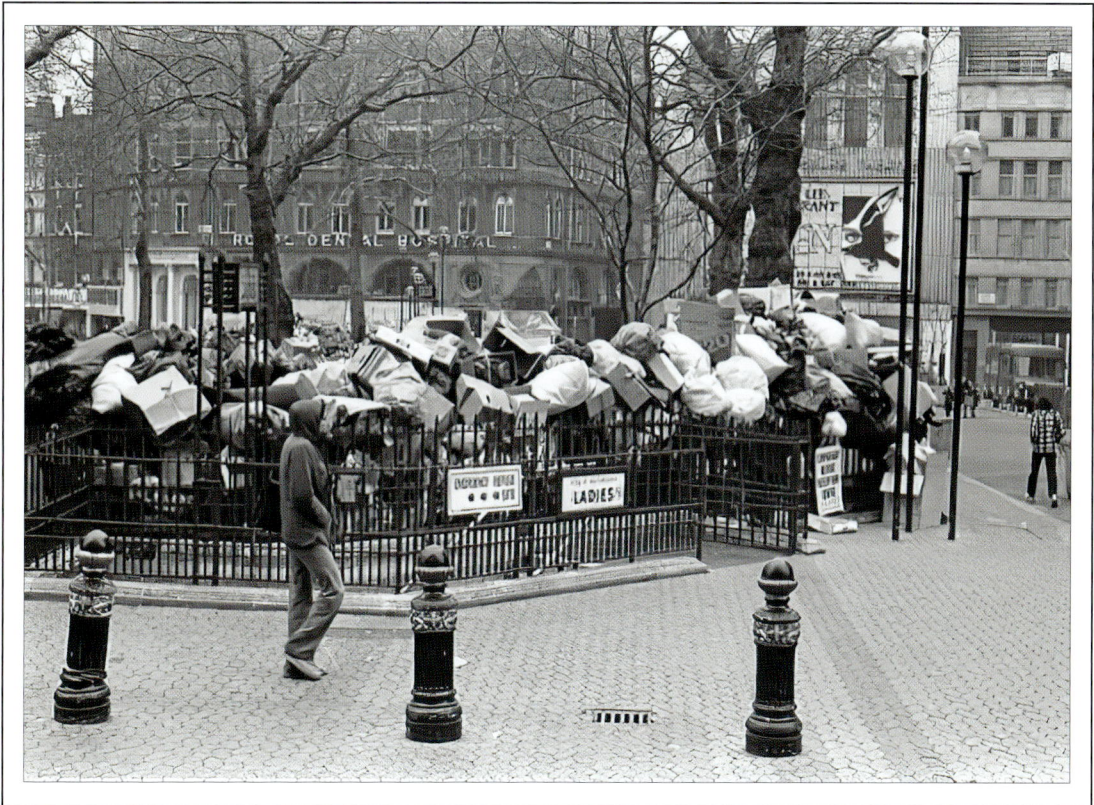

Chapter Seventeen

Life in the 'Twilight Zone'.
Towards a new chapter in my life.

So in March, 1990 I arrived job-hunting in Sydney. A good omen, for me, was seeing Eric Clapton browsing books at W.H. Smith at Heathrow Airport.

Gerri Dibsdall, my headhunter, had found me a room to rent in Cammeray with a woman who worked in the business as a Suit.

I then started on a round of interviews and they all said "love the work" and "Clemenger would be perfect for me". The only problem was the Creative Director, Dick Greenlaw, wouldn't deal with Gerri for some reason.

I was at a lunch in Sydney with Simon Collins and a group from Saatchi's London came in with Ron Mather and ended up joining us.

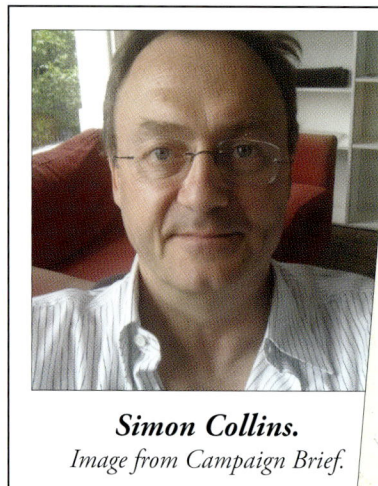

Simon Collins.
Image from Campaign Brief.

Ron Mather.
Image from Campaign Brief.

Ron asked what I was up to and I explained the Clemenger dilemma. Ron said to bring my portfolio into his office the next day. He must have liked what he saw because he rang Dick and I had an interview a day or so afterwards.

Two sketches dashed off by Simon at lunch. Above, Max Henry, and Alan Thomas below. ▶

Lost in North Sydney.

I had been told that the Clemenger offices were on the Pacific Highway. I wandered up and down North Sydney with no sign of the agency. I was already late for the interview. So I found a public phone box and rang the agency.

They apologised and explained that the offices were in St. Leonards a long way up the Highway.

Mike must have done a good sales job and Dick loved the work. He then said there's someone here who knows you besides Richard 'Dickie' Dearing; and Dick's wife, Judy White, came in.

As well as being the agency planner, she and I had worked together on various campaigns at Dorland and, fortunately, had got on really well.

Weeks later, back in the UK, I received confirmation of the job offer from Clemenger.

By September my application to settle in Australia had been approved and we arrived to our new life in November 1990.

We left the UK in a long heatwave and arrived in Sydney to the hottest summer on record. Nothing much changes

*L-R: **Dick Greenlaw** with **David Blackley.** David was to play a part in my life in Oz and who I first met at BBDO in London in the time of Tim Delaney.*

Image: Campaign Brief.

Chapter
Eighteen

1990. The Departure Lounge.

Before we took the great leap south to Australia we had many farewell gatherings. The most popular drink being brought by people was a bottle of Jacob's Creek Australian wine. We must have contributed greatly to their profits that year.

John and Maureen Webster.

The Garrett Clan.

Martyn and Annie Walsh.

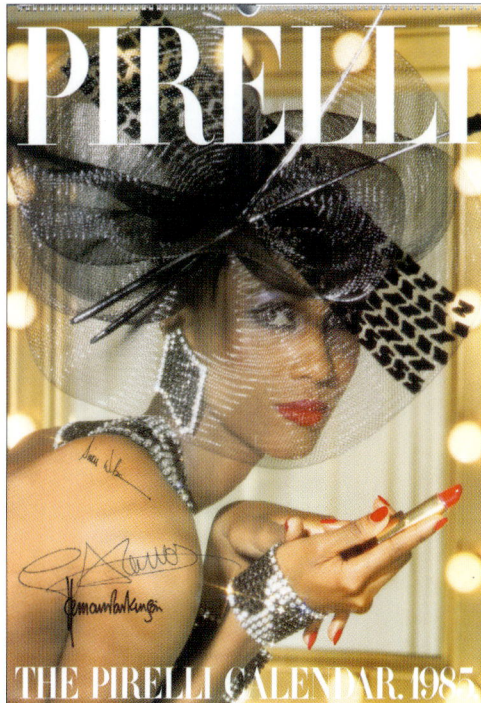

As a leaving the UK present, Martyn gave me this signed copy. Photographer was Norman Parkinson.

Chapter
Nineteen

Awards:

Colin Craig
Joint Creative Director
Cogent Elliott Limited

D&AD Gold Award 1975

Simon Kentish
Art Director/Group Head
J. Walter Thompson
Company Limited

John Mackenzie
Art Director
Saward Baker Advertising
Limited

Michael Doyle
Copywriter
French Gold Abbott Kenyon
& Eckhardt Limited

Bob Isherwood
Art Director
Collett Dickenson Pearce
& Partners Limited

D&AD Gold Award 1974
D&AD Silver Award 1974

John Gorham
Designer

D&AD Executive Committee
1974-1975

D&AD Jury Member
1970-1972

D&AD Silver Awards
1970-1973

Paul Arden
Creative Director
L.A.P. Advertising Limited

1977 judging Direct Mail for D&AD.
I'm the one with the stiped 'kipper' tie. Image: D&AD.

L-R: Colin Craig, Simon Kentish, John Mackenzie, Mike Doyle, Bob Isherwood, John Gorham, Paul Arden.

I got by with a little (and often a lot) help from my friends such as Art Directors, Illustrators, Photographers, Typographers, Commercial Directors, Animators, Suits, Clients and Art Buyers.

Year-Agency	Award	Product
1968-PWP	D&AD	Sandeman Cream Sheery
1970-PKL	D&AD	Harrods
1972-CDP	D&AD	Silver Award, Benson & Hedges (Also chosen as one of the '100 Best Ever Commercials'. Work featured in 'The Commercials Book'.)
	British TV Advertising Awards	Benson & Hedges
1973-CDP	D&AD	Benson & Hedges
1974-CDP	D&AD	National Panasonic Benson & Hedges
1976-SJIP/BMP	Campaign Press Awards	Scotcade Direct Response
1977-FGA	D&AD (Judge (see above) on D&AD Direct Mail/ Sales Promotion Jury	Habitat
1979-BBDO	D&AD	Toyota
1981-Kirkwoods	D&AD	French Wines
1982-W&P	Communication Arts, USA	Miln Masters Seeds
	'The Art of Advertising' Advertising: Reflections of a Century	Benson & Hedges ads from while at CDP from 1973 Benson & Hedges ads (as above)
1983-W&P	Clio	Prime Computers
1984-W&P	Clio	Crown Paints

Accounts I worked on while in the UK:

Alcoholic drinks: Allied Breweries, Budweiser, French Wines, Baden Wines, Taunton Cider, Gaymers Cyder, Tennents Lager, Tolly-Cobbold Brewery, Watney, Mann, Truman Brewery.

Automotive: CarPlan, Citroen, Ford, Land-Rover, Rover, Texaco, Toyota, Volkswagen.

Business to Business: Crown Paints, ICI Agricultural, Securicor, Manpower, Miln Masters Seeds Merchants.

Charities: Oxfam, UNICEF.

Computers/IT: Apple, Apricot, Prime.

Cosmetics/Personal Care: Bud Deodorant, Halston Perfumes, Orlane, Shulton's Oriental Spice, Tampax.

Finance: Abbey Life Insurance, First National Securities (CreditPlan), Legal & General Insurance, National Provincial Bank, Royal Bank of Scotland (RoyScot.

Food: Allied Bakeries, Homepride Bakeries, Homepride Cook-in-Sauces, Smiths Snacks, Lifesavers Bubble Yum, Midland Counties Ice Cream, Realeat VegeBurgers.

Government: Health Education Authority (Skin Cancer), The European Movement, The Post Office.

Hotels/Holidays/Airlines: Aer Lingus, Grand Metropolitan, Hilton, Ladbroke Holidays, Lufthansa, Sheraton.

Household: Crown Paints, Dixons, Hotpoint, Ronson, National Panasonic, Polycell NPD, Rowenta, Saisho, Sony, Scotcade Direct Response, Technics, Zanussi.

Media: Sunday Telegraph.

Pharmaceutical: Ciba-Geigy (Do-Do, Proflex).

Photographic: Agfa Film & Cameras, Saisho, Sankyo.

Retail: British Home Stores, Dunhill Menswear, Habitat, Harrods, Hepworths Menswear, Western Jeans.

Telco: British Telecom.

Tobacco: Benson & Hedges (Special Filter and Mellow Virginia).

Watches & Accessories: Bulova, Citizen, Filofax.

Index.

A concise bibliography.

Proof.	The Magazine of the LCP, 1965.
DDB Annual Report.	1967.
DDB News, Volume 7, Issue 3, 5, 6, 7.	1968.
The Art of Writing Advertising.	NTC Business Books.
D&AD Annuals.	Booth-Clibborn Editions. Thames & Hudson. 1968 to 2000.
100 Great Advertisements.	Times Newspapers Ltd,1978.
The Art of Advertising.	William Heinemann 1982.
Advertising: Reflections Of a Century.	William Heinemann1982.
Remember those Great Volkswagen ads?	Merrel 1982.
Pipe Dreams by Mike Dempsey.	Pavilion Michael Joseph, 1982.
Thirsty Work, Ten Years of Heineken Advertising by Peter Mayle.	Macmillan 1983.
Ogilvy on Advertising by David Ogilvy.	Pan Books Ltd 1983.
Bill Bernbach's Book.	Villard Books 1987.
The Saatchi & Saatchi Story by Philip Kleinman.	Pan Book Ltd 1987.
So Far, The First Ten Years of a Vision, by Rob Price,	Apple Computer 1987,
The One Show.	Rotovision S.A. Geneva1989.
Bill Bernbach said…	DDB Needham 1989.
Up the Agency by Peter Mayle.	Pan Books Ltd 1990.

Language & Typography by Cal Swann.	Lund Humphries 1991.
Commercial Break, the Inside Story of Saatchi & Saatchi by Alison Fendley.	Hamish Hamilton 1995.
IA book about the classic Avis advertising campaign of the 60s by Henri Holmgren & Peer Eriksson.	HHAB Askungevagen 1995.
Inside Collett Dickenson Pearce by John Salmon & John Ritchie.	B. T. Batsford 2000.
Well-written and red by Alfredo Marcantonio.	Harriman House 2002.
John Webster. The Earth People's Ad Man.	DDB UK 2012.
Hegarty on Advertising by Sir John Hegarty.	Thames & Hudson 2011.
Hegarty on Creativity by Sir John Hegarty.	Thames & Hudson 2014.
The Real Mad Men by Andrew Cracknell.	Quercus 2011.
Be The Worst You Can Be by Charles Saatchi.	Booth-Clibborn Editions 2012.
The Art Deco Poster.	Thames & Hudson 2013
Who Shot the Pregnant Man? by Alan Brooking.	Sans Souci Associates 2018.
The Copy Book. How some of the best advertising writers in the World write their advertising.	D&AD, Taschen, 2018.

I must also give credit to The Hidden Persuaders *by Vance Packard, published by Penguin in 1957.*

This pioneering and prescient work revealed how advertisers use psychological methods to tap into our unconscious desires in order to "persuade" us to buy the products they are selling.

Another influential book was Madison Avenue U.S.A. *by Martin Mayer, published by Penguin in 1961. The inside story of what really goes on in the advertising business: the agencies, the clients, the personalities who ruled America's buying habits.*

Finally...

Here's to the crazy ones.
The misfits, the rebels, the
troublemakers. The round pegs
in the square holes. The ones
who see things differently.
They're not fond of rules.
And they have no respect for
the status quo. You can quote
them, disagree with them,
disbelieve them, glorify or
vilify them. About the only
thing that you can't do, is
ignore them because they change
things. They invent. They imagine.
They heal. They explore. They
create. They inspire. They
push the human race forward.
Maybe they have to be crazy.
Because the ones who are crazy
enough to think that they can
change the world, are the ones
who do.

Jack Kerouac

Acknowledgements.

Last, but not least, I would like to acknowledge all the great help I received from Richard Kelley (now part of our great diaspora and living in New York State) in the preparation and production of this book. He truly is my other 'Best Man', not forgetting Graeme Robertson, of course. Richard has written many books himself.
I also received great advice from Aslan Brooking and George Lois.

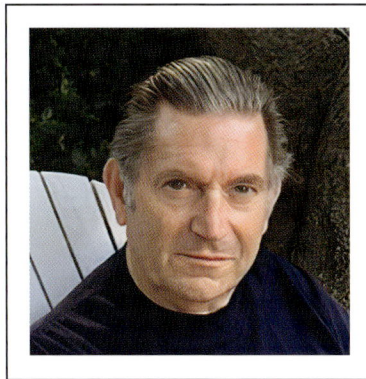

Finally, I would also like to give thanks to my wife for putting up with me over all these months and providing an honest and critical eye over the content. Also thanks to Paul Fonteyne for reviewing the copy and keeping me honest and respectful.

The following (in alphabetical order) reviewed content relevant to them via email: Keith Benton, Alan Brooking, Terry Bunton, Mike Everett, Paul Garrett, Sir John Hegarty, Cathy Heng, Alan Lofthouse, George Lois, Caroline O'Byrne, Mike Stephenson, Dave Trott, Barry Woodcraft, Johnny Wright. Also help from John O'Driscoll on various details. Many images were supplied (again in alphabetical order): Larry Franklin, Caroline O'Byrne, John O'Driscoll, Paul Walter, Barry Woodcraft.

Paul Carpenter deserves a gigantic thanks for coming up with, what I think, is a great cover design. He could have said "no" when I asked but then as my Mum might have said, 'If you don't ask you don't get."

Next stop, Sydney. See Book Two.